Red Planets

Marxism and Culture

Series Editors:
Mike Wayne and Esther Leslie

Marxism and the History of Art:
From William Morris to the New Left
Edited by Andrew Hemingway

Philosophizing the Everyday
The Philosophy of Praxis and the Fate of Cultural Studies
John Roberts

Marxism and Media Studies
Key Concepts and Contemporary Trends
Mike Wayne

Red Planets

Marxism and Science Fiction

Edited by
MARK BOULD AND CHINA MIÉVILLE

First published 2009 by Pluto Press
345 Archway Road, London N6 5AA

www.plutobooks.com

Copyright © Mark Bould and China Miéville 2009

The right of the individual contributors to be identified as the authors of this
work has been asserted by them in accordance with the Copyright, Designs
and Patents Act 1988.

British Library Cataloguing in Publication Data
A catalogue record for this book is available from the British Library

ISBN   978 0 7453 2731 0   Hardback
ISBN   978 0 7453 2730 3   Paperback

10   9   8   7   6   5   4   3   2   1

Designed and produced for Pluto Press by
Chase Publishing Services Ltd, Sidmouth, England
Typeset from disk by Stanford DTP Services, Northampton, England

Printed and bound by CPI Group (UK) Ltd, Croydon, CR0 4YY

in memory of Bill Burling
a dear friend

CONTENTS

SERIES PREFACE

There have been quite a number of books with the title 'Marxism and...', and many of these have investigated the crossing points of Marxism and cultural forms, from Fredric Jameson's *Marxism and Form* to Terry Eagleton's *Marxism and Literary Criticism*, Raymond Williams' *Marxism and Literature*, John Frow's *Marxism and Literary History* and Cary Nelson and Lawrence Grossberg's *Marxism and the Interpretation of Culture*. These titles are now all quite old. Many of them were published in the 1970s and 1980s, years when the embers of 1968 and its events continued to glow, if weakly. Through the 1990s Marxism got bashed; it was especially easily mocked once its 'actually existing' socialist version was toppled with the fall of the Berlin Wall. Postmodernism made Marxism a dirty word, and class struggle a dirty thought and even dirtier deed. But those days that consigned Marxism to history themselves now seem historical. The president of France spoke fearfully of the return of the spirit of 1968 at the end of 2008, when Athens was burning and the anomalous wave rippled through Italy. The crash of neo-liberalism in a now global economy has trashed many so-called certainties about the superiority of capitalism. A new spirit of critical questioning is emergent. Marxism, however critically its inheritance is viewed, cannot be overlooked by the increasing numbers who make efforts to provide an analysis and a consequent practice.

Our series 'Marxism and Culture' investigates Marxism as a method for understanding culture, a mode of probing and explaining. Equally, our titles self-reflexively consider Marxism as an historical formation, with differing modulations and resonances across time – that is to say, as something itself to be probed and explained. The first two books in the series address popular or mass culture. Mike Wayne's *Marxism and Media Studies* outlines the resources of Marxist theory for understanding the contemporary mediascape, while also proposing how the academic discipline of Media Studies might be submitted to Marxist analysis. John Roberts' *Philosophizing the Everyday* uncovers the revolutionary origins of the philosophical concept of the everyday, recapturing it from a synonymity with banality and ordinariness propounded by theorists in Cultural Studies.

A volume on *Marxism and the History of Art* shifted the attention to 'high culture'. Taking into its broad scope the insights of a number of key figures in Marxist aesthetics, the volume reveals the pertinence of Marxist theory to manifold aspects of the art world: the materiality of art; the art market and the vagaries of value; the art object as locus of ideology; artists, art historians and art critics as classed beings; art and economy; art as commodity; the analogism of form and historical developments.

This latest book in the series is devoted to the exploration of science fiction, a mass culture genre which has produced an identifiable tradition of novelists with explicitly socialist commitments, going back at least as far as William Morris, who wrote *News From Nowhere* (1890), a story that imagines a future communist society where work is a pleasurable creative activity. Science fiction has also attracted considerable interest from Marxist critics, drawn to a genre in which the dynamics between technology, social relations under capital, and the human body are explored and experimented with. As a result, a very strong tradition of Marxist SF criticism (in both literature and film) has emerged and developed within academia in the last 40 years or so. This anthology draws on the debates that have taken place within this tradition, provides a critical assessment of current Marxist approaches to the genre, and opens up new perspectives and paths for Marxist SF criticism to explore. It remains absolutely essential, if we are to break with the horizon of capital, both to imagine alternative models of social being and to critically decode the ways in which those alternative models remain tied, by the sticky threads of ideology, to the horizon of capital. This book makes a contribution to that important task.

Mike Wayne and Esther Leslie

INTRODUCTION

ROUGH GUIDE TO A LONELY PLANET, FROM NEMO TO NEO

Mark Bould

For most of the eighty or so years since science fiction (SF) was identified and named as a distinct genre,[1] it has typically been dismissed as the infantile excrescence of a stultifying mass culture, a literature doubly debased by its fantastic elements and mediocre prose. Whenever an SF novel – such as George Orwell's *Nineteen Eighty-Four* (1949), Thomas Pynchon's *Gravity's Rainbow* (1973), Margaret Atwood's *The Handmaid's Tale* (1985) or Molly Gloss's *Wild Life* (2000) – is found to contradict such expectations, it is generally treated as 'not really SF' or as somehow 'transcending the genre'. The same is true of SF in other media, with films such as *Alphaville* (Godard, 1965), *2001: A Space Odyssey* (Kubrick, 1968), *Solaris* (Tarkovsky, 1972), *Possible Worlds* (Lepage, 2000) or *Le Temps du Loup* (Haneke, 2003) often regarded as the works of an 'auteur' rather than the products of a genre and industry. Such a position is as ill-informed about the nature, breadth and variety of SF as it is transparent in its cultural politics of taste. This is not to claim that all SF is good (whatever that might mean), but that the genre is deserving of more serious attention than common stereotypes suggest. And even if this were not true of individual SF texts and practices,[2] it would be true of the genre's cultural reach and impact. For example, the two highest-grossing films of 2008 – Christopher Nolan's *The Dark Knight* and Steven Spielberg's *Indiana Jones and the Kingdom of the Crystal Skulls* – were science-fictional, each taking US$1 billion globally (before revenues from merchandising and ancillary sales to DVD, television, and so on); a group of SF writers, including Larry Niven, Jerry Pournelle and Greg Bear, originally proposed the Strategic Defense Initiative to Ronald Reagan in the early 1980s, and these writers are now part of the Sigma group, whose motto is 'Science Fiction in the National Interest', and advise the US Department of Homeland Security on the so-called War on Terror;[3] and while millions of people belong to science-fictional religions, such as the Church of Scientology, many others claim to have been abducted by aliens. Even if one were to find all SF texts to be without value or interest, one surely cannot dismiss such instances of the genre's cultural significance.

SF began to receive serious academic attention in the late 1950s. SF studies emerged as a (primarily literary) discipline in the 1970s and, since the postmodern turn of the 1980s, it has developed to include cultural studies, film studies, television studies, game studies, and so on. It has long been allied with Marxist, feminist and queer theory, and increasingly with critical race studies, as politically engaged theorists and critics have found in the genre the radical potential for thinking differently about the world. In this volume, we have brought together the work of a number of explicitly Marxist thinkers who engage with SF, ranging from the most established to the newest figures in the field. In the remainder of this introduction, I will outline one of the reasons why Marxists should care about SF (and SF about Marxism), before briefly introducing their contributions to this vital and growing body of criticism.

Fredric Jameson argues that William Gibson's *Pattern Recognition* (2003) and Bruce Sterling's collection *A Good Old-Fashioned Future* (1999) are manifestations of the contemporary 'geopolitical Imaginary'. In addition to illustrating 'the inner networks of global communication and information' and surfing the entre-preneurial excitement 'of the money to be made' from developing and exploiting them, these recent fictions by the two figures most responsible for the emergence and visibility of cyberpunk in the 1980s also express 'the truth of emergent globalization' and provide 'a first crude inventory of the new world system'.[4] But

Jameson deploys an oddly anachronistic allusion – 'a Cook's tour of the new global waystations'⁵ – which suggests that SF has long been doing these things.

In an earlier essay, Jameson entertained the position that 'there has always been globalization': 'trade routes have been global in their scope' since the Neolithic, 'with Polynesian artifacts deposited in Africa and Asian potsherds as far afield as the New World'.⁶ Cook's tours, however, originated in the mid nineteenth century, close to the dates commonly associated with the birth of SF.⁷ Thomas Cook was ten years old when Mary Shelley published *Frankenstein, or the Modern Prometheus* (1818). He made his first commercial arrangement with a transport company to carry a group of passengers he had organised in 1841, the year of Edgar Allan Poe's 'A Descent into the Maelström'. This relationship with Midland Counties Railway became permanent in 1844, the year of Poe's 'A Tale of the Ragged Mountains' and 'Mesmeric Revelation', leading Cook to found his company and begin, in 1845, the year of 'The Facts in the Case of M. Valdemar', to organise trips further afield. In 1872, the year of Jules Verne's *Around the World in Eighty Days*, Cook began his own round-the-world tours, although in the opposite direction to that taken by Phileas Fogg and Passepartout, and taking three times as long. By the time of Cook's death in 1892, the year of Konstantin Tsiolkovky's 'On the Moon' and the first *Frank Reade* dime novels, his company was selling over 3 million tickets per year. In the preceding year, new author H.G. Wells had published 'The Rediscovery of the Unique', an essay arguing that 'Science is a match that man has just got alight' but 'around him ... darkness still';⁸ in 1893 he had published 'Man of the Year Million', whose speculations on future human evolution underpinned his design of the Martians in *The War of the Worlds* (1898), and, in 1894 and 1895, different versions of his first novel, *The Time Machine*. When Wells died, in 1946, Thomas Cook & Son was no longer a family business, but owned by four railway companies.

Fantastic fictions of various sorts and across multiple media can easily be read as expressions of – and are sometimes concerned with – capitalist modernity. In broad terms, supernatural horror depicts pasts that refuse to die (haunting, legacies, degenerations) and subjects made monstrous (vampires, werewolves, zombies), while fantasy emphasises endangered feudalism (aristocratic elves leave Middle Earth to petit bourgeois hobbits, who will be supplanted by humans, whose proletarian nature is foreshadowed by orcs). On some level, then, both genres are also about changes within – or of – the mode of production and their consequences.

All of the fantastic genres require and allow imaginary world-building: none of them take place in a world which pretends to straightforward mimesis (although this does not prevent them being, in various senses, verisimilitudinous, realistic or mimetic). SF world-building is typically distinguished from other fictional world-building, whether fantastic or not, by the manner in which it offers, however unintentionally, a snapshot of the structures of capital. (This is not always or exclusively the case, and may often be unintentional; and it is important to recognise that it is a difference of degree rather than of kind.) This is perhaps best explained by metaphor. In the metal-working process called 'bossing', a piece of sheet metal is placed against a shot bag – a soft leather bag not quite stuffed with shot or sand – and gently hammered with a bossing mallet so as to curve the metal into the desired shape. When one removes the finished artefact, it leaves behind a rough impression, a negative space, in the bag. Because SF requires the writer to structure plausible worlds and futures, the innovations which she integrates into a model of social totality impact against material reality. When the fictional world is held up for our regard, a pristine and total creation, it has nonetheless left behind a negative space. And because such fictions rarely address the economic dimensions of social totality, that negative space is often primarily, if unwittingly, bound by the structures, potentials and limits of capital. To demonstrate this capacity – which is not a definition – of SF, I will turn to two works with much in common: Jules Verne's *Twenty Thousand Leagues under the Seas* (1869) and the *Matrix* trilogy (Wachowski brothers, 1999, 2003, 2003).

I will begin with three uncontentious points about Verne's fiction. First, as Pierre Macherey argues, 'the *subject* of all Verne's work' is 'Man's domination of nature': 'science will eventually know and transform nature entirely'.[9] Second, Verne frequently catalogues the world through which his characters pass, drawing extensively on and 'restat[ing], rewrit[ing] or recycl[ing] knowledge gleaned in the scientific, geographical and historical reviews of the day',[10] leading Darko Suvin to observe that the 'world of Verne's early books is ... more *interpolated* than extrapolated from the imaginative space of textbooks of exotic geography, zoology, mineralogy'.[11] Third, as Marc Angenot notes, Verne's narratives are 'narratives of circulation'[12] – hence Suvin's observation that Captain Nemo was almost crushed beneath the Antarctic ice as a punishment for daring to stop at the South Pole, 'the still point of the whirling globe'.[13] Despite Angenot's suggestive comments – 'Verne portrays expense, not accumulation; circulation, not surplus value'[14] – the connection between this circulation and capital remains relatively unexplored, especially in relation to these other characteristics of Verne's work.

Twenty Thousand Leagues starts with a synopsis of maritime encounters with a gigantic, fast-moving hazard in the Pacific and Atlantic oceans, beginning the novel's mapping of the transport and communications networks of the emerging world market. The encounters never just happen at sea, but at specific grid references on the global map; and the ships involved are never merely ships, but the property of commercial shipping ventures (or occasionally navies). In addition to a brief history of the Cunard Line, the first two chapters also mention the Calcutta and Burma Steam Navigation Company, the West India and Pacific Steamship Company, the French Line, the Royal Mail, the Inman Line, the Montreal Ocean Company and the San Francisco–Shanghai line, clearly indicating the flows of global commerce. As reports of brushes with this nautical anomaly arrive 'hot on the heels of one another', so the supposed

> monster came into fashion in all the big cities: it was sung about in the cafés, jeered at in the newspapers, acted out in the theatres. The *canards* had a perfect chance to lay whoppers of every hue. Each imaginary gigantic creature resurfaced in the papers.[15]

The actual destination of this flow of information remains unspecified, creating a sense of a rhizomatic communications network without a centre. This resonates strongly with the 'communicational concept of globalization' which, Jameson suggests, leads 'into a postmodern celebration of difference and differentiation: suddenly all cultures around the world are placed in tolerant contact with each other in a kind of immense cultural pluralism'.[16] Some trace of this is evident in the first meal Nemo serves aboard the *Nautilus*, which includes 'fillet of turtle', 'dolphin livers', whale's milk, seaweed sugar and 'a sea slug jam that a Malay would declare without equal'.[17] However, the economic concept of globalisation produces a sense of 'a world-system from which "delinking" … is henceforth impossible and even unthinkable and inconceivable'.[18] While the failure to designate the reports' destination(s) might imply the absence of a centre, it equally suggests the invisibility of the system's fundamental dissymmetry to those at its core: the identities of the presumptively European and North American 'big cities' are so obvious as not to require naming. Likewise, despite the apparent neutrality of the grid of longitude and latitude, its origins and purpose are to be found in the projects of imperial and economic expansion and integration. Consequently, in *Twenty Thousand Leagues* the world often seems reduced to, or captured within, a grid of equivalised positions across which commerce flows, like version 1.0 of the internet.

Martin Willis notes that the supposed 'sea serpent', actually the *Nautilus*, 'enters the world of imagination before it reaches science, becoming a song, a piece of prose, a sketch, and a myth before any scientific system is brought to bear';[19] but more significant is its entry into the world of information, promptly and widely commodified before its existence is even verified. Its integration into global capital proceeds apace. Following its collision with Cunard's *Scotia*, 'maritime losses from unknown causes were simply attributed to the monster', leading to a panic about 'travel between the various continents … becoming increasingly dangerous': insurance companies threaten 'to raise their premium rates' and 'industrial and commercial journals' argue for the need to 'purge the seas of this redoubtable monster, in order to safeguard cross-ocean communications'.[20] As Professor Aronnax explains, the crew of the vessel upon which he and his companions were pursuing the *Nautilus* thought they were hunting 'some powerful marine monster, which it was necessary to rid the ocean of at any cost'.[21]

Nemo himself embodies many of the contradictions of the emergent world market. On the one hand, he wishes thoroughly to de-link himself from the human world. He declares himself 'a man who has broken with humanity' and 'not what you call a civilized being'; elsewhere he refuses to distinguish between 'savages' and other men, or between surface men and sharks.[22] He rhapsodises about the sea's peacefulness and lack of tyrants – on the oceans' 'surface immoral rights can still be claimed, men can fight each other, devour each other, and carry out all the earth's atrocities. But thirty feet below the surface their power ceases, their influence fades, their authority disappears' – and imagines 'founding cities in the sea, agglomerations of underwater dwellings which ... would come up to breathe on the surface of the oceans each morning, free cities if ever there were any, independent cities!'[23] Although Nemo's hatred of despotism and yearning for independence is given no specific motivation,[24] he strongly identifies with anti-colonial struggles. He recognises a Sinhalese, 'the inhabitant of an oppressed country', as a 'compatriot ... to my last breath'.[25] He secretly finances Crete's rebellion against the Turks. He pays tribute to the wreck of the *Vengeur* and decorates his cabin with portraits of republican, anti-colonialist, nationalist and abolitionist leaders. However, Nemo's support for such causes also prevents his de-linking from the global economy. Not only does he take sides in various struggles; his vast wealth is itself derived from colonial plunder (he loots sunken Spanish treasure ships and other wrecks). Moreover, the *Nautilus* is assembled from components custom-made by various companies, each 'sent from a different point on the globe via a forwarding address'.[26] The companies, which Verne names, are located in Le Creusot, Essen, Glasgow, Liverpool, London, Motala, New York and Paris. While the island to which these components are delivered and on which the *Nautilus* is constructed appears to be at the centre of a commercial web, a confluence of mail and cargo delivery networks, this is merely – as these named locations indicate – the temporary activation of a network centred in northwest Europe and the US. The *Nautilus*'s construction exemplifies the 'rocketing exportation of heavy machinery from the industrial core countries, which characterized the extended economic boom of the 1850s through the early 1870s that decisively established capitalism as the single unifying world economy',[27] and also provides a model for increasingly common production practices in which subcontractors remain ignorant of the overall project towards which their efforts contribute – a relationship homologous to that between the capitalist and the alienated proletarian. This in turn suggests another contradiction: Nemo's longed-for separation from the emerging world market can also be seen as exemplifying capital's own desire for transcendence.

Jameson suggests that, when we try to think of globalisation as a 'purely communicational concept, we begin to fill in the empty signifier with visions of financial transfers and investments all over the world, and the new networks begin to swell with the commerce of some new and allegedly more flexible capitalism'.[28] Likewise, SF's depictions of cyberspace, 'the information space "behind" computer screens, networking together Information and Communications Technologies', tend to work as a euphemism or 'metaphor for dematerialised, immaterial or friction-free capital-in-circulation'.[29] The seas through which Nemo circulates – 'Mobile in the mobile element'[30] – often function in a similar way. Midway through his disquisition on the ocean's circulation, Nemo himself describes the sea, in its planetary homeostatic function, as the 'stabilizer of the overall economy of the globe',[31] while the descriptions of the marvels Aronnax and his companions observe are clearly lifted from articles, encyclopaedias and textbooks: just as the *Nautilus*'s massive windows 'turn the ocean into a vast aquarium',[32] so this relentless cataloguing replaces nature – and the sea in particular – with a realm of information. Nature, information, capital and commodities are mapped together in Aronnax and Conseil's discussions of the submarine world: typically, the former 'looks on in wonder', while the latter 'lists, categorizes, and classifies species'.[33] It requires no great leap to recognise that this scientific colonisation is equally capital's colonisation of nature,[34] or to reformulate Aronnax's rapt gaze and Conseil's cataloguing as twin operations of the commodity form: one fetishises, the other equivalises. The game is further given away on those occasions, of which they are nearly a dozen, on which Aronnax slips from contemplation to the assigning of exchange-value, attaching prices or market values to various creatures or their parts.[35] Such transpositions sometimes take on epic proportions – 'The Gulf Stream is a huge reservoir of heat' which 'would provide enough calorific value to maintain in fusion a river of molten iron as big as the Amazon or the Missouri' – but are more generally invoked so as to naturalise the commodification of the world, as when Conseil notes petrels 'are so oily … they would … make perfect lamps! The only thing one could ask is that nature herself provide them with a wick!'[36]

This fantasy of informationalisation, which seeks to disavow the processes of commodification it euphemises, is paralleled by a fantasy of linguistic dematerialisation, which seeks to disavow human intersubjectivity. Not only are Nemo's crewmen devoid of any physical sign or token of their specific national origins, they also speak a language unknown to the surface world and presumably invented by Nemo. Both of these fantasies operate homologously to, and share in, the 'abstraction of social products and practices from the laboring bodies that generate them'.[37] This abstraction operates across all levels, from the fetishisation of the commodity that obscures the social relationships of production to the 'bipolar opposition between Net and self' that Manuel Castells argues increasingly structures our societies.[38] Information technology infrastructure, developing from such early ventures as the transatlantic telegraph cable to which Verne's novel devotes a couple of pages, has enabled the world to become 'truly global', aiding capital's dream of endless expansion; but while 'capital is global, and core production networks are increasingly globalized, the bulk of labor is local. Only an elite specialty labor force, of great strategic importance, is truly globalized'.[39] Thus, Castells argues, 'capital and labor increasingly tend to exist in different spaces and times: the space of flows and the space of places, instant time of computerized networks versus clock time of everyday life': capital now circulates – or appears to circulate – in the timeless time of instantaneous transactions and the spaceless space of instant communication, while humans must struggle to accommodate themselves to a network logic which breaks down *the rhythms, either biological or social, associated with the notion of a life-cycle*.[40]

This tension between human rhythms and capital's globalised space-time is evident from the moment Aronnax and his companions board the *Nautilus*. When their first meal is slow in coming, proletarian harpoonist Ned Land grows angry, while the bourgeois professor and his valet counsel uncomplaining subordination of the body to the submarine's schedule: 'I imagine that our appetites are ahead of the chef's bell', Aronnax comments, to which Conseil replies, 'So we'll simply have to reset them to the right time'.[41] Nemo soon reveals that the *Nautilus* runs on the 24-hour clock: 'for me there is neither night nor day, sun nor moon, but only the artificial light which I carry with me'.[42] In these class-hierarchical relationships to embodiment and time is the seed of the world Castells describes, but Nemo's identification with capital goes further than his mere kinship with the globalised professional class. On the one hand, he is concerned with reducing all materiality to a space of undifferentiated flow – a tendency best captured in his experiment to find the depth at which the sea 'possessed a constant temperature ... whatever the latitude'.[43] On the other hand, he seems to become like capital itself. His submarine, a vessel 'a century ahead of its time',[44] crosses through a channel beneath the Suez isthmus in just 20 minutes, and is thus simultaneously identified with a natural world always-already awaiting commodification *and* situated in the future of then-current commercial–imperial endeavours to carve out the Suez canal.

This sense of leaping over restrictions – over material constraints, knowledges, technological cutting-edges – and of constant striving to collapse the future back into the present is typical of Verne's fiction. For example, in *The Steam House* (1880), Captain Hood prognosticates about future human endeavours – journeys to the poles, the ocean depths, the centre of the Earth – until he goes too far, predicting voyages to the planets: 'Man, a mere inhabitant of the earth, cannot overstep its boundaries', the narrator objects, without effect.[45] Hood's opinion is shared by Michael Arden in *Around the Moon* (1870), who argues that distance effectively does not exist; it is also mapped onto the practice of science in *Journey to the Centre of the Earth* (1864), in which Professor Lidenbrock explains that 'Science ... is composed of errors, but errors that it is right to make, for they lead step by step to the truth'.[46] This passing-over of boundaries at which others have fallen forms the very structure of *The Adventures of Captain Hatteras* (1864), in which the progress of the polar expedition is marked by, and depends upon, the failure of earlier explorers. *Twenty Thousand Leagues* repeats this in miniature when Nemo recites the history, from 1600 onwards, of the most southerly positions reached by European and American vessels, each exceeding the one before it, and culminating in his own arrival at the South Pole.

There are strong affinities between this recurring pattern in Verne and Marx's description of the logic of capital, which is driven by 'contradictions which are constantly overcome but just as constantly posited'; indeed, 'in as much as it both posits a barrier *specific* to itself, and on the other side equally drives over and beyond *every* barrier, [capital] is the living contradiction'.[47] As Michael A. Lebowitz explains,

> capital *succeeds* in driving beyond all barriers and ... its development occurs through this very process. This contradiction within capital, in short, is an essential part of its movement, impulse and activity. Thus, the creation of the specifically capitalist mode of production, the growing place of fixed capital, the growth of large firms, increasing centralization of capital, development of new needs and of the world market – all these critical developments emerge as the result of capital's effort to transcend its barriers, to negate its negation.[48]

In Marx, Lebowitz argues, the (Hegelian) Limit to this potentially infinite expansion of capital is the working class – not the Abstract Proletarian, the 'subject-for-capital' that Marx modelled for analytical reasons in *Capital* – but full human beings, 'subjects-for-themselves'. Verne, however, despite his growing ambivalence about imperialist–industrial capitalist modernity, rarely even notices the working class – an absence most evident, perhaps, when Phileas Fogg and Passepartout cross France just a year after the Paris Commune and only glimpse the city, it is retrospectively reported, 'through the windows of a hackney cab and in the pouring rain', from '7.20 to 8.40 a.m., between the Gare du Nord and the Gare de Lyon'.[49]

More than a century after the publication of *Twenty Thousand Leagues*, the *Matrix* trilogy offers a similar snapshot of the structures of capital, outlining in Jameson's word the 'truth' of globalisation. In an unspecified future, the machines farm humans as an energy source. Kept perpetually unconscious, these humans, unaware of the real situation, are plugged into the Matrix, a virtual-reality world that resembles our world. Modern SF's spatialisation of class, familiar from Wells's *The Time Machine* (1895) and Lang's *Metropolis* (1926), is evident in the contrasts between the postmodern architecture of the virtual city's downtown and the subterranean existence of the last group of conscious humans. But the contradictions within *The Matrix*, and within and between its sequels, render it more complex, in a manner consonant with late-capitalism and Castells' bipolar split. This is most apparent in the films' fantasy of disembodied flight, of leaving behind what Agent Smith (Hugo Weaving) describes as the rotting flesh and stench of the human zoo. It can also be observed in the films' more general somatophobia: for example, it is all right for Trinity (Carrie-Anne Moss) to look sexy in skin-tight leather while engaged in slow-motion action sequences, but on the occasions we see characters wearing bondage gear – and who look like they might actually engage in BDSM – they are reduced to sinister signifiers.

In the context of the communicational concept of globalisation, which tends to see intra-, inter-, cross- and trans-cultural contacts as a progressive proliferation, producing 'an immense global urban intercultural festival without center',[50] many have argued for the trilogy's multiculturalism – in its conceptualisation, production, casting, audio-visual field and global success. This multiculturalist utopianism is often associated in particular with *The Matrix Reloaded*'s dance-party in Zion, the subterranean city of the last free humans: a multitude of bodies – youthful, tattooed, pierced, predominantly non-white – rave to tribal drums and techno-beats; individuals become one in defiance of the machines' imminent onslaught. It is, perhaps, the working class that Verne could not depict – not reduced to subjects-for-capital but living as subjects-for-themselves. One can even read the protagonist, Neo, in this positive light, since he is played by Keanu Reeves, a Lebanon-born Canadian Asian-Pacific passing as white in a role originally written for an African-American (Will Smith), which involves learning to fight like a Chinese (specifically, Jet Li as choreographed by Yuen Woo-Ping), and yearning to be as black – as cool – as Laurence Fishburne, who plays rebel commander Morpheus. But one can also see in these moments and images Hollywood's longstanding practices of incorporation, whereby it scavenges successful elements from other cinemas which are then sold back to the cultures from which they have been appropriated.

Reeves' ethnicity has never been an issue – he is to all intents and purposes always-already 'white' – but the *Matrix* films commodify 'blackness' and other ethnicities as images of resistance so as to allay the whiteness of Neo-the-messiah.[51] Likewise, while the non-white revolutionaries are technologically competent, thus seeming to mitigate the racial logic which typically depicts blackness as 'always oppositional to technologically driven chronicles of progress',[52] the trilogy nonetheless also replicates it: Zion's control room is, in contrast to every other human space, a dazzling white; the Architect (Helmut Baikatis) of the Matrix appears as a white man in a white suit, found in a white space after passing through a white light, while his opponent, the Oracle (Gloria Foster, Mary Alice), is a wise old black woman occupying brown/green domestic or public spaces; and Neo, who can outperform everyone else in the Matrix and is ultimately able to manifest his powers in the real world, is, of course, white, regardless of how black his clothing, accessories and comrades might be. This fundamental dissymmetry can also be seen in the dance-party, which becomes a site of public black passion between Link (Harold Perrineau) and Zee (Nona Gaye), and which is inter-cut with – and forms a backdrop for – the white romance and private lovemaking between Neo and Trinity. Zion might be the opposite of Babylon, but it is always also some New – and distinctly un-Blakeian – Jerusalem.

While much of this is undoubtedly a consequence of the racist structures of the western imaginary, it must also be seen in terms of the global economy, which has itself always been caught up in the (re)production of this imaginary. The multiculturalism of the *Matrix* films is, in Slavoj Žižek's words, 'the cultural logic of multinational capitalism' – that is,

> a disavowed, inverted, self-referential form of racism, a 'racism with a distance' – it 'respects' the Other's identity, conceiving the Other as a self-enclosed 'authentic' community towards which he, the multiculturalist, maintains a distance rendered possible by his privileged universal position. Multiculturalism is a racism which empties its own position of all positive content (the multiculturalist is not a direct racist, he doesn't oppose to the Other the *particular values* of his own culture), but nonetheless retains this position as the privileged *empty point of universality* from which one is able to appreciate (and depreciate) properly other particular cultures – the multiculturalist respect for the Other's specificity is the very form of asserting one's own superiority.[53]

This dynamic is evident in *The Matrix*'s stripping-out of certain kinds of specificity. Shot in Sydney, it suppresses the city through tight control of framing, depth of field and shifts in focus so that only a local would recognise it (the sequels ultimately replace it with CGI long shots of some über-Manhattan). Arguably nothing more than an attempt to produce a 'generic' city appropriate to the function of the Matrix, it is also typical of Hollywood production practices when financial considerations dictate shooting US-set films in Canada or overseas. This would also explain the suppression, within and without the Matrix, of local accents in favour of a 'universalised' American-ish one. Likewise, Neo can do 'his Superman thing' but he is never compared to, say, Ultraman, Diabolik or Santo. As in Verne, there is an unspoken centre, a point of 'universality'.

Such recurring tensions between fixity and fluidity are a crude impression of the uneven consolidation of the world market. On the one hand is the fantasy of a world transformed into information-capital – not only is the diegetic world of the Matrix composed entirely of code, represented by lines of digits cascading down computer monitors outside the Matrix and becoming visible to the resurrected Neo within it, but also extra-diegetically of digitised images on the cinema screen itself – and on the other is a longing for certainty, whether of premodern religion (prophecies, Zion's temple, Gnostic allusions) or rational, modern space-time.

Jameson suggests that the appearance of spatial discontinui-ties – 'doors that literally open onto other worlds, that connect radically distinct types of spaces whose difference can range from worldly to otherworldly' – characteristic of A.E. van Vogt's 'Golden Age' SF can be read 'as a virtual allegory of the brutal and abrupt world-displacements of Americans at war' to which van Vogt's own 'displacements, from western Canada to [Ottawa], and thence to Los Angeles, sensitized him in advance', or as creating an effect of juxtapositions with other worlds, 'something like tourism before the Second World War'.[54] With post-war consolidation of the world market, these disjunctions seem to become increasingly part of everyday life. Unsurprisingly, then, they are common in the trilogy: between the Matrix and the world; between the world and other simulated spaces (the dojo, weapons shop, station platform); in the corridor of backdoors into the Matrix programme; and in the frantic pursuit of the Keymaker (Randall Duk Kim), who can open doors onto other spaces which then disconnect when the door is closed. Similarly, the films also play across discursive levels. One soon learns that all dialogue is to be taken literally: the dead metaphors that clutter language unnoticed are retro-activated by later events, while the figurative dimension often turns out to have been evacuated. Character names seem to possess allegorical meaning, but never do more than merely invite one to read the films allegorically.[55] Such lit-eralisations and pinnings-down promise certainty; their constant refusal tends instead to destabilise. Consequently, in its recurring non-contiguities and unreliabilities, the trilogy appears as yet another allegory of the experience of unmappable late-capital: an era in which colonial structures might be perpetuated but in which there are now 'only colonies, no colonizing countries', and in which capital has become effectively 'an anonymous global machine blindly running its course'.[56]

Intertwined with this tendency towards equivalisation, in which everything becomes a dematerialised value in circulation – evoked by Agent Smith who, having freed himself from the machines, reproduces without limit or control – is the yearning for knowability. Within the Matrix, the rebels communicate via cell phones, mobile and thus effectively placeless nodes in a centreless network; but they depend upon geographically specific phones – fixed landlines – in order to enter and exit the virtual world; and when they race through the maze of building interiors and rooftops, they rely upon an 'operator' outside the Matrix who can map their place within it. Neo ultimately arranges peace with the machines – fixed entities – by removing the threat posed to them (and the humans) by the infinitely replicable Smith, who has even found a way out of the Matrix into the physical world – like capital crossing yet another barrier specific to itself.

These contradictory tendencies are evoked in *The Matrix*'s conclusion. After Neo has achieved the impossible, gaining perfect knowledge of the system while situated within it, he takes to the air to the sound of Rage Against the Machine's 'Wake Up'. This track evokes the modern guitar-based rock of earlier moments of countercultural resistance, but its reliance on digital recording technologies shifts its signification, rendering it postmodern information-capital. According to the Architect, previous versions of the Matrix failed because of a residual human element that resisted the perfection of the virtual world. That trace is audible in 'Wake Up': in the space between the sound of rebellious pleasure and the sound of cash registers, and between community and community, the communicational and the economic, use-value and exchange-value, the self and the Net. It is the sound of the subject-for-itself – the Limit at which capital fails.

These accounts of *Twenty Thousand Leagues* and the *Matrix* trilogy are not intended as interpretations so much as observations of the negative space they leave behind in the shot bag of the world in which they were produced, circulated and consumed. Despite this common capacity of SF, there is no necessary relationship between Marxism and SF – although there has always been a close one. The 'most important figures in the development of Anglophone SF ... between the mid 1880s and the beginning of the First World War – Edward Bellamy, William Morris, H.G. Wells and Jack London – were all socialists',[57] a trend continued in the UK through the mid-century writers Olaf Stapledon and George Orwell, the various leftists and anarchists associated with Michael Moorcock's *New Worlds* magazine in the 1960s and 1970s, and current writers such as Iain M. Banks, Gwyneth Jones, Ken MacLeod and China Miéville. In the US in the late 1930s and 1940s, the New York-based SF fan group, the Futurians, were often just as concerned with radical politics, and included in their number major writers of the next two or three decades (Isaac Asimov, James Blish, Damon Knight, Cyril M. Kornbluth, Judith Merril, Frederik Pohl); later writers of note include Samuel R. Delany, L. Timmel Duchamp, Eric Flint, Ursula K. Le Guin, Marge Piercy, Mack Reynolds, Kim Stanley Robinson and Joanna Russ.[58] Moreover, from the emergence of SF studies as an academic discipline in the 1970s, Marxism has provided a major critical–theoretical lens through which to understand the genre.

By the late 1960s, less than a dozen critical books on SF, including collections of essays and reviews by Blish and Knight, had been published in the US. There had also been letters, editorials and reviews in the SF magazines, and critical commentary in fanzines, for over four decades, and, since 1959, the *Newsletter of the Conference on Science Fiction of the MLA*, which became the journal *Extrapolation*. The Science Fiction Research Association and the Society for Utopian Studies were founded in 1970 and 1975, respectively. In the UK, the Science Fiction Foundation was founded (1971), and launched *Foundation: The Review of Science Fiction* (1972).[59] Tom Moylan, reflecting on the 'political and intellectual milieu' of this period, sees it as one in which 'democratic opposition to the system of postwar capitalism and contending superpower bureaucracies [was] relatively more substantial, and occupied greater "liberated zones" of praxis, before the ravages of counter-revolution in the 1980s'.[60] He describes a vast 'array of intellectual and cultural activity', from neighbourhood organisations and film societies to festivals and rock bands – and to universities, where 'inter-, cross- and transdisciplinary work in African-American, gay and lesbian, Third World, women's and other "Studies" programmes emerged as the intellectual and pedagogical dimension of the political struggles for self-determination'.[61] Curricula began to take greater account of popular culture. Leftist theory and criticism were reinvigorated, including 'a refunctioned critical Marxism, a new wave of Marxist or socialist feminism and gay and lesbian studies, the maturation of critical ecological studies, and expanding anti-, non- and post-Western scholarship'.[62]

This was the state of play when 'the Suvin event' occurred.

December 1972 saw the appearance of Suvin's 'On the Poetics of the Science Fiction Genre' – later subsumed into his *Metamorphoses of Science Fiction: On the Poetics and History of a Literary Genre* (1979). In 1973, with R.D. Mullen, he launched and edited *Science Fiction Studies*, the most theoretically sophisticated of the SF journals, with strong Marxist and feminist tendencies. From that moment on, SF theory and criticism have inhabited – not by any means always contentedly – the Suvin event horizon, or attempted to escape it.

Suvin argued that SF is the 'literature of cognitive estrangement', a 'literary genre whose necessary and sufficient conditions are the presence and interaction of estrangement and cognition, and whose main formal device is an imaginative framework alternative to the author's empirical environment' and which is 'distinguished by the narrative dominance or hegemony of a fictional "novum" (novelty, innovation) validated by cognitive logic'.[63] One might question the efficacy, even the possibility, of defining a genre. One might point to the many problems with Suvin's definition, such as its replication of Althusser's distinction between science and ideology, or its exclusion from the genre of many of the works popularly considered to be SF. One might argue, like Edward James, that ultimately it merely 'rephras[es] the stance of the past rather than establishing totally new grounds on which to base [SF] criticism' but does so in 'quite a different register'[64] (whether in terms of its angular and 'difficult' prose, imbued with European critical theory, or of the cultural capital it accrued when published in book form by Yale University Press). One might develop alternative approaches to the genre, such as H. Bruce Franklin's or John Rieder's explorations of SF's complicity in empire, or Delany's leftist post-structuralism, or Donna Haraway's ironic socialist–feminist thick descriptions of techno-scientific culture. One might, like Carl Freedman, even consider Suvin's definition as 'not only fundamentally sound but indispensable'.[65] However one responds to it, Suvin's definition (and its elaboration) itself arrived like a novum, reordering SF theory and criticism around it, idiosyncratically and contingently wedding SF to Marxism.

The essays that follow wrestle, in various ways, with the Suvin event.

Red Planets is divided into three sections: 'Things to Come', 'When Worlds Collide' and 'Back to the Future'. The first is concerned with the utopian trace of Ernst Bloch's Not-Yet. Matthew Beaumont distinguishes two kinds of SF text – those set in other worlds and those in which another world intrudes into our own – which challenge our perception of the real without falling into the irrationalism typically associated with fantasy or horror. He pays particular attention to Ian Watson's 'Slow Birds' (1983), which is set in an alternate Earth into which elements of our own intrude and from which they return, occasionally bearing traces of this other Earth – a dialectical traffic that brings alterity into being. William J. Burling considers the representation of the work of art within utopian SF from the perspective of social relations. The fictional arts in novels by Ursula K. Le Guin and Kim Stanley Robinson constitute a *mise en abyme* of the utopian text's own struggle to imagine a world beyond capital. Carl Freedman contrasts film noir's deflationary tendency with SF's inflationary tendency as a kind of corollary of Marxism's intertwined project of analysing the logic of capital and struggling for revolutionary liberation. He focuses on SF's drive to transcend the mundane empirical norm, to uncover the richness and depth of reality beyond constraint, drawing out the (often critically suppressed) visionary tradition out of which SF has grown within the Suvinian paradigm. John Rieder contests Freedman's influential argument that the tension between literary SF's cognitive estrangement and cinematic SF's spectacle renders cinematic SF 'intrinsically impossible'.[66] While *Until the End of the World* (Wenders, 1991) both elaborates and succumbs to this tension, he argues, its mapping of colonialist and anti-colonialist discourses onto this fracture functions to critique SF's complicity in colonialism, while opening the prospect of a future beyond it.

'When Worlds Collide' points towards Haraway's contention that SF is good for thinking with, bringing SF texts and Marxist theory into collision so as to help us conceptualise, and act within, the current conjuncture. Steven Shaviro examines recent SF about life after the Singularity – the supposedly imminent moment in which the line charting technological progress goes vertically off the graph. Considering the work of futurists such as Ray Kurzweil and Hans Moravec alongside Charles Stross's novel *Accelerando* (2005), he suggests the extent to which this 'rapture of the nerds' is a fantasy of capital, and that the Singularity might already have happened. Sherryl Vint treats SF prose fiction not in terms of traditional literary study, but as a core component of the western technological imaginary. Inspired by Cordwainer Smith's stories about animals engineered into sentience but denied human status, and drawing upon work from the emerging inter-discipline of animal studies, she uses SF to reconsider the labour theory of value. While the concept of 'animal labour power' is a non sequitur in orthodox classical Marxism, Smith's stories demonstrate that Marx's concept of labour *is* based upon a speciesism that contemporary science is increasingly calling into question. Recognition of the labour power and alienation of animals as well as humans, and of the social relations that we share, points to political allegiances necessary in the ongoing global extinction event *and* to a route out of our alienation from nature. Phillip Wegner analyses the complex formal and thematic structure of Ken MacLeod's *Fall Revolution* quartet (1995–99), which is organised so as to render impossible final judgements on the actions it depicts *and* to demonstrate that foreknowledge of consequences is impossible. He reads these novels – and the period of their composition, between the fall of the Berlin wall and the fall of the twin towers – in terms of Georg Lukács's *Augenblick*: that is, the moment that is open to revolutionary action, whose very existence demonstrates that things do not need to turn out the way that they did, and which demands that we act as if the Not-Yet could arrive, enter history, transform the world.

'Back to the Future' returns us to the Suvin event, suggesting that SF studies could be very different to the SF studies we have. Iris Luppa considers critical reactions in Weimar Germany to the SF films of the period, especially Fritz Lang's *Frau im Mond* (1929), which most leftist critics dismissed as a sentimental potboiler betraying its own rational, utopian, technological imaginary. Greater attention to its popularity, and to the popular culture it exemplifies and self-reflexively represents, might have enabled more fruitful interactions between the intellectuals and the masses with whom they needed to ally. For those familiar with Suvin's *Metamorphoses* (which does not really consider any twentieth-century writers to emerge from the American pulp and paperback tradition) and the Marxist canon of 'critical utopians'[67] (Delany, Le Guin, Piercy, Russ) that emerged in the 1970s, this situation is extremely resonant. Rob Latham maps the more-or-less simultaneous emergence of Marxist geography and New Wave visions of the future city. He shows how the contradictions of Thomas M. Disch's *334* (1972) reveal the dystopianism of the 'empirically' real world from which the SF text is supposed to distinguish itself. SF's ability to think about the same kind of urban spaces and problems analysed by David Harvey and Manuel Castells suggests a potential dialogue that Marxist criticism never pursued. Darren Jorgensen, engaging more directly with 1970s Marxist SF theory and criticism, argues that it is haunted by – and predicated upon – the failures of May 1968 that are evident in the canonisation of Philip K. Dick and Ursula Le Guin and in the SF theory of Suvin and Jameson. Considering a pair of Jameson's essays on these authors that were central to the development of SF studies in the 1970s (and which appeared in a journal edited by Suvin), he argues that a more radical understanding of SF – one capable of aiding the development of revolutionary consciousness – would have emerged from the 'scientific Marxism' of Louis Althusser (against which Jameson argued in his *The Political Unconscious: Narrative as a Socially Symbolic Act* (1981)). He contends that we need to reconnect with revolutionary struggle, to re-imagine what we do in terms of revolutionary experience and possibility, rather than of failure. Andrew Milner locates the Suvin event within its specific historical conjuncture, exposing the logic of its prescriptions and opening up the tensions between the two halves of Suvin's *Metamorphoses* – the poetics and the history of SF. Drawing on Raymond Williams' concepts of 'selective tradition' and 'structure of feeling', he urges Marxist critics to turn to SF as it exists in the world and is commonly experienced across a range of media.

Some speculate that, if one could plunge through the heart of a black hole, one might emerge in a different universe. Rather than trying to escape the Suvin event horizon, China Miéville's afterword pursues Suvin's logic with utter fidelity, just to see where it might take us.

The editors would like to thank their contributors and other comrades who have always welcomed, with great generosity, our engagements with both Marxism and SF. Special thanks to John Newsinger, who gave us a title.

Notes

1. In Hugo Gernsback's editorial introduction to the first issue of the American pulp SF magazine, *Amazing Stories* (April 1926).
2. For a sense of the range of forms of SF, see the opening section of Mark Bould, Andrew M. Butler, Adam Roberts and Sherryl Vint, eds, *The Routledge Companion to Science Fiction* (London: Routledge, 2009).
3. See Mimi Hall, 'Sci-fi writers join war on terror', *USA Today* 29. Available at www.usatoday.com/tech/science/2007-05-29-deviant-thinkers-security_N.htm (accessed 7 January 2009).

4. Fredric Jameson, *Archaeologies of the Future: The Desire Called Utopia and Other Science Fictions* (London: Verso, 2005), pp. 384–5.
5. Ibid., p. 384.
6. Fredric Jameson, 'Notes on Globalization as a Philosophical Issue', in Fredric Jameson and Masao Miyoshi, eds, *The Cultures of Globalization* (Durham: Duke University Press, 1998), p. 54.
7. John Rieder's *Colonialism and the Emergence of Science Fiction* (Middletown: Wesleyan University Press, 2008) outlines what is involved in the emergence of a genre and lays to rest the distracting notion of a single, originating text (pp. 15–21).
8. H.G. Wells, 'The Rediscovery of the Unique'. Available at http://gaslight.mtroyal.ab.ca/rediscnq.htm (accessed 18 July 2008).
9. Pierre Macherey, *A Theory of Literary Production*, transl. Geoffrey Wall (London: Routledge & Kegan Paul, 1986), p. 166.
10. Timothy Unwin, 'The Fiction of Science, or the Science of Fiction', in Edmund Smyth, ed., *Jules Verne: Narratives of Modernity* (Liverpool: Liverpool University Press, 2000), p. 46.
11. Darko Suvin, *Metamorphoses of Science Fiction: On the Poetics and History of a Literary Genre* (New Haven: Yale University Press, 1979), p. 150.
12. Marc Angenot, 'Jules Verne: The Last Happy Utopianist', in Patrick Parrinder, ed., *Science Fiction: A Critical Guide* (London: Longman, 1979), p. 19.
13. Suvin, *Metamorphoses*, p. 153.
14. Angenot, 'Jules Verne', p. 25.
15. Jules Verne, *Twenty Thousand Leagues under the Seas*, transl. William Butcher (Oxford: Oxford University Press, 1998), pp. 6, 7.
16. Jameson, 'Notes on Globalization', pp. 56–7.
17. Verne, *Twenty Thousand Leagues*, pp. 67–8.
18. Jameson, 'Notes on Globalization', p. 57.
19. Martin Willis, *Mesmerists, Monsters, and Machines: Science Fiction and the Cultures of Science in the Nineteenth Century* (Kent: Kent State University Press, 2006), p. 144.
20. Verne, *Twenty Thousand Leagues*, pp. 10, 11, 15.
21. Ibid., p. 62.
22. Ibid., pp. 62, 63, 153, 177.
23. Ibid., pp. 68, 121.
24. Verne's publisher, Pierre-Jules Hetzel, vetoed casting Nemo as a Polish nobleman who had lost family, friends and nation to Russian despotism, but the novel retains traces of this sentiment, as well as of similar anti-American, anti-Austrian, anti-British and anti-Turkish

feeling. *The Mysterious Island* (1874–75) construes Nemo as a victim of British imperialism in India.

25. Verne, *Twenty Thousand Leagues*, p. 206.
26. Ibid., p. 87.
27. John Rieder, *Colonialism and the Emergence of Science Fiction* (Middletown: Wesleyan University Press, 2008), p. 28.
28. Jameson, 'Notes on Globalization', p. 56.
29. Sherryl Vint and Mark Bould, 'All That Melts Into Air Is Solid: Rematerialising Capital in *Cube* and *Videodrome*', *Socialism and Democracy* 42 (2006), pp. 218.
30. Verne, *Twenty Thousand Leagues*, p. 54.
31. Verne, *Twenty Thousand Leagues*, p. 120. This is also part of the novel's proto-ecological sensibility: Aronnax refers to an 'inexhaustible' nature 'beyond man's destructive bent', but is gradually persuaded otherwise by Nemo's refusal to hunt whales (p. 287) or walruses (p. 308) for sport; Aronnax notes geothermal cooling across geological timescales (p. 240), but also that the Gulf Stream is believed to be changing 'speed and direction' on a historical timescale, with 'changes of an unforeseeable nature' for 'the climate of Europe' (p. 349).
32. Willis, *Mesmerists*, p. 157.
33. Ibid., p. 154.
34. Indeed, his supposed ambition 'to summarise all the knowledge – geographical, geological, physical, astronomical – accumulated by modern science, and to recast in an appropriate form, the history of the universe' was even formulated in the ballyhoo with which his publisher prefaced the first volume of Verne's complete works (see Macherey, *Theory of Literary Production*, p. 163).
35. See, for example, Verne, *Twenty Thousand Leagues*, pp. 74, 75, 115, 189, 192–5, 202, 305, 309.
36. Ibid., pp. 350, 304.
37. David McNally, *Bodies of Meaning: Studies on Language, Labor, and Liberation* (New York: SUNY Press, 2001), p. 1.
38. Manuel Castells, *The Information Age: Economy, Society and Culture, Volume I: The Rise of the Network Society*, second edn (Oxford: Blackwell, 2000), p. 3.
39. Castells, *Information Age*, pp. 101, 131.
40. Ibid., pp. 506, 476; italics in original.
41. Verne, *Twenty Thousand Leagues*, p. 56.
42. Ibid., p. 79.
43. Ibid., p. 163. Macherey's description of this dialectical process of winning 'rectitude' from 'a radical diversity' (*Theory of Literary Production*, p. 182) resonates with the 'standardization on an

unparalleled new scale' that Jameson associates with the consolidation of the world market ('Notes on Globalization', p. 57).

44. Verne, *Twenty Thousand Leagues*, p. 212.
45. Cited in Macherey, *Theory of Literary Production*, p. 167.
46. Jules Verne, *Journey to the Centre of the Earth*, transl. William Butcher (Oxford: Oxford University Press, 1992), p. 146.
47. Karl Marx, *Grundrisse* (New York: Vintage, 1973), pp. 410–11, 421; italics in original.
48. Michael A. Lebowitz, *Beyond Capital: Marx's Political Economy of the Working Class*, second edn (Houndmills: Macmillan, 2003), p. 13.
49. Jules Verne, *Around the World in Eighty Days*, transl. William Butcher (Oxford: Oxford University Press, 1995), p. 32.
50. Jameson, 'Notes on Globalization', p. 66.
51. Arguably, the presence of Cornel West – as Councillor West in the sequels and on DVD commentaries – similarly functions as a celebrity endorsement for certain market segments, just as Susie Bright did for *Bound* (Wachowski brothers, 1996).
52. Alondra Nelson, 'Introduction: Future Texts', *Social Text* 71 (2002), p. 1.
53. Slavoj Žižek, 'Multiculturalism, Or, the Cultural Logic of Multinational Capitalism', *New Left Review* 225 (1997). Available at www.newleftreview.org (accessed 27 July 2008).
54. Jameson, *Archaeologies*, pp. 320, 323, 70.
55. On such 'postmodern allegories', see Brian McHale, *Postmodernist Fiction* (London: Methuen, 1987).
56. Žižek, 'Multiculturalism'.
57. Istvan Csicsery-Ronay, Jr., 'Marxist Theory and Science Fiction', in Edward James and Farah Mendlesohn, eds, *The Cambridge Companion to Science Fiction* (Cambridge: Cambridge University Press, 2003), p. 114.
58. For a more detailed account, see William J. Burling, 'Marxism', in Bould et al., *Routledge Companion to Science Fiction*, pp. 236–45.
59. See Edward James, 'Before the *Novum*: The Prehistory of Science Fiction Criticism', in Patrick Parrinder, ed., *Learning from Other Worlds: Estrangement, Cognition, and the Politics of Science Fiction and Utopia* (Liverpool: Liverpool University Press, 2000), pp. 19–35.
60. Tom Moylan. '"Look into the dark": On Dystopia and the *Novum*', in Parrinder, *Learning from Other Worlds*, p. 51.
61. Ibid.
62. Ibid., p. 52.
63. Suvin, *Metamorphoses*, pp. 4, 7–8, 63.

64. James, 'Before the *Novum*', pp. 32, 33.
65. Carl Freedman, *Critical Theory and Science Fiction* (Hanover: Wesleyan University Press, 2000), p. 17. Freedman goes on to offer a major corrective to Suvin's definition, shifting its emphasis from cognition to the text's 'cognition effect'.
66. Carl Freedman, 'On Kubrick's *2001*: Form and Ideology in Science-Fiction Cinema', in Freedman, *The Incomplete Projects: Marxism, Modernity, and the Politics of Culture* (Middletown: Wesleyan University Press, 2002), p. 111.
67. See Tom Moylan, *Demand the Impossible: Science Fiction and the Utopian Imagination* (London: Methuen, 1987).

Part I

Things to Come

1

THE ANAMORPHIC ESTRANGEMENTS OF SCIENCE FICTION

Matthew Beaumont

Linear Perspective is a machine for annihilating reality, an infernal yawn that swallows everything wherein the vanishing-point functions. Conversely, reverse perspective, like a fountain of reality spurting into the world, serves to generate reality, extract it from non-being and advance it into reality.

Pavel Florensky[1]

Perhaps the most famous UFO to appear in the history of European painting is the saucer-shaped object that slices silently across the pictorial space of 'The Ambassadors' (1533). Hans Holbein the Younger's double portrait of Jean de Dinteville and Georges de Selve is a meditation on the intellectual and artistic accomplishments of Europe in an epoch of imperial expansion. The luxuriously robed table at the centre of the composition, framed by the casually posed forms of the French ambassadors themselves, is artfully heaped with exquisite objects pertaining to the disciplines of geometry, astronomy, mathematics and music. The instruments of enlightenment that are at once understatedly and ostentatiously displayed in this picture – the terrestrial and celestial globes, for example – are thus also the instruments of colonial domination. Holbein's tableau is a complicated, perhaps contradictory celebration of the apparently unassailable cultural authority that these Catholic statesmen embody. It emanates a sense of calm, almost sanctimonious command that discreetly conceals the messier economic and political premises of this cultural authority, even as it ultimately advertises them. Holbein sublimates the ambassadors'

Jean de Dinteville and Georges de Selve ('The Ambassadors'),
by Hans Holbein the Younger (© The National Gallery)

power in the familiar double sense of both elevating or exalting it
and making it seem socially acceptable.

The surface of the portrait participates in this process of
signification, deploying the comparatively recent techniques of oil
painting both to spiritualise the objects it depicts and to emphasise
their materiality. Holbein's reproduction of the different textures
that define these objects, which enables the spectator to appraise
them sensuously as well as visually, mimes the combination of
expensive materials and specialist, skilled labour that comprises
them, and thus represents their status as commodities. As John
Berger points out, in the sixteenth century the increasingly popular
techniques of oil painting publicised the emergence of capital
accumulation, 'which was dynamic and which found its only

sanction in the supreme buying power of money'; oil paintings therefore 'had to be able to demonstrate the desirability of what money could buy'.[2] Of course, in addition to demonstrating that the objects they depicted were commodities, oil paintings increasingly advertised themselves as commodities. The richly delicate surfaces of the scientific and artistic instruments exhibited on the table are contained and comprehended by the richly delicate surface of the composition itself. Insofar as it implicitly insists on a formal analogy between these instruments and the ornamented, framed oak board on which they are painted, 'The Ambassadors' therefore also insists on a material analogy. It celebrates the commodity status of painting itself at the same time as it claims that painting is the supreme medium for sanctifying the accoutrements of secular authority.

So Holbein identifies the spectator standing before this portrait as someone for whom the consecrated objects soliciting attention from the centre of the composition, and the cultural values inscribed in them, are in the end purchasable, possessable commodities. 'The Ambassadors' is, then, an allegorical painting about the spectator's accumulation, in the epoch of nascent capitalism, of what Pierre Bourdieu called 'symbolic capital' – if this formulation is understood to mean 'economic or political capital that is disavowed, misrecognized and therefore recognized, hence legitimate, a "credit" which, under certain conditions, and always in the long run, guarantees "economic" profits'.[3] It dramatises the dialectical relationship between symbolic and economic capital whereby each appears to be the precondition of the other. And it does so partly through the spectator's identification with Dinteville and Selve: the spectator stands opposite the table situated between them, so as to complete a triangular relationship that institutionalises inclusion in the social sphere that they occupy and to which the spectator aspires. Their coolly inclusive gaze, both seductive and faintly defiant, reinforces the sense that the spectator is a tolerated presence in this sphere. Holbein's painstaking reconstruction of the three-dimensional space inhabited by the ambassadors – which is based on an elaborate application of perspective, as the geometric patterns on the mosaic floor most obviously indicate – also contributes to this process of identification, because it extends to the spectator the sense of effortless command that these statesmen emblematise. In the virtual space mapped out by this composition the spectator is transmuted into a proprietor potentially in command of its constituent objects. The painting thus 'recruits' the spectator, to put it in Althusserian terms, transforming the individual into a subject.[4] Specifically, it transforms the spectator into a bourgeois subject (in contradistinction, for instance, to a christian one).

To pursue this interpretation is of course to ignore the most striking element of the portrait: the alien image that slides across the picture's surface and inauspiciously ruptures its perspective. Bruno Latour vividly describes its distortive impact on the spectator's relationship to the painting:

> If the attendants at the National Gallery of London allow you to kneel down at the painting's left side, your face as if touching the varnished pigment, this unidentified flying object will appear to be a skull – the accepted symbol of the many memento mori painted at the time. But then, how will the fiery Ambassadors appear? As a grotesque and distorted medley of bright and meaningless shapes. If the Ambassadors are straightened up, the skull is skewed. If the skull is rectified, the two Frenchmen are slanted, fleeing away like flying saucers.[5]

The image of the skull introduces into the composition an optic that is incompatible with that of the stable spectator constructed by the laws of perspective: to reconfigure the incomprehensible image as one that is mimetic of a recognisable object, the spectator must scrutinise it from an angle that violently disfigures the ambassadors and the instruments that symbolise their achievements. In forcing the spectator into this contorted, almost abject posture, Holbein deliberately undermines the illusion of solid, three-dimensional reality that he has so carefully organised. The composition is dramatically decomposed and its ideological premises – in particular the assumption that the economic and symbolic forms of capital it depicts can in some uncomplicated sense be claimed or attained – are completely upset. From this perspective, reality itself appears as a smear.

The death's head thus makes the cultural and political ambition to which the spectator had initially accommodated himself seem meaningless. It does so not by emblematically reminding the spectator of death, as in the conventional inclusion of a memento mori (the ornament on Dinteville's hat does this, but the abstractness, and hence inadequateness, of its allusion to death is underlined by its near-imperceptibility). Instead, the skull that slants across the surface of Holbein's painting aggressively defamiliarises and radicalises the tradition of the memento mori. Its superficial abstraction is in fact an index of its concreteness, its almost excessive immediacy. It introduces the idea of death at the level of form rather than content. The spectator is forced physically to transform, even to abase, herself in the face of this death's head. Rather than communicate death's dominion algebraically, deploying a traditional emblem drained of signification, Holbein communicates it poetically, as Victor Shklovsky might have put it, by inscribing it on the spectator's body.[6] The monstrous, distorted skull does not so much represent as enact death's ontological interruption of life.

The perspectival device so adventurously used by Holbein to distort the death's head in 'The Ambassadors' has since the early seventeenth century been known as *anamorphosis* (from the Greek meaning to 'form again' or 'transform'). Jurgis Baltrušaitis emphasises its philosophical as well as optical importance for the history of representation:

> Anamorphosis ... plays havoc with elements and principles; instead of reducing forms to their visible limits, it projects them outside themselves and distorts them so that when viewed from a certain point they return to normal. The system was established as a technical curiosity, but it embraces a poetry of abstraction, an effective mechanism for producing optical illusion and a philosophy of false reality.[7]

It is as a philosophy of false reality, or, more precisely, a poetics of alternative realities, that anamorphosis interests me. An anamorphic image posits the coded presence of an almost unimaginable reality that momentarily obtrudes on ideologically constituted reality, thereby rendering it arbitrary, ontologically inconsistent. Holbein's skull, for example, is metonymic of a domain in which the commodities that advertise the ambassadors' economic, political and symbolic capital have neither exchange-value nor use-value. From an anamorphic perspective, the empirical reality so painstakingly reconstructed in this painting is emptied of signification and forced to compete with an almost completely incompatible alternative that threatens to be even more compelling. The effect of anamorphosis, philosophically speaking, is therefore that of extreme relativisation. Anamorphic perspective radically subjectifies the act of seeing, and so exposes the fact that linear perspective, dependent on the notion that there is one, motionless point from which the subject can adequately perceive the object, is far from objective. Anamorphosis is an immanent critique of perspective, creating what Daniel Collins calls an 'eccentric observer', a spectator whose dynamic, tangential relationship to the picture plane undermines 'those one-eyed regimes built upon singular assumptions about the proper point of view'.[8] It demonstrates that the dominant perception of reality is not natural but cultural; and this, potentially, is politically enabling, because it reveals that reality can be altered.

Anamorphosis was first employed as a pictorial effect in the early sixteenth century, by both Erhard Schön, a student of Albrecht Dürer, and Holbein – although in the late fifteenth century Leonardo da Vinci had in his notebooks described anamorphic deformations of perspective. It became a particularly modish form of optical experimentation from the mid seventeenth century, when cylindrical mirrors and other catoptric devices were popularly used to create its characteristic effects. Jean-François Niceron, adopting Gaspar Schott's neologism, theorised anamorphosis in *La Perspective curieuse* (1638), defining instances of it as 'figures belonging to normal vision and which, away from the predetermined view-point, seem distorted and nonsensical, but seen from the proper view-point will appear correctly proportioned'.[9] Niceron and his associates at the French convent in Rome also explored its metaphysical implications, using anamorphic representations to interpret 'the hidden spiritual order of God's creation, which to the casual eye merely seems a chaos of disparate forms'.[10] Thereafter, anamorphosis appeared as little more than an artistic curiosity, an archaic technical device for producing amusing optical illusions.

However, this process of prettification was significantly challenged by avant-gardists in the early twentieth century. The surrealists, whose 'fondness' for 'The Ambassadors' has been documented,[11] implicitly restored the political dimension of anamorphosis in the 1920s. Surrealist artists effectively questioned the Cartesian assumption that there can be a 'proper view-point', and so emphasised that anamorphosis is only an extreme example of the arbitrariness of perspectival rules.[12] For example, the violent distortions of Salvador Dalí's *Baigneuse* (1928) dramatise the impossibility of arriving at a supposedly rational or objective representation of reality. Arguably, this surrealist reclamation of anamorphic forms prompted the resuscitation, in the last half-century, of the concept of anamorphosis in the context of philosophical discourse about the subject. In the 1970s, Jacques Lacan – a friend of Dalí and in some senses himself a surrealist – and Jean-François Lyotard, influenced by the publication of Baltrušaitis' monograph about anamorphic art, which had appeared in Paris in 1955, produced books that used 'The Ambassadors' for the cover.[13] Lyotard's *Discours, Figure* (1971), which discusses the painting as an exemplum of his thesis that the representational planes of paintings are necessarily non-identical to themselves, reproduced a detail of the anamorphic skull in its 1978 second edition.[14] Lacan's *The Four Fundamental Concepts of Psychoanalysis* (1973), which directly compares this skull to 'Dalí's soft watches', reproduced the image in its entirety and argued that Holbein uses the anamorphic perspective of the 'gaze', identified with *objet a*, to make visible 'the subject as annihilated'.[15]

More recently, this thesis has been elaborated by Slavoj Žižek in relation to the Lacanian concept of the 'Real'. He emphasises, for example, that the anamorphic stain on the surface of 'The Ambassadors' upsets the spectator's neutral pose, 'pinning [the spectator] to the observed object itself': 'This is the point at which the observer is already included, inscribed in the observed scene – in a way, it is the point from which the picture itself looks back at us'.[16] I do not propose to reconstruct these positions in further detail, but silently to lean on them to the extent that they can illuminate the logic of estrangement characteristic of anamorphosis. For my hypothesis is that, in SF, the representation or inclusion of the alien other functions as a kind of anamorphic stain. The novum, so to speak, constitutes the point from which the SF text looks back at us, radically estranging our empirical, social environment and revealing its arbitrariness, its basic fungibility.

In order to historicise this claim that the defamiliarising devices characteristic of SF are equivalent to anamorphosis, it is necessary briefly to revisit 'The Ambassadors' through Stephen Greenblatt's interpretation of it in relation to Thomas More's *Utopia* (1516). Greenblatt argues that the portrait, painted half a decade after More had ceased to be Holbein's official patron, though from inside precisely the same social milieu, 'plunges us, with the sensuous immediacy and simultaneity that only a painting can achieve, into the full complexity of More's estrangement', and that it is formally analogous to *Utopia* because, in the shape of its anamorphic stain, and the esophoric perspective that it actualises, it creates a 'non-place' from which 'normal vision' is rendered impossible. This non-place, like the non-place that is the island of Utopia, reaches out and touches 'phenomenal reality, infecting it with its own alienation'.[17] The narrative displacements of More's book – more complicated than its division into halves implies – are thus the textual equivalent of those shifts in perspective that reinvent the act of representation in Holbein's painting:

> Like 'The Ambassadors', *Utopia* presents two distinct worlds that occupy the same textual space while insisting upon the impossibility of their doing so. We can neither separate them entirely nor bring them into accord, so that the intellectual gratification of radical discontinuity is as impossible to achieve as the pleasure of wholly integrated form.[18]

This dialectical relationship between 'two distinct worlds', I propose, also typifies SF's textual dynamics.

No doubt it is too simplistic to posit *Utopia* as the point of origin of SF, as of utopian fiction itself, but its importance to the emergence of the genre cannot be overstated. As the totalising attempt to imagine a perfectible society that implicitly or explicitly exposes the limits of the empirical present, utopian fiction probably takes precedence over competing literary forms – fairytales, classical myths, earthly paradises, folk stories about cockaigne, extraordinary voyages, millenarian fantasies, philosophical dialogues, technological blueprints, political manifestoes and satires, in addition to comparatively recent inventions like historical novels and gothic fictions – that helped create the preconditions for the appearance of SF as a singular phenomenon at the end of the nineteenth century. The social vision characteristic of utopian fiction, like that of SF, is the imaginative product of an epoch in which it is at least technically possible to conceptualise society, for all its contradictions, as a totality. 'It is precisely this category of totality that presides over the forms of Utopian realization', Fredric Jameson announces (assimilating SF to the notion of a utopian realisation).[19] The possible worlds devised by the older, cognate formal archetypes catalogued above are, by comparison, piecemeal.

From its inception in the early sixteenth century, utopia is imprinted by the character of capitalism, to the extent that this social formation, in contrast to feudalism, is itself increasingly totalising. 'Utopic discourse makes its appearance historically only when a mode of capitalist production is formed', Louis Marin states (though he seems to conceive of capitalism as an event rather than a process).[20] The advent of capitalism, in spite of its fitful, uneven development, provides the fundamental conditions of possibility for the utopian form, which defamiliarises society insofar as it is able to totalise it and totalises it insofar as it is able to defamiliarise it. In the dream of utopian communism that shapes *Utopia*, More universalises the class position of small independent producers who were relatively detached from the decline of feudalism, and therefore acutely conscious of its effects.[21] The ideal model of society that More constructed consequently appeared to an unprecedented extent as a totality apprehended as if from the outside. It is this emphasis on totality, enabled by the articulation of two distinct worlds occupying the same textual space, that makes utopian fiction the most important precursor to SF.

The doubled, dialectical perspective that defines both these forms constitutes a challenge to the singular, integrative perspective of realism, an aesthetic that evolved initially in painting and then in literature. Realism – the development of which was inseparable from the rise of Renaissance humanism, and especially its intellectual commitment to understanding history as a continuous process – is linear and chronological in its approach to representation. It unifies time and space. As Elizabeth Ermarth argues, 'fictional realism is an aesthetic form of consensus, its touchstone being the agreement between the various viewpoints made available by a text'.[22] Realist literature constructs its reader as the site at which this consensus about what can be identified as objective, in fictional terms, is imaginatively coordinated; and in this respect it is like realist painting, which exploits perspective to position the spectator at the point at which it is possible to achieve an illusion of objectivity. In both cases, the apparent selfsameness of the empirical world is reinforced. 'The consensus of realism', Ermarth continues, 'produces in literature a rationalization of consciousness analogous to the rationalization of sight evident in realistic painting'.[23] Utopian fiction and SF, which are themselves of course partially predicated on this realist consensus, nonetheless complicate it, more or less effectively, by introducing an anamorphic perspective. If *Utopia* 'both uses and abandons techniques proper to realism'[24] at the moment of its emergence, then so does the tradition of SF that descends from it. SF, which enters its formative phase in the late nineteenth century, as the realist aesthetic atrophies, undoubtedly relies on its techniques for rationalising consciousness; in addition, though, it de-rationalises consciousness. It uses the anamorphic perspective inscribed in its representation of other times, other spaces, to de-realise this time, this space.

How then do anamorphic estrangements function in SF? Anamorphosis generally assumes two different forms in the history of painting, and this distinction is reproduced in SF. In the more common form, the entire composition is anamorphic

– as in Niceron's experiments in perspective, which effectively involved taking an image in the shape of a square and re-plotting its coordinates in the shape of a trapezoid. This composition can be identified as *an anamorphosis*. In the less common form, the composition is dominated by linear perspective but incorporates one anomalous, anamorphic image – as in 'The Ambassadors'. This image, as a component of the composition, can be identified as *an anamorph*. The distinction roughly corresponds to the difference between SF set excusively (or almost exclusively) in an 'unfamiliar' or irrealist world and SF set in a 'familiar' or realist world that nonetheless contains traces of an ineluctable otherness.

This schema might be clarified in relation to Darko Suvin's influential concept of the novum:

> One should say that the necessary correlate of the novum is an *alternative reality*, one that possesses a *different historical time* corresponding to different human relationships and sociocultural norms actualized by the narration. This new reality overtly or tacitly presupposes the existence of the author's empirical reality, since it can be gauged and understood only as the empirical reality modified in such-and-such ways.... [SF's] specific modality of existence is a feedback oscillation that moves from the author's and implied reader's norm of reality to the narratively actualized novum in order to understand the plot-events, and now back from those novelties to the author's reality, in order to see it afresh from the new perspective gained.[25]

This passage vividly sketches the defamiliarisation device that is characteristic of SF. It fails, however, to discriminate carefully enough between a novum that overtly 'presupposes the existence of the author's empirical reality' and one that does so 'tacitly'. In the terms that I am adumbrating, the former is an anamorph (the author's empirical reality is explicitly present in the text, and the novum is the presence of an alternative reality embedded in it) and the latter an anamorphosis (the novum is the alternative reality portrayed by the text, and the author's empirical reality, which it more or less systematically distorts, is only implicitly present).

This can be illustrated, preliminarily, through a simple comparison of two 'fantasias of possibility'[26] by H.G. Wells.

When the Sleeper Wakes (1899), in which the protagonist falls into a cataleptic sleep in 1897 and comes to consciousness again in 2100, is set almost exclusively in an unfamiliar society. In this novel, the dystopian future that Wells composes, which is a systematic estrangement of the author's present, itself constitutes an anamorphosis. So the reader, processing that future from a realist perspective, is implicitly positioned in a skewed, defamiliarising relationship to this present. In contrast, *The War of the Worlds* (1898), in which the protagonist narrates a Martian invasion of contemporary England, is set exclusively in a familiar society. However, the apocalyptic present that it depicts contains an anamorph in the form of the Martians themselves. These aliens – shapeless masses that 'heaved and pulsated convulsively' – are the anamorphic stain on Wells' portrait of *fin-de-siècle* England. 'Vital, intense, inhuman, crippled and monstrous', they are the element of the *unheimlich* excavated in England's so-called home counties. The Martians inspire 'disgust and dread' in the protagonist when he sees them creeping from 'the Thing' in which they have landed, and in an insane panic he attempts to make an escape – 'but I ran slantingly and stumbling', he reports, 'for I could not avert my face from these things'.[27] That slanting movement, caused by an obscene fascination with the aliens, perfectly describes the anamorphic perspective that this archetypal science fiction instates. The reader's attempt to comprehend these aliens, like that of the protagonist, effects an estrangement of the novel's contemporaneous setting; and this estrangement is analogous to the violent decomposition of the ambassadors and the objects beside them that occurs when the spectator is compelled to reconfigure the image of the skull from the margins of Holbein's painting.

Fredric Jameson has explored the spatial disjunction characteristic of A.E. van Vogt's narratives, in which the representations of 'two distinct spaces are like the juxtaposition of two sentences from utterances absolutely distinct and heterogeneous'. He offers the example of 'The Weapon Shop' (1942), in which the eponymous building appears abruptly in somebody's backyard one night; and he describes it in terms of 'the sudden intrusion, into normal everyday space, of a new object, whose inner volume does seem distinct from the outside world, but not yet altogether abnormally so'.[28] As an intrusion into everyday life that decisively estranges it, the shop is an anamorph. It is on such figures in SF that I finally want to focus in detail, emphasising in particular that, in spite of Jameson's description of 'the new object' in van Vogt's story as not completely abnormal, it generally assumes a more or less alien form. The inner volume of the anamorph, it might be said, has a habit of expanding, so that, even if its outer appearance does not dramatically alter, it finally incorporates 'normal everyday space'. Like the 'Blochian Novum' defined by Carl Freedman, it 'is never a single new element inserted into an essentially unchanged mundane environment, but is instead such a *radical* novelty as to reconstitute the entire surrounding world and thus, in a sense, to create (though certainly not *ex nihilo*) a new world'.[29] Once internalised, the anamorphic perspective irrevocably transforms the normal.

A good example of the spatial tension diagnosed by Jameson is *Roadside Picnic* (1972), by Arkady and Boris Strugatsky, in which the Zone – its atmosphere toxic, its rough territory dotted by exotic, incomprehensible debris – is the site of an inexplicable alien visitation. Likened by one character to the polluted spot on which travellers randomly traversing the cosmos once carelessly picnicked, it is the novel's anamorph, and from the anamorphic perspective it sets up, the empirical reality portrayed by the Strugatskys is estranged. The relationship of these competing realities is that of contiguous spaces that, in Jameson's formulation, are absolutely distinct and heterogeneous. The Zone's inner volume, though, is apparently assimilating the outside world, almost imperceptibly, so that individuals living in its environs are susceptible to experiencing it existentially, as a kind of psychotic episode. In the following passage, Redrick, one of the stalkers who scavenges for the alien objects that lie scattered inside the Zone, seems suddenly to internalise its sheer otherness as he crosses a street to reach a hotel (as if he has suddenly stepped into one of Philip K. Dick's contemporaneous novels):

He had never experienced anything like this before outside the Zone. And it had happened in the Zone only two or three times. It was as though he were in a different world. A million odors cascaded in on him at once – sharp, sweet, metallic, gentle, dangerous ones, as crude as cobblestones, as delicate and complex as watch mechanisms, as huge as a house and as tiny as a dust particle. The air became hard, it developed edges, surfaces, and corners, like space was filled with huge, stiff balloons, slippery pyramids, gigantic prickly crystals, and he had to push his way through it all, making his way in a dream through a junk-store stuffed with ancient ugly furniture … It lasted a second. He opened his eyes, and everything was gone. It hadn't been a different world – it was this world turning a new, unknown side to him. This side was revealed to him for a second and then disappeared, before he had time to figure it out.[30]

Here, it is not the stalker that is in the Zone, but the Zone that is in the stalker. Redrick momentarily glimpses 'this world' as it can be grasped from the anamorphic perspective of 'a different world'; and in this respect his hallucination allegorises the reader's experience of SF. The Zone, seen from the viewpoint of empirical reality that is embodied in the stalker's outer vision, is (to cite Wells' description of the invading Martians) 'vital, intense, inhuman, crippled and monstrous'. Conversely, empirical reality itself, seen from the viewpoint of the Zone that is realised in the stalker's inner vision, is vital, intense, inhuman, crippled and monstrous too. Holbein's anamorphic skull, which has these same irreducibly alien attributes, effects an equivalent transformation. From the perimetric point at which the stain on the composition seems comprehensible, the normal everyday space of the ambassadors appears vitally, inhumanly, monstrously other, and the objects that fill it are metamorphosed into so much exotic, incomprehensible debris.

I want to explore the operation of the SF anamorph in one final example. Ian Watson's 'Slow Birds', first published in *The Magazine of Fantasy & Science Fiction* in 1983, is a political fable about the Cold War. It is set in an unfamiliar pastoral England that is implicitly parallel to the familiar, if highly technologised England that the author extrapolates from his empirical present. The rural landscape of this superficially idyllic England, which is shaped by an archipelago of pre-industrial villages, is on closer inspection scarified by lakes of glass that lie scattered across the plains (as if the setting of Hardy's bucolic novels has been subjected to the entropic processes portrayed in Ballard's apocalyptic novels). It is the sporadic explosion of so-called 'slow birds' that causes this creeping vitrification. Slow birds are unfathomable forms with tubular metal bodies that make sudden, random appearances, travelling at an almost infinitesimally slow pace and eventually either disappearing abruptly or exploding. Each slow bird that destroys itself leaves 'a flat, circular sheet of glass', 'a polarized limited zone of annihilation' (distantly recalling *Roadside Picnic*); and these sinister spaces consequently threaten to connect up, enveloping the entire landscape in a lifeless vitric substance.[31] It transpires that the mysterious floating phenomena nicknamed 'slow birds' are nuclear Cruise missiles, deployed in a conflict between 'Russ and 'Merica. They have been diverted through this innocuous parallel universe because, characterised as it is by the extreme viscosity of its time and space, it enables them to evade being captured or neutralised. The slow birds thus 'ignore gravity', and 'dodge in and out of existence': 'They were something irrational, something from elsewhere'.[32]

The missiles, which with one exception remain inscrutable to the inhabitants of this landscape, are an anamorphic stain on this Constableseque England. Like the skull in Holbein's painting, these unidentified flying objects cast profound, penetrating shadows across the normal everyday space they traverse. They denote death of course; and the nuclear warhead is in this sense only an ancient death's head reconsituted in the peculiar socio-economic conditions of the late twentieth century. They also represent the anamorphic point from which the stabilities of this parallel, pre-industrial earth are undermined, and its pretty landscape is reconfigured, in a quietly, intermittently cataclysmic process, as an ugly smear. The unpredictable materialisation of the slow birds makes the ontological foundations of this society seem insubstantial. They are spectral – if spectrality, as Jameson has claimed, is 'what makes the present waver: like the vibrations of a heat wave through which the massiveness of the object world

– indeed of matter itself – now shimmers like a mirage'.[33] But if on the one hand the fantastical, pastoral reality constructed for the reader threatens to die out because of the destruction gradually leaking from the author's empirical, hyper-industrial reality, then on the other hand the former promises to redeem the latter. At one point a child is maliciously strapped to one of the slow birds, and consequently disappears when it dematerialises; and it is this child who, on his reappearance, explains that in a parallel universe riven by war 'the missiles shunt to and fro through time'. He describes the world to which he has abruptly returned home as the 'other possibility-world', because it represents potential redemption. 'I brought them great hope, because it meant that all life isn't finished,' he says; 'Life can go on.'[34] If the missiles constitute an anamorph in the pastoral world, the child constitutes an anamorph in the hyper-industrial world.

'Slow Birds' thus dramatises a double estrangement. Its setting is an anamorphosis in that it is an almost completely self-contained, more or less systematic distortion of the author's empirical reality; and it therefore performs an anamorphic defamiliarisation of this reality. But it also contains an anamorph, in the form of the missiles; and this anamorph therefore restores a sense of estrangement to the fantastical reality it depicts. At the same time, the missiles open up a portal. On its other side, in a symmetrical process, the world of the Cold War, 'a board game run by machines', is already anamorphically estranged.[35] And it too contains an anamorph, in the form of the child who accidentally slips from one time–space continuum into the other. So, in a complicated doubling of anamorphic perspectives, Watson brilliantly exploits the anamorph both as a dystopian figure and a utopian one. If it is a death's head from one perspective, it is an emblem of redemptive life from another. For the reader of this narrative, who must imagine herself into the position in which she is in fact already situated – that is, a capitalist society torn apart by inter-imperial conflict – the child, as a kind of ana-anamorph ('like a fountain of reality spurting into the world', in Pavel Florensky's poetic formulation), 'serves to generate reality, extract it from non-being and advance it into reality'.[36]

Notes

1. Pavel Florensky, 'Reverse Perspective', in Nicoletta Misler, ed., *Beyond Vision: Essays on the Perception of Art* (London: Reaktion, 2002), p. 212.
2. John Berger, *Ways of Seeing* (London: BBC & Penguin Books, 1972), p. 91.
3. Pierre Bourdieu, 'The Production of Belief: Contribution to an Economy of Symbolic Goods', in Randal Johnson, ed., *The Field of Cultural Production: Essays on Art and Literature* (Cambridge: Polity, 1993), p. 75.
4. Louis Althusser, 'Ideology and Ideological State Apparatuses: Notes towards an Investigation', in *Lenin and Philosophy and Other Essays*, transl. Ben Brewster (New York: Monthly Review Press, 2001), p. 118.
5. Bruno Latour, 'Opening One Eye While Closing the Other ... A Note on Some Religious Paintings', in Gordon Fyfe and John Law, eds, *Picturing Power: Visual Depiction and Social Relations* (London: Routledge, 1988), p. 16.
6. Victor Shklovsky, 'Art as Technique', in *Russian Formalist Criticism: Four Essays*, transl. Lee T. Lemon and Marion J. Reis (Lincoln: University of Nebraska Press, 1965), pp. 3–24.
7. Jurgis Baltrušaitis, *Anamorphic Art*, transl. W.J. Strachan (Cambridge: Chadwyck-Healey, 1977), p. 1.
8. Daniel L. Collins, 'Anamorphosis and the Eccentric Observer: Inverted Perspective and Construction of the Gaze', *Leonardo* 25: 1 (1992), p. 77.
9. Quoted in Baltrušaitis, *Anamorphic Art*, p. 164.
10. Martin Kemp, *The Science of Art: Optical Themes in Western Art from Brunelleschi to Seurat* (New Haven: Yale University Press, 1990), p. 211.
11. Elizabeth Cowling, 'An Other Culture', in Dawn Ades, *Dada and Surrealism Reviewed* (London: Arts Council of Great Britain, 1978), p. 460.
12. I use the adjective 'Cartesian' advisedly. Lyle Massey complicated the presupposition, influentially articulated by Erwin Panofsky, that perspective is paradigmatic of Descartes' rationalism, in 'Anamorphosis through Descartes or Perspective Gone Awry', *Renaissance Quarterly* 50 (1997), pp. 1148–89.
13. See Martin Jay, *Downcast Eyes: The Denigration of Vision in Twentieth-Century French Thought* (Berkeley: University of California Press, 1993), p. 48.
14. Jean-François Lyotard, *Discours, Figure* (Paris: Editions Klincksieck, 1978), pp. 376–9.

15. Jacques Lacan, *The Four Fundamental Concepts of Psychoanalysis*, transl. Alan Sheridan (London: Hogarth Press, 1977), p. 88.
16. Slavoj Žižek, *Looking Awry: An Introduction to Jacques Lacan through Popular Culture* (Cambridge: MIT Press, 1991), p. 91.
17. Stephen Greenblatt, *Renaissance Self-Fashioning from More to Shakespeare* (Chicago: University of Chicago Press, 1980), p. 21.
18. Ibid., p. 22.
19. Fredric Jameson, *Archaeologies of the Future: The Desire Called Utopia and Other Science Fictions* (London: Verso, 2005), p. 5.
20. Louis Marin, *Utopics: Spatial Play*, transl. Robert A. Vollrath (Atlantic Highlands: Humanities Press International, 1984), p. 198.
21. See Christopher Kendrick, 'More's Utopia and Uneven Development', *boundary 2* 13: 2/3 (1985), pp. 233–66.
22. Elizabeth Deeds Ermarth, *Realism and Consensus in the English Novel: Time, Space and Narrative*, second edn (Edinburgh: Edinburgh University Press, 1998), pp. ix–x.
23. Ibid., p. 4.
24. Ibid., p. 13.
25. Darko Suvin, *Metamorphoses of Science Fiction: On the Poetics and History of a Literary Genre* (New Haven: Yale University Press, 1979), p. 71.
26. H.G. Wells, *When the Sleeper Wakes* (London: Everyman, 1994), p. 3.
27. H.G. Wells, *War of the Worlds* (Harmondsworth: Penguin, 2005), pp. 21–2.
28. Jameson, *Archaeologies of the Future*, pp. 321, 319.
29. Carl Freedman, *Critical Theory and Science Fiction* (Hanover: Wesleyan University Press, 2000), p. 69.
30. Arkady and Boris Strugatsky, *Roadside Picnic*, transl. Antonina W. Bouis (London: Victor Gollancz, 2007), p. 67.
31. Ian Watson, 'Slow Birds', in *Slow Birds and Other Stories* (London: Victor Gollancz, 1985), p. 12. I am grateful to Chris Marsh for pointing me to this text.
32. Ibid., p. 28.
33. Fredric Jameson, 'Marx's Purloined Letter', in Michael Sprinkler, ed., *Ghostly Demarcations: A Symposium on Jacques Derrida's Specters of Marx* (London: Verso, 1999), p. 38.
34. Watson, 'Slow Birds', p. 32.
35. Ibid., p. 32.
36. Florensky, 'Reverse Perspective', p. 212.

2

ART AS 'THE BASIC TECHNIQUE OF LIFE': UTOPIAN ART AND ART IN UTOPIA IN *THE DISPOSSESSED* AND *BLUE MARS*

William J. Burling

Yet it is in this kind of attention to precise material articulations – in which and only in which specific consciousness, specific feeling is realized – that the true social practice and analysis of art must begin.

Raymond Williams[1]

Utopian novelists since at least the late nineteenth century have been interested in what the function of the arts might be, what forms art might take and, by extension, what the role of the artists might be in utopian society. Edward Bellamy and William Morris devoted considerable attention to the arts, and more recently Samuel R. Delany and Marge Piercy offer sophisticated, detailed representations of utopian arts. Few critics, however, have considered this component of utopian representation, despite artistic production standing in a privileged relationship to utopian ontological issues. Indeed, Fredric Jameson observes that 'the test of the imaginative qualities of a given utopian text' is its 'capacity to imagine properly utopian art works', and elsewhere remarks that 'the work of art within the work of art ... becomes the miniature glass in which Utopia's most glaring absences are thus reproduced with minute clarity'.[2] Neither Jameson nor any other utopian theorist, however, has proposed a methodology for interpreting 'the miniature glass' in utopian fiction.

This essay outlines such a theoretical model, offering interpretations of Ursula K. Le Guin's *The Dispossessed* (1974) and Kim Stanley Robinson's *Blue Mars* (1996). Le Guin's novel features two important concerns of her fiction which may be usefully extended to utopian fiction in general: the implications of form and function of the arts *in utopia* (utopian art); and the critical significance of art *about utopia* – that is, the representation of the arts as a usefully revealing benchmark of utopian fiction's latent, as opposed to manifest, ideological assumptions.

Le Guin is perhaps the most persistent of all authors to explore the conditions, social function and meaning of artistic practice in utopian SF. Novels and stories such as *The Left Hand of Darkness* (1969), 'The New Atlantis' (1975) and *Always Coming Home* (1985) exemplify her commitment to the centrality of the arts to meaningful human identity, both personal and collective. Her most complex and conflicted utopian meditation, however, is *The Dispossessed*, which addresses one of the fundamental challenges of utopian thinking: how to imagine and represent the *forms* the arts might take when neither religion nor commodity exchange constitutes the foundation of the arts – specifically of music, that most abstract of practices. Although she is not entirely successful in her project, its shortcomings suggest criteria for assessing the ideological integrity of any utopian representation.

The Dispossessed manifestly emphasises the centrality of the arts to collective and personal life. The narrator remarks of Anarresti (socialist) society, 'No distinction was drawn between the arts and the crafts; art was not considered as having a place in life, but as being a basic technique of life, like speech'.[3] This situation sharply opposes Urrasti (capitalist) society, where the arts are depicted purely in exchange values that have been mystified as idealist aesthetics. Art as 'basic technique of life', therefore, specifies far more than mere personal practice, entailing a collective social and cultural logic, as opposed to the dehumanising isolation resulting from commodity exchange. However, Le Guin's ostensibly progressive and humanising assumptions regarding the arts entail a fundamental ideological contradiction.

Perhaps the greatest challenge for the utopian novelist is to represent how an alternative economic system might affect other segments of the social formation, such as the arts. One way to theorise the relationship is through Marx's fundamental analytical categories for the analysis of any mode of production: the *means* and *relations* of *production* and *consumption*. With special emphasis on the arts, Bertolt Brecht modified Marx's economic apparatus to clarify how artistic and economic practices connect, and so I will employ his notion of the material apparatus to explore the production issues, while drawing from Étienne Balibar and Pierre Macherey's 'On Literature as an Ideological Form' (1974)[4] and the work of Slavoj Žižek to theorise consumption issues, especially the key philosophical category of reflection. After outlining Brecht's model and applying it to the representation of the arts in *The Dispossessed* with reference to music, I discuss 'reflection as consumption', the novel's ideological blind spot. The representation of music in Robinson's *Blue Mars* (1996) is then offered as a contrasting example, and I conclude by theorising how utopian fiction might overcome the barriers of ideological mystification in order to imagine post-capitalist social formations and the arts.

The Apparatus and the Arts

Brecht's concept of the apparatus provides a useful model for understanding the significance of form as the bearer of ideological tendencies in utopian fiction, and by extension in all art. Brecht is not the only theorist to emphasise form in this manner (Adorno, for example, commented that 'form – the social nexus of everything particular – represents the social relation in the artwork'),[5] but he does offer a particularly clear theoretical means to demythologise the claim that aesthetics is the most important factor in understanding the arts. His radical assertions that '[a]rt is merchandise, only to be manufactured by the means of production (apparati)' and that artists must not imagine 'that they have got hold of an apparatus which in fact has got hold of them' serve to ground the two main issues with which I am concerned in relation to utopian fiction.[6] By 'the apparatus' Brecht means: 1) the ways in which artistic practice conforms to and is limited by the conditions of material production specific to capitalism, which, in the main, defines the artwork as a commodity; 2) the process by which art's status as commodity defines its *formal relationship* to the dominant mode of production.[7] In other words, any work of art reproduces the assumptions underlying the social means and relations of production and consumption of capitalism – the need to generate a profit – no matter what the content might represent. The implications of social relations, in particular, are significant for interpreting Le Guin's sense of utopian art.

While Brecht is concerned with the artwork only within the capitalist mode of production, his emphasis on how the apparatus is always silently inscribed in the ontological sense of what is meant by 'the arts' can logically be extended to any other mode of production, socialist or otherwise, such as is frequently represented in utopian fiction. Form must not be understood, however, solely as the imaginative product of solitary artistic genius. Rather than being an 'object', as Raymond Williams notes, form represents 'the relations between social (collective) modes and individual projects'.[8] Form is thus a mediated process, a strategy of representation that arises spontaneously in response to the complex, evolving material and social demands of the dominant culture. The degree to which the forms of the arts, rather than their content, silently reproduce the latent 'social nexus' of capitalism when represented in the proposed utopian non- or post-capitalist mode of production serves as my analytical touchstone.

The post-capitalist society on Anarres is represented as dedicated to creating a whole new way of life based on a radical redefinition of 'common sense' that maximises mutual aid, human potential and freedom, as opposed to the contrasting Urrasti self-interest, exploitation, commodity exchange and material accumulation. Thus *The Dispossessed* connects material issues of production and consumption to the respective social formations and their arts. We must be precise, however, with respect to Le Guin's orientation. Anarres's anarchical society, where the bureaucratic mechanisms of the state have been pared to an absolute minimum, bears strong affinities to anarcho-syndicalism, rather than being an instance of Marx's 'withering away of the state'.[9] While of no impact at the initial level of analysis, this distinction eventually becomes important in its bearing on the ontological underpinnings of Le Guin's representation of the arts. Anarresti society is shown as dedicated to a definition of ideological 'common sense' that strives to maximise human potential and freedom. The Anarresti consciously refashion many elements of their former ontological paradigm (for example, a whole new language), with the result that their post-capitalist 'organic economy was too essential to the functioning of the society not to affect ethics and aesthetics'[10] – and, indeed, every other aspect of social relations. Le Guin invokes here, of course, the fundamental Marxian notion of the interrelatedness of all components of the social formation, with an emphasis on economics.

The notion of 'organic economy' is key. Le Guin implies that her vision of Anarresti society will represent a radically new sense of relations of production affecting such factors as respect, freedom and imaginative expression. Work and private life are far more highly integrated, producing pointedly utopian, non-alienated and collective effects in both individual consciousness and social relations. Let me repeat that my entire line of reasoning rejects the presumed priority of the idealist analytical category of 'aesthetics', though Le Guin herself embraces the concept, and to this point I will return in due course. With this collective 'organic economy' and concomitant apparatus of production in mind, therefore, let us examine the depiction of Anarresti music with respect to the demands of production and consumption in order to lay bare that economy's latent ontological assumptions.

Music on Anarres

The social context of music on Anarres differs strikingly from that on Urras, the latter representing our own commodity-exchange status quo. Indeed, the conditions on Urras do not require specific illumination, as we will recognise them by their opposite number on Anarres. Shevek, the protagonist, states,

> Music is a cooperative art, organic by definition, social. It may be the noblest form of social behavior we're capable of. It's certainly one of the noblest

jobs an individual can undertake. And by its nature, by the nature of any art, it's a sharing. The artist shares, it's the essence of his act.[11]

On Anarres, therefore, music is represented as cooperatively social, not individualistic and isolating, and certainly not subject to individual material ownership. Thus, neither Shevek nor any of his comrades is shown as claiming music as a personal material possession, but, as we shall see, for all of its presumed social purity, Anarresti music maintains a *latent* propertarian relationship through the process of reflection. First, however, I will outline Le Guin's successful *manifest* re-contextualisations of music's form and purpose when it is freed from capital's *production* apparatus.

On Anarres, the conditions and relations of musical production are striking. Music is a live performance medium, entailing no social network of management and labour, and never reproduced via technology: no 'Hit Parade', no virtuoso specialists, no egotistical celebrity artists, no exploitative managers or record companies, no product sales, no media hype – in short, no commodity 'product' whatsoever. In all of these *manifest* ways Le Guin has represented faithfully the formal requirements of production. The apparatus model further enables us to establish and clarify the additional, fundamental *latent* meaning of artistic form: on Anarres the underlying form is that of an interactive *event*, while on Urras, as in our culture, music is understood as *intellectual property* whose meaning emerges through commodity exchange. The mechanism of production is the crucial factor respecting art's form. Variations of content, while interesting, have a far lesser ideological significance for art than those of form. As Adorno notes, 'the relation of art to society is not to be sought primarily in the sphere of reception. This relation is anterior to reception, in production'.[12] Seen in this light, for art to be utopian, it must transform the social relations of its production, or, in other words, transform the apparatus.

The interactive experience of making and listening to live music on Anarres is therefore intensely social in ways rare both on Urras and in our own society. For clarification, one need only consider two films about cultures not based on capitalist assumptions: *Atanarjuat: The Fast Runner* (Kunuk, 2001) depicts in passing how music functions in Inuit culture; and *Songcatcher* (Greenwald, 2000) renders well a pre-capitalistic sense of music practice in early-twentieth-century Appalachia. In both cultures, there are no privileged performance experts with accompanying elitist status – any and every person could and did routinely improvise personal songs on the spot for specific applications, such as expressions of anger, frustration or courtship, but also maintained a large inventory of collective tunes for general social use, as in religious ritual; and the idea of regarding a song as either personal property or material product is ontologically unimaginable, a non sequitur.

Anarres, however, is an ambiguous utopia that has not yet rid itself of all potentially crippling practices, and Le Guin openly depicts sticky points. One of her most successful, probing criticisms occurs through the crisis faced by Shevek's friend Salas, who is represented as unable to secure a labour posting from Divlab (the ostensibly egalitarian and non-authoritarian coordinating agency for worker assignments) as a composer, despite having created a large body of original music. The surprising reason for the rejection is 'I write dysfunctional function'.[13] The irony that music can ever be considered 'dysfunctional' in a supposedly anarchical and libertarian society reveals a disturbing ideological flaw embedded in Anarresti culture. Bedap, another of Shevek's friends, explains the situation: Divlab

> can justify it because music isn't useful..... The circle has come right back around to the most vile kind of profiteering utilitarianism. The complexity, the vitality, the freedom of invention and initiative that was the center of the Odonian idea, we've thrown it all away. We've gone right back to barbarism.[14]

Bedap refers here to the liberatory philosophy of Odo, which forms the ontological basis for Anarresti society and which fiercely asserts complete personal freedom for all citizens – a fundamental principle Divlab compromises in its concerns for collective survival on a planet with a harsh environment and severely limited natural and labour resources.

On Anarres, then, utopian personal freedom is undermined by collective material and logistical problems, which, while banal, are also undeniably threatening and socially influential. Thus, Le Guin forthrightly explores the conflict of interests by depicting the treatment of a composer whose creative work falls beyond the pale of even this most progressive of utopian societies.

Reflection as Ideological Hallucination

Although Le Guin frees music (and other specified arts) from commodity exchange status, a resilient element of capitalist ontology latently resides in her otherwise well-informed and nuanced representation of Anarresti music. In what at first appears to be an unexceptional, even 'natural' detail, Shevek remarks that he has 'discovered, at last, His art'.[15] Why the need for the possessive pronoun? Why does Le Guin assume that the Annaresti consume and possess art at the level of personal reflection? Why does she assume that reflection as perception of art is a universally transcendent experience? The answer, I propose, is that the prescriptions of capitalism's commodity experience of consumption have been mystified through the ontological presumption of 'human nature'. For all of her efforts to recast music in a non commodified form, Le Guin is unable to recognise and move beyond one of the most powerful, pervasive, insidious, and yet subtle areas of capitalist ideological penetration: psychic reflection.

As Balibar and Macherey insist in an assertion that can be extended to all the arts, 'to understand this category [reflection] is therefore the key to the Marxist conception of literature'.[16] The 'Marxist category of "reflection" is quite separate from the empiricist and sensualist concept of the image, reflection as "mirroring". The reflection, in dialectical materialism, is a "reflection without a mirror"', or, rather, a *projection* 'of the "real" in the manner of an hallucination'.[17] This tendency to hallucinate is quintessentially an effect of collective ideological orientation, but is not perceived as such by the individual consciousness. The mechanisms of reflection silently replicate the underlying assumptions of the prevailing mode of *production* within the social relations of *consumption*. The operations of this latent mechanism can be theorised – indeed, even recognised – only by a materialist theory of reflection.

Le Guin unknowingly internalises the cultural logic of capital in ways which operate at the latent level described by Jameson's concept of the 'political unconscious'.[18] To be more specific: capital's consumers assume that the music's form is *aesthetic* and its purpose is *pleasure*, but the presumption that the experience of art be pleasurable is strictly historical and unique to our own era: 'indeed, as components of ritual [religious] praxis the predecessors of art were not autonomous [from social function]; yet precisely because they were sacred they were not objects of enjoyment'.[19] Adorno expands this insight by identifying the underlying distinction: 'The bourgeois wants art voluptuous and life ascetic; the reverse would be better'.[20] Anarresti art is exactly voluptuous through the assumed notion of aesthetic pleasure. To repeat the relevant quotation: 'organic economy was too essential to the functioning of the society not to affect ... aesthetics'.[21] Le Guin (and our culture) fails to recognise that to achieve a wholly new identity, art must transcend the commodity assumptions of both material production (which Le Guin rightly understands) *and* reflective consumption (which she does not).

Theorising the connection between pleasure and the operations of reflection is difficult, yet crucial. The reified logic of capitalist consumption dictates that the pleasure value of art is always and precisely *personal*. Thus Le Guin must not be criticised for imagining that the problem of the relationship of art to life under capital can be solved by simply recasting art in non-commodified and hence socially organic relations of production. Indeed, her representation of art as freed from commodity exchange is progressive, but her definition of art itself is idealised and not historically valid. It assumes a specious, falsely nostalgic notion of aesthetically transcendent 'pure art' of the sort produced in small-scale village and even tribal cultures.

Pleasure as replicated ideology is also theorised by Slavoj Žižek, who argues that 'enjoyment is sustained by a severe superego imperative'.[22] He suggests that interpretations such as Freud's and Marcuse's notions of the 'pleasure principle', which tie enjoyment (understood as synonymous with pleasure) to the body and hence to the id, are either wrong or vastly insufficient. Rather, enjoyment is a matter of consciousness and 'in its innermost status [is] something imposed, ordered – when we enjoy, we never do it "spontaneously," we always follow a certain injunction'.[23] Žižek outlines the mechanism by which this injunction to enjoy operates. In short, 'enjoyment' is an inverted psychic projection that one quilts from 'heterogeneous material into a unified ideological field' by imagining *the way I see the others seeing me*.[24] Enjoyment is therefore the experience of taking pleasure in what I think others would insist that I enjoy – a line of argument consistent with Balibar and Macherey's sense of reflection as ideological hallucination, and with Marx's assertion that 'Life is not determined by consciousness, but consciousness by life'.[25]

To summarise: the enjoyment of art is the psychic replication of socially assumed mandates – in other words, of ideology – governing all pleasure through two separate but related areas. The first is the need to identify and embrace certain forms of cultural production as belonging to the socially constructed and privileged category 'art'. As Adorno, Jameson, Eagleton, Williams, Brecht and Benjamin suggest, art itself has taken on a very specific historical meaning since the medieval period. Thus, art as we understand it did not exist prior to the advent of capitalism; that which is construed as art under capital is a heavily loaded category that has no similar meaning, and would be unrecognisable, under any other mode of production. Therefore Shevek's notion that music is 'his art' is historically specific in assuming that music even qualifies as 'art'.

The second component involves the assertion that the artwork produces pleasure. The experience of enjoying art is not naturally occurring, but rather an entirely learned behaviour. The particular response is generated in accordance with the historical moment's symbolic order, the latter conforming to the particular ideological imperatives of the mode of production but misrecognised by the psychic subject as 'natural' (that is, conforming to the ontological paradigm of what is 'known to be the truth'). As Jameson reminds us, pleasure is always dialectical, always historical and always a 'socially symbolic experience'.[26] In the era of capitalism, pleasure, as Adorno teaches us, is best understood as having a psychic 'disciplining function' by which exchange value 'disguises itself as the object of enjoyment'.[27] On this view pleasure is 'disguised' as taste, which Adorno further declares 'is itself outmoded'[28] simply for the fact that taste is learned exchange-value behaviour, not naturally occurring innate personal preference.

To return to Žižek, the experience of encountering the artwork is a combination of 'the Imaginary ... hooked on the Symbolic',[29] so that conformance to social expectations through the superego is the very essence of ideology. The enjoyment resulting from the fusing of the Imaginary and the Symbolic in the superego, now understood as the embodiment of ideology, may perhaps be more usefully termed social allegory. By allegory, Žižek means a given ideological field which 'encloses itself [and] effaces the traces of the material process which generated it', while Jameson terms allegory 'the thematizing of a particular pleasure as a political issue'.[30] These two senses strongly reinforce each other and serve well to argue for pleasure as a mandated, internalised socio-political fiction.

Further, this allegory of enjoyment varies according to the social (class) relations of consumption in any given mode of production. Pierre Bourdieu's work on social and symbolic spaces suggests that what one considers a personal pleasure is highly class-specific, and nothing other than what one has learned and internalised as pleasurable. Likewise, what one disdains becomes 'proof' of the 'natural' difference – and thus inferiority – of the social Other. For example, in French social practices, piano music is associated with the largest accumulations of cultural and actual capital, while accordion music is the 'preference' of those with far fewer resources and lower status.[31] This differentiation of what various classes consider 'pleasurable' extends to sport, hobbies and beverages, as well as the arts, and is translatable into political positions.

The very idea of Shevek having 'his art' is therefore an excellent example of the 'imaginary solution' that reveals an irresolvable social contradiction. According to the theoretical assumptions of Anarresti culture, notions of personal ownership and social class of any kind should be nonexistent. On the one hand, music is depicted as a learned collective and non-classist social pleasure, and yet on the other the phrase 'his music' must mean 'the art form preferred by Shevek and others like him', implying the unacknowledged existence of class distinctions and, presumably, even residual class struggle.

To the objection that surely humans can and do express personal preferences and enjoyments, I suggest that whatever 'truth' is contained in the assertion of 'natural personal pleasure' is precisely that which is challenged by Lacan's notion of pleasure as social injunction. Of course, observation will show us that people do 'enjoy' the arts, but the pleasure they experience, I argue, is innately ideological. 'Therefore', Žižek comments, '"criticism of ideology" consists in unmasking traditional allegory as an "optical illusion" concealing the mechanics of modern allegory',[32] echoing Balibar and Macherey's perception of 'the real' as hallucination and Adorno's notion of 'disguise'. In other words, what we have long imagined as personal pleasure in the arts as 'natural human experience' is one allegory among many that serves to conceal its own 'space of ideological narration'.[33]

To clarify even further what might be gained by interpreting representations of utopian art from the perspective of the apparatus, let us turn to Robinson's *Blue Mars*, which contrasts sharply with Le Guin's in its recognition of the space of ideological narration.

'The Sheffield Sound': Music on Mars

Robinson represents numerous episodes concerning art forms in *Blue Mars*, including architecture, film, theatre, opera and dance. Two of these, involving music, demonstrate important utopian dynamics. The first is a relatively short and hence simple example, the second much more complex.

Nirgal, a native-born Martian, has temporarily joined 'the ferals', a purposely non-technological social group living as close to the natural world as possible, and representing what Marx terms the tribal or primitive mode of production: 'A group of them picked up some stones and began to hit them together in rhythm, all their different patterns meshing bass to treble. The rest of them began to dance around the bonfire, hooting or singing or chanting.'[34] A tribal culture depicted as engaging in rhythmic percussion and dancing is unremarkable from the traditional aesthetic perspective, inasmuch as one would not expect such a society to be capable of producing or practising 'civilised' complex musical forms. In fact, the resulting sound lacks such components as melody and form. The formal properties gain considerable ideological interest in two ways, however, when approached from materialist (non-aesthetic) perspectives generated by the demands of the apparatus: 1) the relationship between the primitive (pre-capitalist) mode of production and the purpose of music; and 2) the ways in which music is produced and consumed as related to the culture's framework of social relations.

In every sense Robinson is faithful to the social relations relative to and required by the artificially re-enacted primitive mode of production. As opposed to the capitalist sense of music as 'intellectual property' – as a commodity whose use is intended to maximise gain for the owners of the music, who are often not its creators – Robinson's feral music exists in a non-commodifiable form as an event: a collective, dynamic social experience outside material exchange in which anyone and everyone can play (another example of which is the group drumming practised today in our culture as anachronisms). This means that there is no labour category of 'musician', no separate category of 'audience', and no special instruments (which would require specialist labour to produce and would become commodities bought and sold within an exchange network of ownership demarcating hierarchical social status). An emphasis on the apparatus rather than on traditional aesthetic categories such as technical proficiency allows the ontological (ideological) assumptions of musical practice to emerge.

The second episode appears as a minor digression in the plot, but is useful for more directly interrogating the novel's utopian integrity with respect to the arts. In a section primarily concerned with depicting political debates about immigration policy, the characters, following a day of heated discussions, congregate at a dancing venue. Maya, Vendana and Athos wander downtown 'until they passed a large band playing what they called the Sheffield sound. This music was only noise to Maya: twenty different drum rhythms at once, on instruments not intended for percussion or even for musical use'.[35] Despite the fact that this episode is situated within a highly technological urban setting, the apparatus requirements of musical production and consumption are met. Thus, as with the ferals, musical practice exists formally outside of the commodity framework, and emphasises egalitarian social relations – though this time not in a tribal mode of production, but rather in a post-capitalist economy. In other words, both groups share the same non-capitalist and hence non-hierarchical social relations that are embedded in their practice of music.

Robinson deploys the music and dancing as an analogue to amplify the concomitant political implications of the chapter. In other words, the music and dance scene serves metaphorically to meditate on how 'twenty different' drummers can produce a satisfying and useful collective result. Maya at first is said to think of the result as 'noise', which is, of course, an aesthetic response grounded in the capitalist sense of pleasurable reflection, but is later represented as thinking 'it made a kind of sense; not musical sense as she understood it, but rhythmic sense'; and when confronted by someone who remarks, 'I thought you didn't like this kind of music', responds 'Sometimes I do'.[36] In other words, Maya, as one of the 'First Hundred' settlers, and thus still carrying the ideological baggage of Terran, capitalist aesthetic assumptions, begins to grasp, if in only a partially conscious way, what is for the native-born Martians the new internalised ontological logic of egalitarian practices of both music and politics. Hence, while Robinson intends the Sheffield

Sound to serve as a metaphor for the newly emerging political sensibilities on Mars, that very political reality in turn generates the conditions for a new form of music. The relationship is solidly reciprocal in the most credible sense.

Challenges to Imagining Utopian Arts

The Dispossessed reminds us that the current sense of 'art' is a complex and ever-changing cluster of definitions and practices emerging out of and serving in turn the ideological purposes of the feudal and capitalistic modes of production, which in their turn will not be viable under future modes of production. Furthermore, there is no possibility of returning to some a priori 'true' notion of art as practised by 'tribal' or 'primitive' societies because: 1) no such practice as Le Guin represents ever existed; and 2) primitive social contexts of expression through song, dance, painting and so on never contained any transcendent essence that has been degraded in modern times. Surviving objects and practices of tribal and primitive cultures served far different social purposes that are routinely re-valued today through the mechanisms of ahistorical, aesthetic and ontological conceptions that silently serve capitalist ideology: tribal artefacts for personal consumption, either for elite collector commodity exchange value or to satisfy rarefied personal 'aesthetically culinary tastes', the latter always entailing some variety of elitist cultural (or actual material) capital. Le Guin has therefore rightly identified the significance to the arts of the production side of the capitalist commodity-exchange apparatus, but has not recognised the similar importance of the relations and means of consumption.

We are now in a position to address briefly a broader theoretical implication – namely the ideological blockages that prevent utopian imagination in the first place. If the ideology of the status quo is pervasive, how can the utopian novelist possibly imagine alternatives? Adorno states the honest but brutal truth that 'thoroughly non-ideological art is indeed probably completely impossible', virtually invalidating any attempt 'to sketch the form of art in a changed society', for the simple reason that we do not and cannot know what art would mean or require in some future post-capitalist mode of production.[37] As Perry Anderson likewise remarks, utopias 'retain, for all their potential luxuriance of detail, at root a stubborn negativity, an emblem of what, despite everything, we *cannot* grasp or imagine, and which the characteristic oscillations and oppositions within the utopian repertoire bespeak'.[38] An understanding of the seminal importance of the apparatus, however, may provide at least an initial strategy for imagining the supposedly unimaginable.

Instead of focusing on this or that new form of art from the perspective of idealist aesthetics, particular styles or techniques, or even particular manifest forms – such as Walter M. Miller, Jr's decidedly reactionary depiction of mechanistic 'autodrama' in the Hugo Award-winning 'The Darfsteller' (1955) – the demands of the apparatus require us to rethink form, and especially utopian form, from the perspective of social relations.[39] Thus, Le Guin's depiction of music in *The Dispossessed* does not pass the test of credibility simply because she assumes that our current hallucinatory sense of reflection would be reproduced in the decidedly anarchist and post-capitalistic society of Anarres. Understood in this sense, it does not matter how 'different' Anarresti music is with respect to tonal structures or melodies or any other technical elements, for it is not true to the ideological requirements of its own economic apparatus.

Le Guin's representation of music is, instead, an excellent example of what Raymond Williams calls a *variation* of a presently understood art form, rather than the more properly dynamic and utopian matter of *innovation* that a whole new mode of social relations would require. As Williams writes, 'theory can show that form is inevitably a [social] relationship', with the result that to create art 'in different ways is to live in different ways'.[40] Le Guin manifestly asserts that the arts are 'the basic technique of life', but unfortunately she is invoking historically and theoretically incompatible notions of both 'life' and 'art'. Robinson's depiction of music, in contrast, tentatively but more fully achieves the goal of historically legitimate utopian innovation. His sense of a post-capitalist 'form of art in a changed society' of the sort practised on Mars might never come to pass. Who knows? But Martian art as depicted is at least minimally consistent with the theoretical requirements of its apparatus, and therefore plausible.

Whatever forms and relations 'art' will take under some post-capitalist mode of production, we can assert one general guiding axiom. If the future does produce a far more materially equitable and socially egalitarian society, then all of its practices – in education, public affairs, industrial and agricultural production, the sciences and so forth – will by necessity take quite different forms than those practised under capitalism. So why should not the underlying logic of what we call 'art' also differ? In *Island* (1962), Aldous Huxley, an author deeply concerned with the expression of art under differing social conditions, offers a suggestive insight. Protagonist Will Farnaby learns that Pala's supreme art, which can be practised by anyone, is 'the art of adequately experiencing ... all the worlds that, as human beings, we find ourselves inhabiting'.[41] I will conclude by refunctioning[42] and expanding this passage in the following ways: *a properly utopian art form is a collective social practice that disempowers or exploits no-one, is ideologically transparent, and can be produced and/or consumed by any person in some variation.* This model sharply contrasts with the key assumptions regarding art in the era of capitalism, estranges and challenges the elitist and exploitative bases of our 'aesthetic' assumptions, and points towards innovative conditions of lived social relations, of more truly genuine freedom, that we must first strive to imagine if we are ever to bring into historical existence.

Notes

1. Raymond Williams, *Marxism and Literature* (New York: Oxford University Press, 1970), p. 191.
2. Fredric Jameson, *Archaeologies of the Future: The Desire Called Utopia and Other Science Fictions* (New York: Verso, 2005), pp. 416, 184–5; cf. Robert C. Elliott, *The Shape of Utopia* (Chicago: University of Chicago Press, 1970).
3. Ursula K. Le Guin, *The Dispossessed: An Ambiguous Utopia* (New York: HarperPrism, 1994), p. 156.

4. See Pierre Macherey, *A Theory of Literary Production*, transl. Geoffrey Wall (London: Routledge & Kegan Paul, 1978).

5. Theodor W. Adorno, *Aesthetic Theory*, transl. Robert Hullot-Kentor (Minneapolis: University of Minnesota Press, 1997), p. 255.

6. Bertolt Brecht, *Brecht on Theatre*, ed. and transl. John Willett (New York: Hill and Wang, 1964), pp. 35, 34.

7. For a more complete discussion of Brecht's notion of the apparatus and its implications, see William J. Burling, 'Brecht's "U-Effect": Theorizing the Horizons of Revolutionary Theatre', in Chris West, ed., *Brecht, Broadway and United States Theatre* (Newcastle: Cambridge Scholars Press, 2007).

8. Williams, *Marxism and Literature*, p. 187.

9. Le Guin's exact influence is Peter Kropotkin, particularly *Mutual Aid* (1902), which she calls upon throughout the novel. See Philip E. Smith II, 'Unbuilding Walls: Human Nature and the Nature of Evolutionary and Political Theory in *The Dispossessed*', in Joseph D. Olander and Martin Harry Greenberg, eds, *Le Guin* (New York: Taplinger, 1979), pp. 77–96.

10. Le Guin, *Dispossessed*, p. 98.

11. Ibid., p. 175.

12. Adorno, *Aesthetic Theory*, p. 228.

13. Le Guin, *Dispossessed*, p. 175.

14. Ibid., p. 175.

15. Ibid., p. 157.

16. Étienne Balibar and Pierre Macherey, 'On Literature as an Ideological Form', in Terry Eagleton and Drew Milne, eds, *Marxist Literary Theory* (Oxford: Blackwell, 1996), p. 277.

17. Ibid., pp. 279, 288.

18. See Fredric Jameson, *The Political Unconscious: Narrative as a Socially Symbolic Act* (Ithaca: Cornell University Press, 1981).

19. Adorno, *Aesthetic Theory*, p. 13.

20. Ibid., p. 13.

21. Le Guin, *Dispossessed*, p. 98.

22. Slavoj Žižek, *For They Know Not What They Do: Enjoyment as a Political Factor*, second edn (New York: Verso, 1992), p. 10.

23. Ibid., p. 9.

24. Ibid., pp. 18, 13.

25. Lewis S. Fuer, ed., *Marx and Engels: Basic Writings on Politics and Philosophy* (New York: Anchor, 1959), p. 247.

26. Fredric Jameson, 'Pleasure: A Political Issue', in *The Ideologies of Theory. Volume 2: The Syntax of History* (Minneapolis: University of Minnesota Press, 1988), p. 73.

27. Theodor Adorno, 'On the Fetish Character in Music and the Regression of Listening', in Andrew Arato and Eike Gebhardt, eds,

The Essential Frankfurt School Reader (New York: Continuum, 1982), pp. 270–9.

28. Ibid., pp. 270–1.
29. Žižek, *For They Know Not What They Do*, p. 10.
30. Ibid., p. 19; Jameson, 'Pleasure', p. 73.
31. Pierre Bourdieu, *Practical Reason* (Stanford: Stanford University Press, 1998), p. 8.
32. Žižek, *For They Know Not What They Do*, p. 19.
33. Ibid., p. 19.
34. Kim Stanley Robinson, *Blue Mars* (New York: Bantam, 1997), p. 464.
35. Ibid., p. 573.
36. Ibid., p. 575.
37. Adorno, *Aesthetic Theory*, pp. 236, 260.
38. Perry Anderson, 'The River of Time', *New Left Review* 26 (March/April 2004), pp. 67–8.
39. For a more properly utopian representation of theatre, see Samuel R. Delany's depiction of 'micro-drama' in *Trouble on Triton* (1976).
40. Williams, *Marxism and Literature*, pp. 187, 205.
41. Aldous Huxley, *Island* (New York: Harper Row, 1989), p. 176.
42. I employ here a key term created and used by Brecht, *Umfunktionierung*, variously translated as 'rebuilding', 'readapting' and 'functionally reshaping' in the ideological sense. For a fuller explanation of this term, see Burling, 'Brecht's "U-Effect"'.

3

MARXISM, CINEMA AND SOME DIALECTICS OF SCIENCE FICTION AND FILM NOIR

Carl Freedman

Consider four crucial moments from four well-known movies:

1. A gravely wounded insurance salesman settles behind his desk, and, speaking into a Dictaphone, confesses to murder: 'I killed him for money, and for a woman', he says. 'And I didn't get the money, and I didn't get the woman'.

2. A criminal mastermind, having organised and led a major heist, stands ready to board an aeroplane with his girlfriend and make his final getaway. But in his haste he has stuffed the loot into a rickety suitcase, and, as the suitcase is being loaded onto the plane, it comes apart and the money flies off in all directions, reducing his profit to zero and increasing the likelihood of capture to near certainty.

3. An alien physically indistinguishable from human beings, who has been mortally wounded by a senseless act of earthly violence, emerges revived from his spaceship and proceeds, calmly and with complete authority, to explain to a group of scientists and soldiers that unprecedented opportunities await humanity if it learns how to behave peacefully – but that, if humans threaten to extend their aggressive ways into outer space, then the Earth will be destroyed by the robot police force established by the other inhabited planets.

4. An astronaut, having been sent on a mysterious mission to Jupiter, and then having been diverted by even more

mysterious forces to remote parts of the universe, winds up in an ornately furnished apartment, where he passes through the stages of life from young manhood to extreme old age and is reborn as the 'Star Child' of evidently planetary scope and godlike powers.

The four films referred to are, respectively, *Double Indemnity* (Wilder, 1944), *The Killing* (Kubrick, 1956), *The Day the Earth Stood Still* (Wise, 1951) and *2001: A Space Odyssey* (Kubrick, 1968). The first two are instances of film noir, the second two of SF cinema; and each may be taken as exemplary of its kind. *Double Indemnity* is the most widely praised single example of film noir. Produced relatively early in the original Hollywood cycle, Wilder's film was hugely influential on the genre, helping, for instance, to establish such common noir motifs as the use of voice-over narration and the centrality of the femme fatale. *The Killing* is not commonly ranked quite so high, but is likely to appear on critics' lists of the ten or fifteen best examples of classic noir. It is perhaps the most influential of all heist films, and its continuing vitality is illustrated by (for instance) the impact that its structure has had on such movies as *Reservoir Dogs* (Tarantino, 1992) and, to a lesser degree, *Pulp Fiction* (Tarantino, 1994). *The Day the Earth Stood Still* is probably the strongest instance of Hollywood SF in its original (Eisenhower-era) phase; and its influence on later cinema (for example, in its montage of newscasts during the film's opening sequence) has extended beyond SF. *2001*, as I have argued elsewhere,[1] is something like the permanently definitive masterpiece of SF cinema, with not only no rival but virtually no second.

The two noir scenes described above emphatically proclaim the films in which they are embedded to be *deflationary* in outlook. Walter Neff (Fred MacMurray) begins Wilder's film not simply by confessing to murder, but by admitting that his intricate scheme of grand passion and grand larceny has resulted in complete failure, and will yield nothing but his own destruction. Perhaps most deflating of all for Walter, he now knows that the passion he felt for the stunning Phyllis Dietrichson (Barbara Stanwyck), his partner in crime, was never requited, her apparent interest in him just a cynical pretence to cover her real, and entirely mercenary, motives. The conclusion of *The Killing* is equally, if differently, deflationary. Johnny Clay (Sterling Hayden) is shrewder than Walter Neff, and his main problem is not that he misjudges his associates nor that he underestimates the investigating authorities (as Walter disastrously underestimates Barton Keyes – played by Edward G. Robinson – his best friend and the chief investigator for the insurance company that he and Phyllis attempt to defraud). But Johnny – like Doc Riedenschneider (Sam Jaffe), the master criminal in *The Asphalt Jungle* (Huston, 1950), which had a powerful influence on Kubrick's movie – underestimates something more fundamental and more formidable: the power of sheer blind luck. His criminal scheme is smarter and more complex than Walter's, and, unlike Walter's, is designed to make some allowance for unexpected mishaps along the way. But even Johnny Clay cannot plan for everything, like the way that an intrinsically trivial factor like the flimsiness of a piece of luggage can undo all his brilliant work. For *The Killing*, as for *Double Indemnity*, life has less – much less – to offer than one might have imagined: 'What's the difference?' asks Johnny with weary resignation in the film's final line.

In the SF films, however, life offers much *more* than expected. The humanoid appearance of the alien Klaatu (Michael Rennie) allows him to mix undetected in the mundane affairs of Washington, DC, and so helps *The Day the Earth Stood Still* to provide some fine realistic satire of Cold War America under the Truman administration. The short-sightedness and corruption of much in American life are highlighted, and are condensed in Tom Stevens (Hugh Marlowe), the boyfriend of the lead female character, Helen Benson (Patricia Neal), and a man consumed by petty egoistic motives (and also, like Walter Neff, an insurance salesman by trade). But the film ultimately dismisses Tom; and Klaatu's closing speech makes clear that the global humanitarian perspective of the scientist Jacob Barnhardt (Sam Jaffe), clearly modelled after Albert Einstein, is far more compelling and actual. If the planet faces possible catastrophe, it also enjoys undreamed-of opportunities, as Klaatu invites humanity to save itself and to live in peaceful cooperation with extraterrestrial races of far greater intellectual and moral attainments.

2001 is even more inflationary in outlook, even more insistent that reality is richer and more various than most people assume. As the film begins its second major section, set in the titular year, humanity has reached a crisis of banality, pettiness, corruption and mortal danger. The crisis not only 'rhymes' with the more primitive but structurally similar impasse represented in the film's first part, set during 'the dawn of man', but is also reminiscent of the state of affairs that Klaatu and Professor Barnhardt found so distressing. But Kubrick's film offers a transcendence that is even more extraordinary, visually and thematically, than that provided by *The Day the Earth Stood Still*. In *2001*, the human race is not 'merely' given the chance to join in something like an extraterrestrial version of the United Nations (in its original Rooseveltian conception). Humanity, in the person of the unremarkable astronaut Dave Bowman (Keir Dullea), actually takes a stride forward in physical and spiritual evolution, going 'beyond the infinite' – that is, beyond all supernatural mystifications – in order to arrive, in neo-Nietzschean fashion, at a material and secular state of superhumanity. Dave Bowman begins as an Everyman at the dawn of the twenty-first century – technically competent and physically efficient, but an intellectual, spiritual and aesthetic nullity – and ends as a natural god.

The opposition between the inflationary and the deflationary suggested by these four films provides a cognitive axis along which the cinematic genres of SF and noir can be contrasted. SF of course has its origins in literature – more specifically in British Romanticism, one of the most inflationary movements in cultural history. The most widely accepted and most plausible candidate to be the first major work of full-fledged SF remains Mary Shelley's *Frankenstein* (1818), which tackles the awesomely inflationary theme of the artificial creation of human life (and which was composed under the direct inspiration of Percy Shelley's poetry, commonly regarded as more than usually inflationary even by Romantic standards). This inflationary bent – this cognitive affirmation and aesthetic demonstration that, as Ernst Bloch put it, reality is never merely itself but always means 'reality *plus* the future within it'[2] – becomes the principal (though not the only) tendency in the history of SF. It is particularly in evidence in the strongest works of the genre, from pioneering classics like H.G. Wells' *The Time Machine* (1895) and, even more, Olaf Stapledon's *Last and First Men* (1930) and *Star Maker* (1937), through the main achievements of the 1960s and 1970s – probably the genre's most creative period, owing to such authors as Philip K. Dick, Ursula Le Guin, Samuel Delany, J.G. Ballard, Thomas Disch, Joanna Russ, and many others – to more recent triumphs like Kim Stanley Robinson's *Mars* (1993–96) and China Miéville's *Bas-Lag* (2000–04) trilogies.

As *The Day the Earth Stood Still* and *2001* illustrate, SF cinema continues this inflationary bent in those (relatively few) films that are allied, in cognitive substance and aesthetic integrity, to the main current of literary SF. To be sure, most cinematic productions of the genre tend to degrade the latter through an anti-intellectual obsession with technique and spectacle; and, accordingly, the typical SF movie tends to display a hypertrophy of special effects. Yet something of the inflationary pressure of SF – expressed particularly in the visual dimension – can survive even such degradation. Steven Spielberg's *Close Encounters of the Third Kind* (1977), for example, marshals narrative and thematic resources that are nugatory by the standards of literary SF, not even rising to the level of the mediocre. But the visual splendour of the Mothership – surely cinema's most artfully designed and compelling space vehicle since *2001* itself – maintains, though in purely spectacular terms, the properly science-fictional impulse to transcend the mundane and to imply a depth and richness of reality that go beyond any empirical norm. Even when limited by Spielberg's conceptual banality, SF does not necessarily cease to insist, or at least to suggest, that we need not and should not settle for the familiar contingencies of everyday existence. The typical lifeworld of SF is (to adapt Shakespeare's well-known phrase from the play that marks his own nearest approach to SF) a brave new world.

Settling for the mundane is, by contrast, precisely what film noir is all about. Like the American hard-boiled detective fiction pioneered by Dashiell Hammett and Raymond Chandler, from which film noir partly derives, noir is not, to be sure, invariably cynical. It does not necessarily insist that human beings are driven only by the basest motives, nor that honesty and decency are unattainable. In *Double Indemnity*, for example, Keyes displays even greater acumen and toughness than the gangster anti-heroes for which Edward G. Robinson was famous, while also adhering to a rigorous, if mostly unspoken, code of honour in a manner strikingly similar to that of the ideal detective celebrated in Chandler's influential (and exactly contemporary) manifesto, 'The Simple Art of Murder' (1944).

Nonetheless, if noir men (and, more rarely, women) are capable of honour, it is a difficult and rare achievement. In general, the most widely and reliably operative human motives turn out to be the most obvious, familiar and selfish ones, mainly greed and lust; and, despite the labyrinthine complexity of many noir plots, the lifeworld of noir is fundamentally simple, usually boiling down to a neo-Hobbesian war of each against each and all against all. This leaves a distressingly small margin for human freedom, as people are repeatedly shown to be driven by lust, greed and other such forces that are difficult to resist even when their dangers are at least partly understood: Walter Neff, for example, advances steadily towards his doom in the San Quentin death chamber even while always knowing, at heart, that involvement with Phyllis can lead to nothing but disaster. If not always cynical, noir is deeply pessimistic about human possibility and human happiness in a way that recalls the deflationary determinism of Freud, whose immense popularity in the US during the heyday of classic noir forms an important part of the genre's intellectual background. If you are doing as well as Keyes – engaged, functional, decent, truthful and, if not particularly happy, at least not consumed by crippling misery – then, by noir or by psychoanalytic standards, you are probably doing as well as human beings can reasonably expect to do. Of the characters in the SF films discussed above, the only one who could be a character in film noir is Tom Stevens.

A convenient index of the distance between the two genres is provided by the fact that he is utterly contemptible, hardly worthy even of living in the same solar system as Klaatu and Professor Barnhardt. In noir, though, he would be no worse than average, and perhaps even a little better.

The opposition between the deflationary perspective of noir and the inflationary perspective of SF recalls a dialectical tension at the heart of Marxism, which is inflationary and deflationary at once. The deflationary dimension is represented by the attempt to destroy all illusions necessary or useful to the preservation of class society in general and of capitalism in particular. Such demystification is perhaps most familiar in the form of ideology-critique – that is, the exposure of those networks of habit and belief that capitalist societies generate and that in turn help to sustain capitalism's oppressive practices by inhibiting the development of socialist ideas and attitudes. But it also includes the exposure of those illusions structurally intrinsic to the actual economic mechanisms of the capitalist mode of production – for instance, the way that the formally free contract between employer and employee conceals the coercive threat of homelessness and starvation always, if often implicitly, aimed at those who may consider declining the employer's deal; or the way that the production of surplus-value and the concomitant structure of the wage-relation make it appear that the worker is paid for the entire working day, even though wages compensate the worker for only a fraction of his or her actual labour time. In the spheres of both culture and political economy, the deflation of capitalist illusions is an indispensable part of the Marxist project.

But Marxism ultimately aims at the positive project of human liberation and self-realisation, rather than only at the negative task of destroying capitalism and other forms of class (and other) oppression. For this reason the deflationary moment of Marxism, however necessary, can never be sufficient. Marxism is inflationary as well, insisting that, despite the fact that class oppression is essentially coterminous with the history of the human race, it need not always be so. The overthrow of capitalism, for Marxism, need not result merely in the substitution of one ruling class (or elite) for another, as the overthrow of feudalism (or the advent of Stalinism) did. It can instead be the prelude to the radically democratic self-organisation of the human race, allowing all individuals the maximum possible fulfilment of their creative potentialities: as mankind leaps, in Engels' words, from the realm of necessity to the realm of freedom. Even in *Capital* – not only Marx's most important work but also his most elaborately deflationary – Marx provides positive glimpses of the liberated, classless future that beckons as a concrete possibility after the supersession of the capitalist property relations he exposes. In an important passage in Volume Three, for example, Marx defines the socialist freedom that can be attained when capitalism has been overthrown but scarcity not yet eliminated:

> that socialized man, the associated producers, govern the human metabolism with nature in a rational way, bringing it under their collective control instead of being dominated by it as a blind power; accomplishing it with the least expenditure of energy and in conditions most worthy and appropriate for their human nature.

He then offers a briefer hint of the world of achieved communism and material abundance that may lie even further in the future: 'the *true* realm of freedom, the development of human powers as an end in itself'.[3] For Marxism, visionary transcendence is the necessary completion of astringent demystification.

Clearly, I am suggesting a certain homology between the two sides of Marxism and the antithetical genres of SF and noir. But the matter is too complex to allow for any neat quadripartite symmetry. Quantitatively, the work of Marxism is overwhelmingly on the deflationary side, aiming to produce detailed scientific (which means always provisional) knowledge of the real world. To say that such strenuous investigation into the workings of economic, political and cultural processes is far beyond the ability of film noir is not to condemn the latter, but to acknowledge a vast *generic* difference: patently, *Double Indemnity* is a very different kind of achievement from *Capital*. Yet film noir can be understood as producing what the Althusserian tradition might call a figurative analogue of deflationary Marxist knowledge. For example, the typical noir stress on greed (in the moral sense of individual avarice) is, strictly in itself, a matter of little concern to Marxist historical analysis. But noir representations of individual greed may allegorically *gesture towards* – though not actually produce – the kind of knowledge discoverable through application of Marx's principle of the ultimately determining role of the economy. There is, for instance, an aesthetic and affective link – even though not a fully cognitive one – between, on the one hand, Neff's discovery that Phyllis cared nothing for him and everything for an insurance claim and, on the other hand, the analysis that reveals the armed opposition by Britain and France to the invasion of Belgium at the beginning of World War I to have been based less on human sympathy for a small nation than on the fear that the continued economic exploitation of their own empires might be threatened by German expansionism.

SF, however, may provide something more than an analogue of what the inflationary side of Marxism offers: partly because the latter is itself so fragmentary and impalpable compared to Marxist demystification. It is, after all, impossible to produce the same sort of exacting, detailed knowledge about the potential future as about the actual past and present: and so the moments of inflationary positivity in the Marx–Engels oeuvre, while fascinating and important, amount to a series of brief, sometimes ambiguous passages scattered throughout tens of thousands of pages of mainly deflationary scientific analysis. Since, furthermore, the future is strictly unknowable, attempts to comprehend it must be largely speculative: and in this way the cinematic and literary resources of SF, involving the development of fictional characters within an imaginary narrative framework, may sometimes be more useful than expository statements. *The Day the Earth Stood Still* cannot fully convey what it might feel like to live in the kind of interplanetary cooperative association offered to humanity at the film's end. But Klaatu's unsentimental compassion, along with his authoritative and completely uncynical knowledgeability, provide a suggestive clue.

It should be stressed that inflationary and deflationary perspectives not only combine in Marxism, but form a genuine dialectic: each animates and concretises the other. The production of deflationary Marxist knowledge, even at its most technical and recondite, is thoroughly *political* – even moral – in orientation. Marxism works to deconstruct the conventional middle-class dichotomy between fact and value: so that, for instance, Marx's central analytic discovery of the secret of profit in the structure of surplus-value not only provides scientific knowledge of capitalist production but shows the latter to be based on a certain morally charged practice, namely *theft*. Since the ethical unacceptability of practices integral to capitalist (and other class) societies is an inescapable conclusion of Marxist analysis, the latter necessarily implies some positive transcendence of the actual to be mandatory. Conversely, Marxist transcendence must be solidly based on a scientific understanding of the actual. The positive visions of Marxism must be utopian in the Blochian sense of offering some partial but genuine prefiguration of an unalienated, classless future, without being utopian in the bad sense that Marx and Engels stigmatised in the case of the 'utopian socialists', whose schemes they criticised for being based on wishful thinking rather than on an accurate grasp of capitalist reality. If the deflationary side of Marxism is necessarily moral and political, the inflationary side is necessarily scientific.

Does this dialectic within Marxism have a counterpart in any aesthetic dialectic between SF cinema and film noir? I think that it does, and that the dialectic between noir and SF is to be found above all in Alex Proyas's neglected *Dark City* (1998). But the interaction of the two genres has a history before Proyas, one that might be traced as far back as Fritz Lang's seminal *Metropolis* (1926), which has exercised a huge influence on *both* SF and film noir. Not only is *Metropolis* the first great example of SF cinema, but also, though not an actual instance of noir, perhaps the most influential single production of German Expressionism, whose attitudes and techniques were to prove so important for the noir directors (not least Lang himself, who in his Hollywood phase made many noir movies). Two later films that mix SF with noir, and that were clearly made under the influence of Lang's dark, brooding vision of the ominous city, are *Alphaville* (Godard, 1965) and *Blade Runner* (Scott, 1982); and both point directly towards *Dark City*.

Alphaville is perhaps the first important film to combine noir and SF directly; but its method of composition is more that of pastiche than of the dialectic. The film relates how the hard-boiled secret agent Lemmy Caution (Eddie Constantine) travels – by car, wearing a trench-coat and carrying an automatic pistol – across millions of miles of outer space to the totalitarian city of Alphaville, which is ruled by a new kind of supercomputer. After various noirish adventures, he finally assassinates Professor Von Braun (Howard Vernon), Alphaville's top computer scientist, and flees with his new girlfriend, the professor's beautiful daughter, Natasha (Anna Karina). As might be gathered even from this quick summary, in *Alphaville* noir and SF are not dialectically synthesised but instead (as Dr Johnson might have put it) yoked together by violence. The result is a hilariously self-conscious triumph of pastiche, which not only jumbles together motifs from earlier SF cinema and classic Hollywood noir, but also incorporates all manner of other cultural fragments, drawn (for instance) from the Dick Tracy comic strip and the Heckel-and-Jeckel cartoons, as well as from such loftier sources as Dante, Shakespeare, Pascal, Baudelaire and T.S. Eliot. Again and again the film rejoices in the deliberate absurdity of its own juxtapositions. For instance, as Lemmy and Natasha make their final getaway (in a white Ford Galaxy!), Lemmy comments, in properly noirish voice-over, 'A night drive across intersidereal space and we'd be home' – as though travel between star systems were like taking a spin on the Los Angeles freeways. The detail that two generations of over-earnest SF fans have identified as the film's chief 'mistake' – the use of the term 'light-year' as a unit of time (and later of computing power) rather than of distance – is of course no mistake at all. 'Light year' is used as a comically generic signifier of scientificity, one that Godard gleefully pastes together with all the others in his postmodern collage.

Blade Runner makes a more genuinely dialectical attempt to meld noir with SF.[4] The protagonist, Rick Deckard (Harrison Ford), is a typically hard-boiled noir hero – directly modelled, at least in part, after Humphrey Bogart's characters in *The Maltese Falcon* (Huston, 1941) and *The Big Sleep* (Hawks, 1946) – and his professional assignment to eliminate several out-of-control android replicants provides occasion for a series of noirish adventures that suggest a fairly bleak view of human nature and possibility: not least his encounters with two highly sexualised and deadly dangerous android femmes fatales played by Joanna Cassidy and Daryl Hannah. It is, however, in its setting in the Los Angeles of 2019 that *Blade Runner* is at its most powerfully deflationary. Scott's city is dark, chromatically and otherwise, and presents us with an environment that is futuristic and high-tech yet also rainy, decaying, garbage-littered and lethal. The earth is increasingly inhabited by the dregs of humanity, most of those with the resources to emigrate off-world having done so; and the determinant power of corporate capital and the efficacy of cynical economic motives are growing. Given the exaggeration, through futuristic science-fictional means, of classically deflationary noir motifs, *Blade Runner* might be described as *ultra*-noir.

Yet the dialectical complexity of the film is such that its fusion of SF with noir works not only to intensify the latter but also to open up some antithetical inflationary possibilities. In several particulars – the evidently sincere love, for instance, that the replicant leader Roy Batty (Rutger Hauer) expresses for the 'pleasure model' Pris (Daryl Hannah), or the apparently reciprocated love that the replicant Rachael (Sean Young) feels for Deckard – the replicants that Deckard is charged with eliminating seem disturbingly human. Like *Frankenstein* (and, ironically, unlike *Do Androids Dream of Electric Sheep?*, Dick's 1968 SF novel upon which Scott's film is loosely based), *Blade Runner* thus works to expand the category of humanity itself, suggesting it to be more capacious and less easily defined than common-sense would assume. When Batty utters a dying speech of sublime poetic intensity – a speech that draws upon specifically science-fictional images ('attack ships on fire off the shoulder of Orion') to achieve a Shelleyan visionary force – new possibilities that transcend any simple human/android dichotomy are clearly in sight. This inflationary theme reaches its height in the movie's subtlest (and most hotly debated) element: the hint that Deckard himself is an android.

Dark City clearly owes much to *Blade Runner* (as well as to *Metropolis*), but offers, I think, the most thoroughgoing dialectic of SF and noir yet achieved. As in *Blade Runner* – but more systematically – an ultra-noir quality is achieved through science-fictional means. Perhaps no two-word phrase could more strongly suggest the world of noir than 'dark city';[5] and Proyas's visual depiction of the night-time metropolis with abundant use of shadows and of sharp, diagonal camera angles – techniques that classic noir inherited from German Expressionism – conveys the quintessentially noir sense of alienation, disorientation and claustrophobic entrapment. Yet here the entrapment is taken to a science-fictional extreme and rendered terrifyingly literal. As the protagonist John Murdoch (Rufus Sewell) and the viewer gradually discover, the dark city is always and everywhere dark. It is both perpetual and completely self-contained, in the sense that no means of urban transport seems capable of taking one beyond the city limits; and no one can remember ever actually seeing the daylight. 'There is nothing beyond the city', as the strategically named Dr Daniel Poe Schreber (Kiefer Sutherland) at one point tells Murdoch. The metropolis at night is typically the 'world' of classic film noir, but here it is the world in a precisely literal sense: for it eventually transpires that the city is not located anywhere on earth, but is an immense starship hurtling through outer space. The scene in which Murdoch and police detective Frank Bumstead (William Hurt) tear through a brick wall and find the starry vastness of space on the other side is a narrative masterstroke – at once surprising and yet suddenly making sense of so much that had been mysterious in the film to that point.

Science-fictional means achieve a similarly ultra-noir effect in the film's presentation of human character. If the typical noir protagonist is a man driven by transpersonal forces like greed and lust, and equipped with only a limited grasp of his own motivations and an even more limited ability to determine his own fate, Murdoch is that protagonist raised to a higher power. As the film opens, Murdoch finds himself without memories – for memory is, of course, the indispensable pre-condition for human will or freedom – and wanted by the police in connection with a series of sadistic sex-murders about which he knows nothing. He also finds himself involved in a troubled marriage with a woman who claims to be his adulterous wife (Jennifer Connelly), but whom he cannot recognise. The explanation turns out to be that the city is under the control of a weird cabal of alien beings known as the Strangers, who are conducting experiments on the inhabitants in an attempt to learn about the human soul. The Strangers are constantly wiping out the memories of their captives and replacing them with new memories, so that they can observe how humans behave in a variety of circumstances. The deflationary determinism of noir is thus rendered technological and apparently irresistible. It is noteworthy that the Strangers' 'imprinting' of their human subjects is achieved with old-fashioned hypodermic syringes that are frighteningly large and look extremely painful. Though the archaic hardware does not seem entirely coherent, logically, with the advanced technical achievements of the Strangers (who can travel through outer space and also 'tune' – that is, shape the material world by thought alone), the hypos serve a vital cinematic function as visual signifiers of the Strangers' brutal and oppressive rule.

As an ultra-noir production, then, *Dark City* is deflationary and deterministic in ways that allegorise aspects of both Freudian and Marxist materialism. A psychoanalytic note is explicitly sounded by Dr Schreber's name, which combines the subject of one of Freud's greatest case-histories with the founder of American SF and horror fiction; and the way that the humans of the city are controlled by fluids directly injected into their heads recalls the psychoanalytic determinism that Freud himself always believed would eventually be grounded in the chemistry and biology of the brain. Similarly, the relation between the humans and the Strangers in the dark city provides a quasi-Marxist figure of class oppression. Indeed, the Strangers – with their unruffled sense of absolute superiority, their accents of icy, affectless detachment towards their human captives, and their total lack of moral scruple when it comes to manipulating those under their control – amount to a satiric caricature of a ruling class. The most memorable of the Strangers is their evident leader, Mr Book, played by Ian Richardson; and Richardson borrows heavily for his performance from one of his own finest roles, his then-recent portrayal of the monstrously reactionary and repressive Tory prime minister Francis Urquhart in the BBC's trilogy of miniseries, beginning with *House of Cards* (1990).[6]

Yet *Dark City* as an SF film not only raises film noir to a higher power but also – again, like *Blade Runner*, though again with greater emphasis and rigour – dialectically produces a powerful inflationary, and utopian, theme that is the antithesis of noir. For much of the film, it appears that a utopian alternative to noir actuality might be provided by Shell Beach, a seaside resort that Murdoch remembers as home. It is visually the opposite of the dark city – bright, sunny and colourful, rather than shadowy and monochromatic – and characters besides Murdoch recall it as a place of happiness and pleasure. A taxi driver, for example, remembers Shell Beach as the spot where he and his wife spent their honeymoon, and he thinks he knows right where it is; but, when pressed by Murdoch to describe *exactly* how to drive there, he finds he cannot. It turns out that nobody knows how to get to Shell Beach – the place is clearly marked on a subway map of the city, but it is impossible to find a train that actually goes there – and its utopian promise is as illusory as Marx and Engels maintained the schemes of the utopian socialists to be. For the memories of Shell Beach are false memories: not only in the narrative sense that they have been imprinted on the humans by the Strangers, but also in the larger philosophic sense that no object of mere nostalgia can possess authentic utopian value. Utopia, as Ernst Bloch insisted, is necessarily geared to the future. It is no accident that the visual details of Shell Beach (displayed on postcards and the like) suggest a vacation resort of the American 1950s – the decade that constitutes the privileged image of social harmony for reactionary American ideology since the late 1960s. But such mere regression cannot provide escape from the dark city.

What *does* offer escape – or rather inflationary transcendence – is transformative human labour and action. 'The only place home exists is in your head', as the always shrewd if sometimes traitorous Dr Schreber tells Murdoch. Perhaps more than he himself quite understands, Schreber's words point to the impeccably Marxist–Blochian principle that home – 'homeland' (*Heimat*), as Bloch himself puts it – can never be merely recovered but must be attained through the revolutionary work of social transformation that, as Marx insisted, necessarily begins in the human intellect and imagination. *Dark City* ultimately offers a figure of precisely such revolutionary transformation. About two-thirds of the way through the film, Murdoch, Bumstead and Schreber finally establish some bonds of human solidarity – Bumstead ceases to regard Murdoch primarily as a murder suspect, and Schreber ends his traitorous collaboration – in order to rebel against the Strangers' oppressive rule. Aided by Schreber's inside knowledge of the Strangers and, even more, by Murdoch's ability to tune – a talent that the Strangers had been confident was reserved exclusively to themselves – the humans prevail. Human freedom is possible after all, and the determining power of the ruling class, which had seemed unassailable, is broken.

Dark City is thus, finally, and despite its noir or ultra-noir deflationary aspect, a work in the great inflationary tradition of Blake's *The Marriage of Heaven and Hell* (1790–93), Shelley's *Prometheus Unbound* (1820) and Beethoven's *Fidelio* (1805–14): a story of fetters broken and freedom attained. This upward narrative curve can be traced even in the film's most technical details. Proyas constructs the earlier part of his movie mainly through an accumulation of discrete shots, with little tracking or panning: and the effect is one of stasis, entrapment and determinism. But as the humans assert themselves and move against the Strangers' tyranny, the cameras begin to move as well, and a contrasting effect of progressive flow is achieved. Speaking for humanity, Murdoch – who all along has been a kind of ordinary Everyman – announces his ability to 'make this world anything I want it to be': and he suits his actions to his words. He succeeds in tuning an entire ocean, water being both the indispensable basis of human life and the substance to which the Strangers have the greatest aversion. The film ends in a gloriously bright and colourful ocean-side scene that is as far from the visual style of noir as possible. The tableau recalls the pictures we have seen of Shell Beach; yet the film is careful not to *identify* the two. Shell Beach was a mere regressive wish, but this is the real thing, the real product of human thought and action. We leave Murdoch to begin a love relationship with the Jennifer Connelly character, who is no longer burdened with the false memories of having been Murdoch's cheating wife. It is the sort of visionary, material transcendence that has always been what SF does best – and that, of course, has, at least since the final lines of *The Communist Manifesto*, been the ultimate point of Marxism itself.

Notes

1. See Carl Freedman, 'On Kubrick's *2001*: Form and Ideology in Science-Fiction Cinema', in Freedman, *The Incomplete Projects: Marxism, Modernity, and the Politics of Culture* (Middletown: Wesleyan University Press, 2002), pp. 91–112.
2. Ernst Bloch, 'Marxism and Poetry', in *The Utopian Function of Art and Literature: Selected Essays*, transl. Jack Zipes and Frank Mecklenburg (Cambridge: MIT Press, 1988), p. 163 (emphasis added).
3. Karl Marx, *Capital*, Vol. 3, transl. David Fernbach (New York: Vintage, 1981), p. 959 (emphasis added).
4. My comments on *Blade Runner* refer to the significantly different 1992 'director's cut'; in most discussion of this much-discussed film the latter version is (I think rightly) considered definitive.
5. *Dark City* is, indeed, the title of a film noir, directed by German émigré William Dieterle in 1950.
6. Followed by *To Play the King* (1993) and *The Final Cut* (1995).

4

SPECTACLE, TECHNOLOGY AND COLONIALISM IN SF CINEMA: THE CASE OF WIM WENDERS' *UNTIL THE END OF THE WORLD*

John Rieder

Nearly everyone who has written about Wim Wenders' epic-length 1991 SF film *Until the End of the World* (UTEOTW) has commented upon the global scope of both its production and its plot, and while some praise it as the pinnacle of Wenders' distinguished career, negative opinions range from bemusement over its zany but chaotic energy to condemnation of its Eurocentric exploitation of non-Western landscape.[1] But the way the film's mise-en-scène engages exoticising, Eurocentric discourses is more complex and more critically acute than the film's detractors recognise. For the matter of colonial history is everywhere in Wenders' film – not only in the global crisis that acts as its premise, but also in the corporate competition that motivates the secretive location of a cutting-edge research facility in the Australian outback, in the tensions between therapeutic intervention and invasion that characterise the research project itself, in the dissonance between hospitality and assimilation that bedevils the indigenous Australians who donate space and labour to the project, and in the interweaving of romance and tourism in the adventures of its white protagonists. Moreover, these pervasive colonial references are integral to the film's generic texture. That is, one cannot read the film fully – or even adequately – as long as the colonial matter is taken to be merely the superficial decoration of a road film or the exotic backdrop of a tale of romance and international intrigue.[2] The colonial matter is crucial because such concerns are endemic to SF, and understanding their significance in the film involves attending to its engagement of that generic history. Although the film fails to extricate itself from the ideologies implicit in its colonial premises, neither does it simply rehearse them. It alternately exposes colonialism's durable impact on SF, indulges in colonialist fantasies, and critically subverts the ideological basis of those same fantasies. The film's sustained, ambivalent engagement with SF's generic debt to colonialism makes it both a symptomatic and an estimable work of art.

This argument is worth making not only because it is always worthwhile to extricate a thoughtful work from misunderstanding, but also because of the questions raised by the unevenness and contradictions of the film's production, distribution and reception. The production of *UTEOTW* was something of a fiasco. Wenders exhausted a budget of $20-odd million in the course of filming on four continents, forcing him to abandon the planned finale in Africa. To make matters worse, the film flopped disastrously at the box office upon its release in December 1991. Nonetheless, as the movie made the art-house circuit over the next few years (and as its distinguished soundtrack CD proved to have considerably more commercial appeal than the initial release of the film itself), it began developing a reputation as an underground masterpiece. The film's elite status was further enhanced in the mid 1990s, when Wenders issued a director's cut, screened for carefully selected audiences, that expanded the 158-minute commercial release, produced under his studio contract's stipulations as to length, into a 280-minute trilogy. Currently this version is available on DVD in Europe (as *Bis ans Ende der Welt: Director's Cut*), but contractual issues continue to prevent its release in North America, where the studio cut, once available on VHS, has also gone out of print. The tangle of commercial, legal and artistic issues in this saga suggests that the film's remarkably uneven reception is not simply a result of its internal strengths and defects, but rather conforms to the complicated terrain of its production and distribution.

This suspicion draws added force from Carl Freedman's argument that SF 'cinema is ... structured on an immense and perhaps disabling contradiction' between 'the anti-conceptual bias of its most fundamental formal resource: special effects' and the critical impulses that make SF narrative, at its best, what Darko Suvin calls the literature of cognitive estrangement.[3] The crux of Freedman's thesis is that the spectacle of special effects tends to overpower the cognitive, analytic impulse motivating the effects of estrangement that he, like Suvin, sees as being crucial to SF. If elaborating an estranged but plausible and coherent setting is one of SF's most important formal obligations, the power of spectacle in SF cinema typically threatens to evacuate this procedure of its exploratory, speculative qualities and replace them with mere sensory overload. Instead of being called upon to think, as in Brechtian theatre, the viewer is merely absorbed. Freedman presents this contradiction between cognitive estrangement and special effects in formal terms, but I would ask what substance we can assign to generic form itself, unless it is lodged in the repetitive force of commercial and cultural pressures upon narrative production and reception. Wenders' treatment of setting and special effects bears the burden of such pressures, and his different versions of *UTEOTW* respond to them in tellingly different ways.

SF and the World Market

The plot of *UTEOTW*, with global crisis and panic-driven migrations in the background and its central characters' whirlwind tour from Europe to Asia to the Australian outback in the foreground, maps itself onto a well-established generic and planetary geography of imperial centre and frontier. Just as the emergence and consolidation of industrial economies in Europe and North America is unthinkable without the expropriation of raw materials, the exportation of commodities, and the migration of people from and into territories under western colonial and imperial control, so SF is shaped throughout its history by the imaginary relationship of the European (and later American) economic core to the periphery or 'contact zone' between capitalist and non-capitalist economies and western and non-western cultures.[4] *UTEOTW* enacts this relationship through two well-established SF tropes – the technological breakthrough or fantastic invention, and its counterpart, the plot of technology going out of control and threatening to destroy its makers. The way Wenders handles these two motifs clearly exposes their common ground in the capitalist dynamics of technical innovation, market competition and colonial–imperial governance.

That the breakthrough invention is one of SF's oldest and most durable conventions testifies to the genre's close relationship with industrial capitalism's fierce drive for technical innovation. From its beginnings SF has been fascinated with marvellous machines and problems of engineering. More important than this fascination with gadgetry, though, has been SF's reflection upon the economic and social impact of such innovations – the competitive advantage technical innovation gives its possessors in the market, and the military and political power it gives them over the rest of the world. Thus SF and modern industrial arms races have walked hand-in-hand from their beginnings.[5] Furthermore, one of the keys to SF's imaginary 'contact zone' is the uneven distribution of technology across a spatial geography that the ideology of progress codes as a temporal one. In the ideological environment of the late nineteenth and early twentieth centuries, where the industrially developed world saw non-industrialised cultures as survivals of its own pre-industrial past, possession of the technological breakthrough was tantamount to ownership of the present itself – a logic which relegated those who did not have it to the residual past. For the ultimate nightmare driving the arms races of modernity, dramatised in an invasion fantasy like H.G. Wells' *The War of the Worlds* (1898), is the industrial and imperial core's fear of being turned into the pre-industrial and colonised periphery, and so, according to the temporal logic of the ideology of progress, of being subjugated as inevitably as the future supersedes the past. Therefore the play of inclusion and exclusion, and the fantasies of power and impotence that circulate in the vicinity of the technical innovation, have throughout SF's history lent their ambivalence to the genre as a whole, with its dreams of conquest over space, time, disease, poverty and war always counterbalanced by its Frankenstein monsters, fantasies of invasion and apocalyptic disasters.

The trope of the breakthrough invention governs the foreground of most of *UTEOTW*, dictating the movements of its main characters across Europe and Asia to North America, and finally Australia. The marvellous invention itself is a camera that, instead of recording light, records the neurological impulses of the brain in the act of seeing. The initial goal of the camera's inventor, the conventionally egomaniacal and obsessed Dr Farber (Max von Sydow), is to reproduce images that can be communicated to his blind wife, Edith (Jeanne Moreau). The project of collecting these images leads his son, Sam Farber (William Hurt), on the long journey that turns into the film's extended chase sequence. The disguises and zaniness of the chase rest, finally, on the secrecy Farber has been forced into in order to keep the project focused on his personal goal, and hence to keep the camera out of the hands of the US government, who claim to own it because they at some point sponsored his research. The same secrecy accounts for his relocation to a hidden underground laboratory in the outback. Thus the plot in its entirety moves steadily towards a condensation of the technological frontier – possession and operation of the camera – with the geographical 'end of the world' represented by the Australian laboratory; and it interweaves this movement with the approach of the other end of the world: the apocalyptic catastrophe that looms in the background.

The dynamics of economic competition in the foreground are matched by those of political competition in the background, in which an Indian 'rogue' nuclear satellite has gone out of control and threatens to wreak apocalyptic destruction on the planet, inspiring panicky evacuations in the path of the satellite's possible impact and heated international controversy about how to deal with the threat. One might well compare these disorderly proceedings with the pristine solution to the threat of nuclear aggression offered in *The Day the Earth Stood Still* (Wise, 1951): if Earth's squabbling nations will not abandon their aggression, which is threatening to spill out into space, then the guardian robots of an advanced extraterrestrial civilisation will rain down global destruction. In contrast to the Cold War fantasy of the benevolent super-cop imposing world harmony, the contemporary international world order exposed in *UTEOTW* looks exactly like what Michael Hardt and Antonio Negri a few years later would describe as post-imperialist Empire: an endless exercise in crisis management, with the terrifying wild card of US unilateralism in the place of Leviathan.[6] The tension between the foreground and background plots, then, lays over the entire film a conflict between individual autonomy (both in terms of the market and of individual desire) and collective political determination (a determination as capricious as classical fate). The repeated solution to this conflict is the decision to go off the grid, enacted on the individual level early in the film by Claire Tourneur's (Solveig Dommartin) defiance of her comically insistent dashboard computer's warnings that she is driving off the map; throughout the film by the Farbers' flight to the Australian outback; and, most tellingly, by the explosion of the nuclear satellite in the centre of the film, which temporarily disconnects everyone in the film from the rest of the world – and, for a time, seems to have eliminated the grid itself.

Going off the grid turns out to be impossible, however. The world lives through the nuclear explosion, the US government catches up with Farber, and Claire Tourneur's romantic adventure finally installs her, not outside the grid, but within and against it, operating counter-surveillance of 'environmental crime' aboard a Greenpeace satellite. The ultimate impossibility of extricating oneself from the devices of corporate competition or the international anarchy of contemporary imperialism resounds throughout the film's final movement, when Doctor Farber turns his camera to the task of recording dreams. Farber's inward journey of exploration is both illusory and disastrous. The recordings themselves hardly resemble actual dreams. Instead these completely silent, garishly colored video clips are aggressively stylised constructions that, instead of penetrating the depths, evacuate interiority. Nonetheless, the dream images exercise a narcissistic fascination that wholly absorbs and debilitates the film's internal spectators. Thus the dream recordings – which in their extent, their oblique narrative content, and their overlaying of filmic treatments on landscape footage, forcibly recall the 'light show' sequence at the end of *2001* – precisely depict cinematic absorption overpowering narrative articulation, bodying forth a horrific version of the anti-cognitive tendency of cinematic SF described by Freedman. *UTEOTW* turns the generic, formal contradiction between spectacle and narrative into the internal self-contradiction that the film simultaneously depends upon Farber's invention for its most striking cinematography and condemns it for spreading, as the narrator calls it, the 'disease of images'. But *UTEOTW* also models the congruence of that contradiction with the flows and concentrations of power, capital and populations exposed in its mise-en-scène. The addictive dream recordings, in this light, represent the latest form of capitalist invasion, the penetration of the viewers by what Guy Debord would call 'the pseudoneeds imposed by modern consumerism ... an unlimited artificiality which overpowers any living desire'.[7] Connecting this hyperbolic rendition of passive consumption to the film's engagement with colonial ideology, I now suggest, entails following the thread of Wenders' allusion in the dream scenes to the 'light show' sequence in *2001*.

Progress and Passivity in *2001*

Kubrick's *2001* is a watershed in the history of SF cinema from a technical standpoint, because its production values, and particularly the sophistication of its sets and special effects, set a new standard for the genre. But from an ideological point of view *2001* is less a breakthrough than a culmination of the SF cinema of the 1950s, with its male-dominated military–scientific environment, its fascination with high-tech engineering and, as I will demonstrate, its colonialist ideology. Thus it is not an arbitrary choice, but rather one deeply embedded in *UTEOTW*'s play on colonial themes and its engagement of SF tradition, that makes Dr Farber's blind wife, the supposed beneficiary of his research project, a practitioner of that paradigmatic colonial discipline, anthropology. For *2001* itself begins with an extended exercise in evolutionary anthropology, the prehistoric 'Dawn of Man' sequence. The relation of this opening vignette to the rest of the film is crucial both to its internal thematics and to its bearing on *UTEOTW*.

The problem of interpreting the 'Dawn of Man' sequence is encapsulated in the ambiguity of its famous ending, when the ape-man, having used a bone to club an enemy to death and establish his group's territorial dominance over the local waterhole, flings his weapon into the air in triumph. A shot of the bone in mid-flight cuts to a space station in free-falling orbit around the planet, establishing an identity between the primitive tool and the space station, thereby positing the bone-weapon as the origin and essence of human technology. This identity, stretching across untold thousands of years, stands in sharp contrast to the leap from ape to man we have just witnessed, both unfolding its profound ramifications and preparing the narrative's representation of the next sublime evolutionary leap in the film's finale. Yet the same gesture that equates the most primitive and the most advanced human technology also suggests that the struggle over the waterhole is an epitome of human history, and that the crux of technical innovation and scientific discovery – at the waterhole as in the secretive arrangements that surround the discovery of the monolith on the moon – is the empowerment of its possessors to separate themselves from and dominate their opponents. The cut, then, denotes progress and stasis at the same time, and so injects a certain chilling irony into the 'Blue Danube' waltz of the spaceship into the station.

This contradiction is in one way typical of colonial ideology, and in another way peculiar to this narrative – although this peculiarity partakes of an even more crucial ideological strategy. What is typical, first of all, is the play of identity and difference in the colonial encounter between the civilised and the primitive, such that the primitive, curiously observed in all its bizarre otherness, nonetheless displays the secret of civilisation's primal self. The bone-to-spaceship cut, by capturing that play, powerfully evokes the pervasive ambivalence with which the colonial imaginary invests the exotic other and condenses that ambivalence into the conjuncture of a myth of origins and an ideology of progress. But more to the point is the cut's coherence with the peculiar relation between evolutionary progress and technological innovation in *2001*. The intervention of the monolith has the effect, first of all, of making the ape-man's discovery of tools into a gift. It is, in fact, the gift of development that – like the super-robot of *The Day the Earth Stood Still* – the benevolent, super-civilised aliens bestow upon the primitive, but potentially human (or more-than-human), apes to set them on the path towards civilisation. Therefore, as the cut so economically reveals, the evolutionary path from the waterhole to the space station is plotted from the outset, its teleology inscribed in the gift itself.

This predetermination of the path of evolution leads to a second, more consequential peculiarity in the plot of *2001*: the essential passivity of the human recipients of the gift of development. They are simply following a route laid out for them by the aliens, or rather pointed out by the aliens but channelled in the very structure of things. Humanity will inevitably find the monolith buried on the moon if it follows the true way of development, because the technology of space travel is the preordained apex of this stage of human civilisation, and its driving rationale of territorial expansion is the motor of history and a law of nature. Technology has its own logic, revealed in the bone-to-spaceship cut, and that autonomy of the tool with relation to its user will develop into *2001*'s most gripping episode: the attempted takeover of the Jupiter mission by the computer HAL. The same essential passivity, the near absence of real human agency, accounts, I think, for the utter banality of the bureaucrat Heywood Floyd's (William Sylvester) dialogue and the disturbingly flat affect of the astronauts.[8] The heroes of the middle section of *2001* are the sets, especially the exceptionally well-crafted interiors of the various space vehicles, rather than the humans who inhabit them. From the bone-to-ship cut on, the film develops an intractable doubt as to whether the humans really guide their own journey or whether, not just the various ships and tools, but the entire plot of development traps them inside a vehicle essentially beyond their control. Even Dave Bowman's (Keir Dullea) victory over HAL does not resolve this doubt, because it only delivers him to the passive position of passenger to the next stage of development, recipient of the gift at the end of the road from the waterhole.

The resemblance of this passivity to that of the dream-image addicts in *UTEOTW*, and between the two films' portrayal of the conflict between individual autonomy and collective fate, is based on their shared historical and ideological field. For the plot of *2001* constitutes a rewriting of evolution as colonialism. The epiphanic transformation of apes into humans in the 'Dawn of Man' has nothing to do with natural selection and everything to do with the gift of development. *2001*'s rendering of contact between the indigenous culture of the apes and the technological gifts of the more mobile culture of the aliens repeats a time-honoured rhetorical pattern that combines reification (development is not culturally specific but inscribed in nature) with apologetics (the alien gift-givers are benevolent, disinterested donors who are rescuing the natives from being exiled from history). For all its technical virtuosity, the final section of *2001* does not make any thematic or critical leap beyond its predecessors comparable to Bowman's leap beyond *Homo sapiens*.

What it does accomplish, however, is a startling artistic climax to the film's blending of high art (abstract visual material, the modernist music of Ligeti) with its popular narrative genre (the evolutionary leap as a well-established SF trope) and mass cultural appeal, as witness the audiences who left the film blown away by the 'light show'. That the formal contradiction between cinematic absorption and narrative estrangement should also become vividly apparent in this sequence is no accident, but rather the consequence of Kubrick's success at blending high, popular and mass cultural elements. At the same time, the very obscurity of Kubrick's finale would seem to reiterate the play of inclusion and exclusion that joins the plot of the technological breakthrough to that of the colonial frontier. The stunning power of Kubrick's spectacle (which, according to Freedman, thematises the formal impossibility of cinematic SF) epitomises once again the ambiguous benefits of the gift. Is Bowman as Star-Child a figure of the audience's sublime transformation? Or is he a better figure for what the film denies the audience, his calm gaze so utterly different from the passive, dumbfounded reception the finale inevitably evoked? Freedman is correct that, considered as a pinnacle of cinematic SF, *2001* simultaneously proclaims a kind of generic defeat. Let me add, however, that Kubrick's achievement takes much of its equivocal tenor from its ideological environment, the contact zone of colonial anthropology.

Spectacle and Apocalypse in *UTEOTW*

In a comparison between the dream-machine sequences in the latter section of *UTEOTW* and the light-show sequence in *2001*, Wenders' handling of spectacle certainly emerges as more self-reflexive and critically acute. Instead of *2001*'s mimesis of the alien visitors' humanly incomprehensible forms of travel and communication, *UTEOTW* represents the products of a camera that literally alienates its subjects' dreams, in the Hegelian sense of exteriorising the products of mental labour. This transforms Bowman's passivity in the hands of a transcendent destiny into a clear-cut representation of the audience's absorption in technologically mediated images of their own desire. The gift of development, instead of raising its recipients to the next stage of an evolutionary hierarchy, turns them into addicts, dependent upon the new technology for their abjected self-recognition. In addition, Wenders locates Dr Farber's gift in the context of multinational capitalist R&D and international 'new world order' political crisis management. Bowman's isolation is first an effect of accident, in the drama of HAL's breakdown, and then of distinction, in his final transformation. The isolation of the dream-machine's subjects is instead presented as 'the disease of images'. Their narcissistic, quasi-hallucinatory entrapment suggestively links together Farber's egocentricism, the tainted gifts of development, and the possessive individualism of the market and military competition that has driven Farber's research project itself into the outback.

The same critical edge might be discerned in *UTEOTW*'s version of anthropology, which is so pointedly opposed to that which underlies the plot of *2001* that it would seem to reflect a paradigm shift in the discipline. Edith Farber's work emphasises community and cultural practices (like the recorded song of the African pygmy children that helps to establish the romantic attraction between Sam and Claire) rather than territoriality, dominance and weapons – perhaps in keeping with a late-twentieth-century shift in human evolutionary models that connects sexual choice with linguistic proficiency and gathering skills, rather than with male strength and hunting skills.[9] The relationship she has established with the Mbantua would seem to indicate that, instead of the reified notion of development operating in *2001*, her brand of anthropology recognises cultural difference without assuming it to be hierarchical or inscribing it in a narrative of progress.

Unfortunately, the film does not manage the break from colonial ideology for which all of this might lead us to hope. For example, the film's respect for non-western traditional wisdom is not so much anti-colonial as a nostalgic exercise in which a temporary retreat from modernity helps the tourist subject recover from its deleterious effects – as in the romantic interlude spent by Sam and Claire at a rural inn in Japan, where an old herbalist cures the injuries Farber's camera has inflicted on Sam's eyes.[10] Later, in a similar fashion, Sam's Mbantuan family uses traditional methods to help him recover from the psychological effects of the camera's dream recordings. But the entire rendering of the Farbers' extended Mbantuan family is flawed by an exceptionalism all too familiar to colonial fantasy. Just as Sam and Claire are the only guests at the Japanese inn, and the entire effect of the episode would be ruined if the place were crowded with other white guests seeking herbal cures, the status enjoyed by the Farbers among the Mbantua is more a kind of privileged access to a pre-modern refuge than the formation of an anti-colonial alliance.

That privileged access works to a somewhat more complex effect in the mise-en-scène of Farber's laboratory, so that it discloses the contradictions surrounding colonial ideology, global space and indigenous knowledge in the film. The cave where

Farber has relocated his experiments after fleeing from the US government appears to be, or to have been, a space specially marked by the Mbantua people, since one reaches it via a tunnel decorated with aboriginal pictography. Thus the capitalist and imperialist dynamics that generate secrecy around western technical innovation are almost literally superimposed upon an aboriginal architecture that apparently articulates access to the cave with duties and responsibilities, and perhaps enforces a separation between the sacred and the profane. Although the white scientists are the guests of the Mbantua, the laboratory is a geopolitical space that parasitically attaches itself to and threatens to empty of significance the radically differently configured space of its aboriginal host.[11] The instability of this arrangement eventually asserts itself when the research team falls apart into its white and aboriginal components. From their first appearance, the frock-coated aboriginal technicians in Farber's laboratory look like the subjects of an updated missionary fantasy, proving their humanity by becoming just like the white man, who nonetheless remains superior and in charge. It is entirely to the film's credit that it refuses this resolution of cultural difference by univocal assimilation, and moreover makes it absolutely clear that Farber's refusal of reciprocity – his neglect of the duties of mourning enjoined upon him by Mbantuan protocol after Edith's death – causes the partnership to fail. It is also to the film's credit that this failure does not simply erase the critical potential of Edith's anthropology, but rather defeats it in an open struggle with Farber's bald rationale for ignoring the Mbantuan rites: 'I'm a white fellow, you know'.

It is no coincidence that the host–parasite relation between Farber's project and the Mbantuan cave resembles the tensions between the spaceship and its human inhabitants in the central section of *2001*, because the ambiguous role of the white heroes as guests or invaders matches the ambiguities surrounding autonomy and destiny noted earlier, and all are inherent in the colonial underpinnings of the narratives. Similar host–parasite tensions run through the most thoughtful science fiction cinema of the period between *2001* and *UTEOTW*, such as *Alien* (Scott, 1979) and *Blade Runner* (Scott, 1982). *UTEOTW* cannily makes the colonial dynamics of hospitality, settlement and invasion explicitly and tellingly intimate with the tensions of inclusion and exclusion surrounding the technical innovation. The main figure for this intimacy is the extended Farber–Mbantua family formed out of Edith's anthropological research, but the Farber family itself turns out to be a complex and shifting figure that places the ultimate instability of the Farber–Mbantua partnership in its global context.

There are, in fact, three Farber families, each of which articulates a different aspect of colonial and post-colonial history and ideology. The Farbers' nuclear family, dominated by the Oedipal competition and self-absorbed passions of father and son, is ultimately a figure for the blind colonial settler. The key point here is that Farber – like the patriarch of all mad scientists, Victor Frankenstein – combines his wonderful technical expertise with stunning emotional ignorance, and he ultimately turns this ignorance into the active principle guiding his interactions with the Mbantua. In contrast, the Farbers' extended western family – with its global dispersion motivated, first, by the Nazi holocaust, and more recently by corporate and governmental competition over possession of the camera – exemplifies the crisis-plagued fragmentation and incoherence of the international order. The aboriginal family, finally, offers its hospitality and alternative values as that more or less effective, more or less hallucinatory or impossible, locus of escape from the dominant order – an escape that the indigenous, exotic other consistently signifies in the colonial imaginary.

The three Farber families come together to the best effect in the section of the film between the explosion of the rogue satellite and Edith's death. The key is that the explosion of the satellite suspends all global power relations. The survivors who gather in the Mbantuan refuge do not know whether they are merely isolated temporarily or are already inhabitants of a post-apocalyptic world, living in a new 'Dawn of Man'. The three family networks dictate three distinct responses to this situation. First, the Farber nuclear family goes on in exactly the same mode as before the explosion, ignoring the world at large and moving forward with development of the experimental camera. Second, Edith, having been given the gift of sight in these experiments, surveys her dispersed family and, in reviewing their history and her own, seems forced to recapitulate the ongoing crisis of western modernity – moving from her youth, when she met Farber as a fellow refugee from the Nazi holocaust, through the recent past, when struggles over rights to the camera forced them to go into hiding and lose contact with their children, to the present, when she is surrounded by refugees from the nuclear explosion. She responds by sinking into depression and death. Third, in refreshing contrast to the obsessions and recriminations surrounding the first two alternatives, an odd patchwork community forms among the refugees in the Mbantuan enclave. The main figures Wenders uses for this community are music and storytelling, with the film's narrator, Eugene Fitzpatrick (Sam Neill), serving as spokesman both for the film's optimism and for its generic orientation: 'The present will look after itself, but it's our duty to realise the future with our imagination'.

Of these three responses to the suspension of global territorialisation in the current world order, the director's cut most expands and elaborates upon the third, which is only hinted at in the shorter commercial release. Here is where the political economy of contemporary cinema has its most evident impact on the film. It seems clear that the editing of the commercial version produced a concentrated focus on the Farber family's Oedipal triangle, at the expense of the more diverse unfolding of relationships among the 'secondary' characters that the director's cut elaborates in the Mbantuan refuge. Thus the commercial release focuses steadily on the laboratory and the camera – that is, on the cutting edge of technical innovation and the quasi-heroic action that defines the lab as a colony of the centre settled upon and transforming its peripheral surroundings; whereas the director's cut allows itself to explore much more thoroughly the space of the refuge, where a community is forming that has no ideology of progress, and is not driven by an economic demand for technical innovation, but on the contrary is simply trying to reinvent the possibility of a future in the face of modernity's hitherto self-destructive history. I do not want to exaggerate the critical power of the interlude in the Mbantuan refuge, which also partakes of the touristic logic I have already mentioned. But in the difference between the studio version and the director's cut one can discern contrasting economies of plot and pace that clearly correlate, on the one hand, the expectations guiding production for first-run commercial venues with the aggressive colonial ideology endemic to most cinematic SF, and, on the other, those targeting the restricted audiences who first saw the director's cut with some sort of resistance to it.

This suggests that the formal, aesthetic and thematic differences between the two versions correspond not just to the more or less complete realisation of Wenders' vision, but also to the structural tensions in the field of cultural production between the economies of mass circulation and an 'aristocracy of culture', as Bourdieu calls it, where prestige, scarcity, and distinction outweigh direct monetary benefits.[12] It would seem that, in contrast to Kubrick's success at synthesising such tensions, Wenders' commercial flop/cult masterpiece both elaborates and succumbs to them. Yet his achievement is not merely another symptomatic failure of SF cinema to reconcile the genre's cognitive vocation with the commercial pressures of mass spectacle. Its self-reflexivity, its staging of apocalypse as the border between history and possibility, and its complex engagement with SF's colonial legacy make it one of the most substantial and important SF films of its decade.

Notes

1. See Roger Ebert, 'Until the End of the World', *Chicago Sun-Times*, 17 January 1992, available at http://rogerebert.suntimes.com, and Dimitris Eleftheriotis, 'Global Visions and European Perspectives', in Ziauddin Sardar and Sean Cubitt, eds, *Aliens R Us: The Other in Science Fiction Cinema* (London: Pluto, 2002), pp. 164–80. For a highly positive judgement in the first wave of reviews, see Vincent Canby, 'Review/Film: New Hat for Wenders: Daffy and Lighthearted', *New York Times*, 25 December 1991, available at http://movies2. nytimes.com. Daniel Griffin later wrote that the film contains 'the

single greatest scene concerning nuclear holocaust that I have ever seen' ('Until the End of the World', in *Film as Art: Daniel Griffin's Guide to Cinema*, available at http://uashome.alaska.edu/~jndfg20/website/untiltheendoftheworld.htm), and an anonymous reviewer on IMDb writes, '"Until the End of the World" is one of the most beautiful films of the 20th century. It is the pinnacle of Wim Wenders' career' (BornJaded, 'Breathtaking and Permanent', posted 17 July 2004 at http://www.imdb.com/title/tt0101458/#comment).

2. As in Ebert, 'Until the End of the World', and Eleftheriotis, 'Global Visions', respectively.

3. Carl Freedman, 'On Kubrick's *2001*: Form and Ideology in Science-Fiction Cinema', in *The Incomplete Projects: Marxism, Modernity, and the Politics of Culture* (Middletown: Wesleyan University Press, 2002), p. 107.

4. See John Rieder, *Colonialism and the Emergence of Science Fiction* (Middletown: Wesleyan University Press, 2008).

5. See I.F. Clarke, *Voices Prophesying War: Future Wars, 1763–3749* (New York: Oxford University Press, 1992), and H. Bruce Franklin, *War Stars: The Superweapon and the American Imagination* (New York: Oxford University Press, 1988).

6. See Michael Hardt and Antonio Negri, *Empire* (Cambridge: Harvard University Press, 2000).

7. Guy Debord, *The Society of the Spectacle*, transl. Ken Knabb (London: Rebel Press, n.d.), p. 34.

8. As observed in Vivian Sobchack, *Screening Space: The American Science Fiction Film* (New York: Ungar, 1987) and Freedman, 'On Kubrick's *2001*'.

9. See Donna Haraway, 'The Past is the Contested Zone: Human Nature and Theories of Production and Reproduction in Primate Behaviour Studies', in *Simians, Cyborgs, and Women: The Reinvention of Nature* (New York: Routledge, 1991), pp. 21–42.

10. This is not to mention the egregious stereotyping of the Japanese that also mars the earlier scene in the Tokyo hotel.

11. On the usefulness of the frame of hospitality for analysing colonial encounters, see Paul Lyons, *American Pacificism: Oceania in the US Imagination* (New York: Routledge, 2006).

12. On the 'aristocracy of culture', see Pierre Bourdieu, *Distinction: A Social Critique of the Judgement of Taste*, transl. Richard Nice (Cambridge: Harvard University Press, 1984), pp. 11–96; on the economies of profit and prestige in mass and restricted circulation, see Bourdieu's 'The Field of Cultural Production, or: The Economic World Reversed', *Poetics* 12 (1983), pp. 311–55.

Part II

When Worlds Collide

5

THE SINGULARITY IS HERE

Steven Shaviro

The destiny of intelligent tool-using life [i]s to be a stepping-stone in the evolution of corporate instruments.

Charles Stross[1]

Charles Stross's *Accelerando* (2005) is a post-Singularity novel, the best-known example of a small but growing SF subgenre. Post-Singularity SF endeavours to imagine, and work through the consequences of, what techno-futurists have called the Singularity. This is the supposed – and strictly speaking unimaginable – moment when the human race crosses a technological threshold, and definitively becomes posthuman. According to this scenario, the exponential growth in sheer computing power, together with advances in the technologies of artificial intelligence, nanomanufacture and genetic manipulation, will utterly change the nature of who and what we are. Human beings will either be replaced by sentient machines, or (more likely) merge their brains and bodies with such machines. In addition to *Accelerando*, post-Singularity novels include Vernor Vinge's *Marooned in Realtime* (2004) – Vinge is in fact the inventor of the term and concept of the 'technological Singularity'[2] – and Cory Doctorow's *Down and Out in the Magic Kingdom* (2003).

Of course, SF narratives have played with ideas of super-computers and superhuman intelligences for quite some time. But post-Singularity fiction in the strict sense takes off from the computing technologies of the 1990s and from the speculations of Vinge, Hans Moravec and especially Ray Kurzweil, self-described as 'one of the world's leading inventors, thinkers, and futurists,

with a twenty-year track record of accurate predictions'.[3] Kurzweil
explains the Singularity as follows:

> It's a future period during which the pace of technological change will be so
> rapid, its impact so deep, that human life will be irreversibly transformed
> ... this epoch will transform the concepts that we rely on to give meaning
> to our lives, from our business models to the cycle of human life, including
> death itself ... Within several decades information-based technologies will
> encompass all human knowledge and proficiency, ultimately including
> the pattern-recognition powers, problem-solving skills, and emotional
> and moral intelligence of the human brain itself ... the changes [these
> technological developments] bring about will appear to rupture the fabric
> of human history.[4]

He estimates that this transformation will occur no later than
the year 2049.

Though Kurzweil specifies that the Singularity is 'neither
utopian nor dystopian',[5] the affinity of his vision with utopian
thought is clear. After the Singularity, Kurzweil assures us, health,
wealth, and immortality – not to mention the coolest computer
games and simulations ever – will be available, at no cost, to
everyone. Scarcity will be a thing of the past. All barriers and
binary oppositions will fall: 'there will be no distinction, post-
Singularity, between human and machine or between physical and
virtual reality'.[6] In this sense, the Singularity is about getting rid
of our cumbersome bodies; as Kurzweil puts it, 'our version 1.0
biological bodies are ... frail and subject to a myriad of failure
modes'.[7] A post-Singularity upgrade to version 2.0 will get rid of
most of these bugs; and 'with version 3.0 bodies', Kurzweil assures
us, we will be 'able to morph into different forms at will'.[8]

But it isn't just our own bodies that Kurzweil wants to 'upgrade'
or supersede. The Singularity is really about eliminating the
resistance of the outside world to the instantaneous fulfilment of
all our desires. It promises to overcome materiality in general. No
doubt, Freud would call this an infantile fantasy of omnipotence.
Modern science, from Copernicus to Darwin and beyond, is
commonly seen as refuting such a fantasy by dethroning the
human species from its delusion of 'centrality in the cosmos'.[9]

But the lesson of the Singularity, for Kurzweil, is that the age of such humiliations is over. For 'it turns out that we are central, after all', and the 'accelerating pace' of our technology 'will continue until the entire universe is at our fingertips'.[10]

The Singularity is thus fraught with theological significance. It is something like what Alain Badiou calls an Event: a decisive moment of creation and crystallisation 'which compels us to decide a way of being'.[11] Even before it happens, the mere thought of the Singularity – like Nietzsche's 'abysmal thought' of the Eternal Return, or St Paul's thought of the Resurrection – is a conversion experience that compels us to dedicate our lives to its Truth. 'To truly understand [the Singularity]', Kurzweil says, 'changes one's view of life in general and one's own particular life'.[12] An orientation towards the future – even, or especially, towards an incomprehensible one – must alter your behaviour in the present. Kurzweil himself, for instance, 'takes more than 250 [vitamin] supplements daily, often in doses much larger than the US RDAs' and 'closely monitors or tests at least 50 measures of his own health' on a regular basis.[13] All this is to ensure that he stays alive long enough to make it to the Singularity, when he will be able to upload his mind onto the Net.

Given the sensibility at work here, I can only agree with Tony Girard, the character in Ken MacLeod's *The Cassini Division* (1999) who sarcastically dismisses the Singularity as 'the Rapture for nerds'.[14] Now, Badiou invokes St Paul's conversion not for religious ends, but only in order to mobilise it for a new construction of Leninist revolutionary subjectivity. And such eminent Marxist critics as Fredric Jameson and Carl Freedman have long argued for the political implications – in contrast to religious ones – of the utopian impulse in SF.[15] But where does this leave us with regard to the Singularity? Kurzweil's speculations are certainly utopian, in that they envision a future world without scarcity or deprivation. And Kurzweil is as overtly anti-religious as Badiou or Jameson; the post-Singularity world, difficult as it may be to comprehend, is presented as a 'here and now', rather than as a transcendent afterlife. Yet, in striking contrast to any other utopian fiction, Kurzweil spends scarcely a paragraph in his more than 600-pages-long tome discussing social and political issues. There's a brief passage about the necessity of developing 'smart weapons' for 'cyberwarfare' and an equally brief section about the need to protect 'intellectual property' from unauthorised replication.[16] And that's about it. All the rest is minutely detailed technological discussion, with a heavy dose of extrapolation. Kurzweil's book is classic hard SF, if we leave aside its rather silly claim to be making 'accurate predictions'. But it's so narrow in its technological concerns, and in its single-minded claims for transformation and rupture, that it almost seems an inadvertent parody of the genre.

The curious configuration of *The Singularity is Near* – its apolitical and asocial utopianism, and science- and technology-based millenarianism – is, of course, not accidental. For the whole point of Kurzweil's speculation – its ideological function, if you will – is precisely to bring us to utopia without incurring the inconvenience of having to question our current social and economic arrangements. This is why Kurzweil supposes that the onward march of technology will produce the society of plenitude, all by itself – so long as government bureaucrats and religious fundamentalists do not interfere with entrepreneurial innovation. By a curious sleight of hand, even after a radical 'rupture' in the very 'fabric of human history', we witness the persistence of such features of our society today as private property, capital accumulation, branding and advertising, stringent copyright enforcement and, above all, 'business models' (with which Kurzweil seems curiously obsessed).

The ideology-critique that I have just been sketching out is so obvious as to be scarcely worth pursuing. Except that Kurzweil's rather lame and unwitting attempt at SF only makes explicit a problem that haunts even the most brilliant, adventurous and inventive SF. This has to do with the weakness of the utopian imagination, its failure to extend truly beyond present-day, capitalist horizons. As Jameson laments towards the end of his recent book on utopian and science fiction, we have been plagued by the perpetual reversion of difference and otherness into the same, and the discovery that our most energetic imaginative leaps into radical alternatives were little more than the projections of our own social moment and historical or subjective situation: the posthuman thereby seeming more distant and impossible than ever![17]

Slavoj Žižek makes a similar observation (though he is not referring to SF specifically) when he says that 'today it's much easier to imagine the end of all life on earth than a much more modest change in capitalism'.[18] We have no trouble picturing the catastrophic breakdown of the capitalist order, and the extermination of human life on this planet; but we are scarcely able to envision a tolerable and pleasant world without money, without advertising, without brand names and without the vast inequities that characterise a capitalist economy. Kurzweil's book is only the crass exemplification of a much wider problem: the way that all thought today, even explicitly oppositional thought, has been colonised and appropriated in advance by the flows and metamorphoses of capital.

To explore this dilemma, I turn from Kurzweil's own speculations to Charles Stross's far more interesting reworking of them in *Accelerando*. In this novel, Stross never mentions Kurzweil in particular, but he works with the general assumptions about the Singularity to which Kurzweil offers the best-known expression. Instead of questioning the dubious premises of Singularity thought, Stross pushes them to their most delirious consequences. The book tells the story of the supersession of human intelligence by artificial intelligence, as experienced by three or four generations of the Macx family (the exact number depends on whether you count a clone furnished with the memories, as well as the phenotype, of its ancestor as a separate generation). *Accelerando* starts in Amsterdam in the year 2010 with Manfred Macx, an 'agalmic entrepreneur'[19] who regularly patents business models and then gives them away for free, 'making strangers rich'.[20] Manfred is so dependent upon his 'personal area network'[21] and other wireless online computational prostheses that, deprived of them, he becomes a befuddled amnesiac, barely able to remember his own name, location and intentions. *Accelerando* ends on an artificial asteroid circling a brown dwarf (not-quite-star) called Hyundai$^{+4904}/_{-56}$ sometime in the twenty-third century, with Manfred's great-grandson Manni Macx (the aforementioned clone) existing simultaneously as a physical child, playing S&M war games with his little pals, and as an 'adult ghost', or mature intelligent construct, monitoring everything that happens from a virtual 'mindspace'.[22]

In between these starting and ending points, we get a plethora of florid nerd fantasies and wacky business plans. It is as if Stross had taken all his old issues of *Wired* magazine and run them through the linguistic and conceptual equivalent of a digital music sampler. At one point, Manfred decides to shed his human form, and downloads his mind into a flock of pigeons – which gives a whole new, literal, meaning to the idea of 'distributed intelligence'. At another, Manfred's grandson Sirhan schemes to 'acquire a total lock on the history futures market, by having a *complete* archive of human experiences' on hand and available for download.[23] In the post-Singularity age, sex with strangers is less of a gamble than it used to be, because you can run a simulation and see what it will be like ahead of time.[24] There are also sentient simulated lobster minds running spaceships in the Oort cloud, 'group minds' or 'borganisms'[25] who run other consciousnesses as software within their own, and characters who (thanks to cloning, memory downloading and faster-than-real-time life simulations) end up being older than their own mothers.

In a certain way, *Accelerando* is closer to the space operas of Golden Age SF than it is to the cyberpunk fiction of the 1980s. Of course, Stross's exacerbated self-consciousness and tongue-in-cheek, hip attitude are not very Golden Age. And the novel's characters maintain a remarkable range of manias, tics and obsessions – from masochistic abasement to puritanical fear of sexuality to an almost hysterical lust for novelty – that would never have been dramatised in pre-1960 SF. But at the same time, Stross's revelling in cheesy genre formulas, his love of wacky gadgets and surprising, yet ultimately logical, plot twists, and his book's utter lack of existential anguish or nihilistic posturing all suggest a will to write as if cyberpunk had never happened. It may be that Stross's insouciance and comic detachment, and his rejection of an all-too-human angst and negativity, are necessary strategies in order to come to terms with his subject. 'The rapture of the nerds' – and Stross uses the phrase, borrowed from MacLeod, several times in the course of the novel[26] – does not lend itself to the sort of terminal-wasteland introspection and film noir recyclings that were the stock-in-trade of the cyberpunk writers.

The post-Singularity world of *Accelerando* is therefore not dystopian in the cyberpunk manner. Rather, it's a straightforward techno-utopia. The 'necessary comforts of civilization'[27] – which include neural implants and information access, as well as food, clothing and shelter – are available to everyone. The information network is wired directly into your brain. Thanks to 'programmable matter' and nanomachines, any object you want can be instantaneously constructed with just a snap of your fingers. Poverty and war are eliminated. There are still class differences, as well as religious, ideological and political disagreements. But these never reach the point of actual conflict, since the contending parties find it far easier to ignore one another than to actually fight. (A 'killfile' function works in meatspace as well as VR, so that you can simply render irritating people invisible to you; it's great for cocktail parties.) The plot of *Accelerando* is nonetheless thick with political infighting, legal disputes and underhanded market manipulations; even after the Singularity, some things apparently never change. State and market are never explicitly contested; in the course of the novel, they just gradually wither away. By the last chapter, set in the twenty-third century, all human beings live in a world without scarcity. 'Life is rich ... endlessly varied and sometimes confusing', and grounded – much as it was before the pressures of scarcity led to states and to systematic processes of capital accumulation – in communities of human beings 'living in small family groups within larger tribal networks'.[28]

However, *Accelerando* also contains a counter-narrative, running alongside the melioristic (and vaguely Rousseauian) one that I have just described. The society of abundance envisioned in the novel is nonetheless 'a poverty-stricken backwater compared to its neighbors'.[29] These neighbours are societies composed, not of human beings, but of our 'mind children':[30] sentient, autonomous artificial intelligences (AIs), unencumbered by the limits of carbon-based biology. Stross – unlike Kurzweil, but following the deeper implications of his logic – posits two distinct lines of technological evolution. On the one hand, there are the computationally enhanced human beings who are the main subjects of Stross's narrative. On the other, there are the pure AIs: not cyborgs or hybrids, but an entirely new sort of entity. The human quest for technological enhancement – or, more accurately, for increased profits, since this is what really drives the process – leads to the event that we call the Singularity. But once this event has taken place, human beings are no longer at its centre. The Singularity gives birth to inhuman or posthuman AIs, and they are its true 'historical subject'. The enhancements of human life recounted in the novel are only byproducts of the machinic evolution of artificial intelligence itself.

Kurzweil likes to compare the 'high computational efficiency'[31] of which thinking machines are capable with the 'severe limitations' of the human brain.[32] Such a distinction is taken for granted throughout *Accelerando*. In purely technological terms, the AIs evolve, or develop, much faster and further than is possible for merely enhanced human beings. Very quickly, the AIs exceed our powers of comprehension by several orders of magnitude. They are 'fundamentally better consciousness engines than us merely human types'.[33] This is a qualitative, as well as a quantitative, distinction. It isn't just that we don't know what these AIs want; beyond this, it is literally impossible for us to imagine what they *might* want. For they possess a higher-order consciousness than we do, existing on a meta-level in comparison to us: 'a posthuman can build an internal model of a human-level intelligence that is, well, as cognitively strong as the original. You or I may think we know what makes other people tick, but we're quite often wrong, whereas real posthumans can actually simulate us, inner states and all, and get it right'.[34] So much for the problem of 'other minds'.

Although Stross never spells this out explicitly, these posthuman intelligences are like nothing so much as what we know today as transnational corporations. Of course, corporations have long been considered 'persons' in the eyes of the law, even though they are not (yet) conscious entities (and even though they are exempt – unlike biological persons – from being incarcerated, tortured or put to death). *Accelerando* pushes this situation to its logical conclusion. Early in the novel, several of the characters realise that 'we need a new legal concept of what it is to be a person. One that can cope with sentient corporations' and other artifacts of the Singularity.[35] But it's not just that corporations become sentient. The converse is also the case: after the Singularity, all sentient AIs function as autonomous economic entities, 'slyly self-aware financial instruments'.[36] They exist only to accumulate capital, in the form of endless computation. The AIs have freed themselves from merely human parameters, shed their human origins and emerged as alien, predatory lifeforms. They strive to extract the maximum value (in the form of computational power) from all matter. Their focus is on efficiency and on endless self-expansion. They have no goals external to the processes of accumulation and expansion themselves. No measure of abundance can satiate their rapacious competitive drive. Merely enhanced human beings may have attained a state of abundance; but the posthuman AIs still live in a 'scarcity economy', because neither bandwidth nor matter is truly infinite.[37]

Accelerando provides a Stapledonian vision, albeit in brief, of 'the stellar life cycle', the overall trajectory of AI civilisations.[38] The posthuman AIs quickly dismantle the solar system, pulverising the planets and asteroids in order to convert their 'dumb matter' into 'computronium'.[39] In so doing, they force the remaining (merely enhanced) human beings further and further away from the sun: to Jupiter, then to Saturn, then to the Oort cloud, then finally out of the solar system altogether – which is why the remnants of humanity end up circling Hyundai$^{+4904}/_{-56}$. Ultimately there is not room in the solar system for both them and us. The AIs 'restructure the entire mass of their star system into a free-flying shell of nanocomputers, then more of them, Dyson spheres, shells within shells, like a Russian doll: a Matrioshka brain'.[40] But sooner or later they push their mania for accumulation to the point of implosion and extinction. The entire galaxy turns out to be littered with the ruins of dead or dying superintelligent civilisations: it is 'a howling wilderness of degenerate data, fractally compressed, postconscious processes running slower and slower as they trade storage space for processing power'.[41]

What is the role of (enhanced) human beings – or of any other sentient, biological species that produces a technological Singularity – in all this? We are initially important to the AIs as sources of raw material, informational patterns to be simulated and assimilated. The precise *way* they use the information they extract from us 'is not known. (Possibilities include the study of history through horticulture, entertainment through live-action role-playing, revenge, and economic forgery)'.[42] But whatever may be the case, once our computational surplus value has been fully extracted, we are simply shunted aside by the AIs. In some instances, they still value us as 'sapient currency units', stockpiling us for 'future options trades in human species futures'.[43] But even this sort of utility is fairly limited. Sooner or later, we are slated for

ethnic cleansing ... You take people who you define as being of little worth, and first you herd them into a crowded ghetto with limited resources, then you decide those resources aren't worth spending on them, and bullets are cheaper than bread.[44]

The posthuman AIs have upgraded the old-fashioned 'free market' to 'the so-called Accelerated Salesman Infrastructure of Economics 2.0', a system that is 'more efficient than any human-designed resource allocation schema'.[45] Economics 2.0 'replaces the single-indirection layer of conventional money, and the multiple-indirection mappings of options trades, with some kind of insanely baroque object-relational framework based on the parametrised desires and subjective experiential values of the players'.[46] In Economics 2.0, money has been abstracted to this metalevel in order to serve as a universal equivalent for all computation: 'quantized originality – that which allows one sentient entity to outmaneuver another'.[47] Merely human intelligence is incapable of participating in Economics 2.0 'without dehumanizing cognitive surgery'.[48]

Stross is extrapolating here, I think, from the present-day trade in *derivatives*, 'financial instruments that derive their monetary value from other assets, such as stocks, bonds, commodities, or currencies ... derivatives represent a *metalevel* with respect to their underlying assets, a metalevel created by the fixed temporal interval in which they are exercisable'.[49] Derivatives are inseparable from the latest computing and communications technologies. They presuppose the ability to transmit large financial sums instantaneously across the globe. And they defy any sort of intuitive representation, as they can only be expressed in terms of complex differential equations.[50] Derivatives are supposedly 'hedges' against the risks of turbulent currency markets (which is why the unregulated corporations that trade them are called 'hedge funds'). But in fact, derivatives increase turbulence and risk, and they are largely used for purposes of speculation. In all these ways, derivatives are money and credit raised to a higher power.

Marx, in sharp contrast both to the classical political economists upon whom he drew, and the neoclassical and neo-liberal economists whose views are hegemonic today, always emphasised that money is not a neutral and transparent medium. Money's power of abstraction, its *value-form* as a universal equivalent, places its stamp on everything that is expressed in its terms, exchanged for it, or converted into it. But if money (together with credit) is already an abstraction, derivatives are 'doubly abstract ... abstract not only in the conventional sense of being removed from immediate ordinary reality ... but in the historically specific sense of objectifying different, globally distant, and incommensurable social relations as a single priced thing'.[51] Derivatives represent a higher level of what Marx called the fetishism of commodities, as they reify and commodify not only the social relations of production as manifested in manufactured objects, but a far wider and more diffuse set of social relations, which are all quantified under the rubric of 'risk'.[52]

As a result of this double abstraction, derivatives seem to flow freely in a space of their own, a virtual world of purely quantitative calculations. They seem to exemplify 'financial circulation as a play of decontextualised and naturally occurring market surface forms'.[53] The autonomy of derivatives and financial markets – like the autonomy of technological development in Kurzweil's narrative – is, of course, ultimately an illusion. But it is, you might say, an *objective* illusion, which is to say a fantasy. It is a fantasy that, qua fantasy, actually operates in the world, with consequences that are perfectly real and often quite horrific. Indeed, 'the social and political power of financial derivatives are grounded in great measure on their appearing not to be social or political at all, but to simply express the mechanisms and profit goals of the market'.[54] The double abstraction of speculative financial instruments like derivatives is what gives them the power to devastate whole economies almost overnight (as has happened a number of times in the last decade). Magnified and extrapolated, such is the power of the posthuman AIs wielding Economics 2.0 in Stross's narrative.

The world of *Accelerando* never escapes the horizon of capital and its flows, because it remains circumscribed by the incomprehensible logic of Economics 2.0. The novel's human characters can neither comprehend nor participate in this logic, but they are still subject to its effects. Their experience of relative abundance – which makes capitalist relations unnecessary – remains under siege by forces that seek to appropriate every surplus, thereby transforming abundance back into scarcity. This is why the best these human beings can do is hide in the backwater of a brown dwarf star, and hope that the convulsions that extinguish Economics 2.0 civilisations somehow pass them by. The absurdity, and yet inescapability, of this situation is highlighted when the human protagonists of *Accelerando* finally encounter sentient life from another star system. Not only does the alien entity take on the material form of a gigantic slug, but it turns out to be an 'alien business model' – or more precisely a 'parasitic organism … the Economics 2.0 equivalent of a pyramid scheme crossed with a 419 scam'.[55] Never has the classic SF scenario of First Contact been so ludicrously deflated.

Accelerando is a cynical, yet perversely cheerful, fiction for a time when the utopian imagination seems to have been depleted. The problem is not that we cannot imagine otherness, so much as that whatever otherness we imagine is immediately mobilised as a 'business model', once more serving to promote the accumulation of capital. Capitalism today is itself directly and immediately utopian: and that is perhaps the most terrifying thing about it. The technological Singularity of Vinge and Kurzweil is symptomatic in this respect. For – as *Accelerando* helps to show – the Singularity is actually a fantasy of finance capital, in both senses of the genitive. It is the closest we can come to a master narrative in this neo-liberal, post-Fordist age of flexible accumulation and massive virtual monetary flows.

Although the Singularity undoubtedly occurs sometime in the course of the narrative of *Accelerando*, we never actually 'see' it happening, and we cannot pin down precisely when it takes place. Kurzweil, of course, predicts that the Singularity will occur sometime around the year 2049. One character in *Accelerando* suggests a much earlier date: 'it happened on June 6, 1969, at eleven hundred hours, eastern seaboard time … That was when the first network control protocol packets were sent from the data port of one IMP to another – the first ever Internet connection'.[56] I can suggest a few alternative dates, following the premise that Kurzweil's and Stross's technological fantasy is necessarily also a fantasy of capital. Perhaps the Singularity happened on 15 August 1971, when President Nixon suspended the gold standard, thus opening the way for the phantasmatic flows of currency speculation and trade in derivatives. Or perhaps the more accurate date is 6 October 1979, when Paul Volcker, Chairman of the US Federal Reserve Board, definitively abandoned Keynesianism and adopted monetarism as official policy: 'a policy designed to quell inflation no matter what the consequences might be for employment'.[57] In any case, the flows of Capital have now become autonomous – and strictly speaking unimaginable. They have liberated themselves from any merely human dimensions, and from whatever feeble limits Fordism and Keynesianism might previously have placed upon the single-minded pursuit of capital accumulation. In that sense, the Singularity is already here.

Notes

1. Charles Stross, *Accelerando* (New York: Ace Books, 2005), p. 240.
2. See Vernor Vinge, 'The Coming Technological Singularity: How to Survive in the Posthuman Era' (1993), available at www.ugcs.caltech.edu/~phoenix/vinge/vinge-sing.html
3. See Hans Moravec, *Mind Children* (Cambridge: Harvard University Press, 1990) and the jacket of Ray Kurzweil, *The Singularity is Near* (New York: Viking, 2005).
4. Kurzweil, *Singularity*, pp. 7–9.
5. Ibid., p. 7.
6. Ibid., p. 9.
7. Ibid., p. 9.
8. Ibid., p. 340.
9. Ibid., p. 487.
10. Ibid., p. 487.
11. Alain Badiou, *Ethics: An Essay on the Understanding of Evil*, transl. Peter Hallward (New York: Verso, 2001), p. 41.
12. Kurzweil, *Singularity*, p. 7.
13. Jon VanZile, 'On Building Bridges Toward Immortality: Report on Ray Kurzweil', *Life Extension Magazine* (September 2005), available at www.lef.org/magazine/mag2005/sep2005_report_kurzweil_02.htm
14. Ken MacLeod, *The Cassini Division* (New York: Tor, 1999), p. 115.
15. See Fredric Jameson, *Archaeologies of the Future: The Desire Called Utopia and Other Science Fictions* (New York: Verso, 2005); Carl Freedman, *Critical Theory and Science Fiction* (Hanover: Wesleyan University Press, 2000).
16. Kurzweil, *Singularity*, pp. 335, 339.
17. Jameson, *Archaeologies*, p. 211.
18. *Zizek!* (Taylor, 2005).
19. Stross, *Accelerando*, p. 72.
20. Ibid., pp. 3, 40, 382.
21. Ibid., p. 69.
22. Ibid., p. 370.
23. Ibid., p. 290.

24. Ibid., p. 325.
25. Ibid., pp. 96–7.
26. Ibid., pp. 172–3, 270, 318.
27. Ibid., p. 365.
28. Ibid., pp. 359–60.
29. Ibid., p. 315; cf. p. 364.
30. Ibid., pp. 227, 289 – echoing Moravec's *Mind Children*.
31. Kurzweil, *Singularity*, p. 362.
32. Ibid., p. 8.
33. Ibid., p. 376.
34. Ibid., pp. 376–7.
35. Stross, *Accelerando*, p. 98.
36. Ibid., p. 168.
37. Ibid., p. 229.
38. Ibid., p. 303.
39. Ibid., pp. 14, 248, 251, 341 and passim.
40. Ibid., p. 303.
41. Ibid., p. 289.
42. Ibid., p. 313.
43. Ibid., p. 210.
44. Ibid., p. 289.
45. Ibid., pp. 278, 303.
46. Ibid., p. 321.
47. Ibid., p. 295.
48. Ibid., p. 315.
49. Benjamin Lee and Edward LiPuma, 'Cultures of Circulation: The Imaginations of Modernity', *Public Culture* 14: 1 (2002), p. 204.
50. Edward LiPuma and Benjamin Lee, *Financial Derivatives and the Globalization of Risk* (Durham: Duke University Press, 2004), p. 65.
51. Ibid., p. 30.
52. Ibid., pp. 77–83.
53. Ibid., p. 29.
54. Ibid., p. 29.
55. Stross, *Accelerando*, pp. 301, 295.
56. Ibid., p. 172.
57. David Harvey, *A Brief History of Neoliberalism* (New York: Oxford University Press, 2005), p. 23.

6

SPECIES AND SPECIES-BEING: ALIENATED SUBJECTIVITY AND THE COMMODIFICATION OF ANIMALS

Sherryl Vint

I know I am a machine, and I know that I have known feelings only when I was once a living man. I sometimes wonder if you people might go too far. Too far with us robots. Too far, perhaps, with the underpeople too. Things were once simple, when everything that talked was a human being and everything which did not talk was not. You may be coming to an ending of the ways.

Cordwainer Smith[1]

Animals, Claude Lévi-Strauss contended, in a dictum that has become key to animal studies, are good for thinking with; SF is no less provocative. Its peculiar imaginative resources allow not only the interrogation of cultural assumptions but also the construction of alternative possibilities. By postulating thought-experiments, SF can cast fresh light on theoretical debates and inspire radical praxis. This essay takes several SF texts as starting points from which to re-imagine the social relationships between humans and other species, and the ways in which they are embedded in structures of global capitalism. In an age of environmental destruction, xenotransplantation and the production of human/ animal chimeras, this is an urgent task. Donna Haraway's *When Species Meet* (2007) calls for an updated survey of the structure and consequences of capitalism that could take account of the ways nature, humans and technology have all been changed physically and socially by capitalist technoculture. This essay is intended to contribute to such a project by focusing on the ways in which animals are caught up in human social relations as both commodities and labour-power, and on the implications that their dual role has for thinking about labour in late-capitalism. This essay will reconceptualise orthodox Marxism's labour theory of value by exploring the homologies between capitalism's alienating reduction of people to labour-power and its exploitation of the environment in general (and other species in particular). These concerns should not be seen as competing priorities for the left, but as parts of 'the *laws of motion* of capitalism', thus enabling us to develop a wider understanding of 'the societal logic that links together such disparate phenomena as the impoverishment of the poor, the privatization of life forms, and the destruction of the natural environment'.[2] By moving beyond human exceptionalism, productive opportunities for alliances between Marxists, socialists, and environmental and animal welfare activists become possible.

SF is often fascinated with the alienated being of robots and androids, who – like *Star Trek: The Next Generation*'s (1987–94) gregarious Data (Brent Spiner) and *A.I.: Artificial Intelligence*'s (Spielberg, 2001) maudlin David (Haley Joel Osment) – are all too often obsessed with being human. Focusing on the desire to be human in philosophical or psychological terms, such examples typically suggest that these machines could be fulfilled if only they had access to the affective relationships of human community. Equally common in SF is the fantasy of creating a class of beings to serve humanity. In this dream of plenitude all necessary but unfulfilling labour is done without human effort, performed by machines or manufactured beings, such as Isaac Asimov's regulated robots and Iain M. Banks's god-like AI 'Minds', thereby freeing humans for fuller lives. Such tales reveal the alienated nature of labour under capital and, therefore, the human desire to escape from labour as an expression of utopian longing. Manufactured beings are presumed not to be alienated in this way, their labour conceptualised as analogous to that performed by machines rather than to human labour-power.

This problematic assumption drives many SF plots, drawing attention to the emergent subjectivity of the created being and thus its need for life as something beyond being a tool used for human ends. For example, in Marge Piercy's *He, She and It* (1991), Yod, the cyborg designed to protect the free town of Tikva from the multinational corporation Yakamura-Stichen's predations, is a failure because of conflicts between his programming for defence and his programming for sociality. The programmer who gave him empathy comes to regret this choice, observing that 'the creation of a conscious being as any kind of tool – supposed to exist only to fill our needs – is a disaster', and the novel concludes that 'it was inexcusable to create a sentient being for any other reason than to live its own life'.[3] The term 'robot', derived from the Czech for 'worker', was coined in Karel Čapek's play about alienated labour, *R.U.R. (Rossum's Universal Robots)* (1921) – a concern he developed further in his novel, *War with the Newts* (1936). Preferred by their European exploiters to native labour, the newts – a newly discovered species of giant salamander – are deemed not to possess human status, and thus their employers are freed from moral qualms about reducing them to their labour-power alone. However, this fantasy of maximising the extraction of surplus value – the newts are put to work, displayed in zoos, kept as pets, experimented upon, processed into a cheap, if barely palatable, source of protein fit only for the working classes – continually runs up against the material constraints caused by the fact that the newts are living, sentient beings who learn to defend themselves. Central to the novel is the struggle to determine on which side of the human/animal boundary they belong, since if they are merely animal, they cannot be 'exploited', and thus any degree of exploitation can be justified. Although the newts suffer in ways similar to those in which animals suffer under capital, Čapek does not precisely challenge the human/animal boundary so much as its specific use to exclude certain people from the category of 'human', particularly slaves, workers and the colonised. But his use of the animal Other to do so is instructive. Animals, too, have been exploited as labour-power by capital, curtailing and deforming the social relations possible between humans and other species, and, as John Berger notes,

This reduction of the animal ... is part of the same process as that by which men have been reduced to isolated productive and consuming units. ... The mechanical view of the animal's work capacity was later applied to that of workers.[4]

Cordwainer Smith's *Instrumentality of Mankind* stories (1950–75) draw parallels between the alienated lives of robots and the alienated lives of underpeople, 'animals in the shape of human beings, who did the heavy and the weary work which remained as the *caput mortuum* of a really perfected economy'.[5] Like Čapek's robots, Smith's underpeople stand in for the class of exploited workers alienated under capitalist social relations. At the same time, however, Smith suggests that the underpeople equally and simultaneously represent animal lives alienated and exploited by a speciesist human culture. The *Instrumentality* stories tell of a future human society, the Instrumentality of Mankind, that has overcome poverty and suffering for humans through its reliance on an underclass of workers. Because these underpeople are derived from animal stock, their exploitation need not be recognised as such, and thus they form the perfect permanently impoverished pool of surplus labour that capital requires. In Smith's underpeople, capitalist exploitation operates through a speciesist division of human from animal:

Human beings and hominids had lived so long in an affluent society that they did not know what it meant to be poor. But the Lords of the Instrumentality had decreed that underpeople – derived from animal stock – should live under the economics of the Ancient World; they had to have their own kind of money to pay for their rooms, their food, their possessions, and the education of their children. If they became bankrupt, they went to the Poorhouse, where they were killed painlessly by means of gas.[6]

It is illegal to treat underpeople in hospitals because 'It was easier to breed new underpeople for the jobs than it was to repair sick ones'.[7] Like machines, they are simply discarded and replaced when they wear out. Such measures drastically reduce the sphere of social reproduction that must otherwise exist simultaneously with capital to ensure the labour supply.

Smith's insistence that the exploited labour of the underpeople is more than merely an analogy for the exploited labour of the often-animalised working classes is relatively unique. Unlike the majority of SF, from H.G. Wells' *The Island of Doctor Moreau* (1896) to F. Paul Wilson's *Sims* (2003), Smith invokes not only the history of exploited working-class and colonised subjects, but also the history of animal-kind's service to humanity. Furthermore, while texts such as *War with the Newts* or *Sims* represent their underclasses as a homogeneous mass of the dispossessed, Smith carefully individualises his underpeople as much as his human characters. For example, the partnerships of cats and pilots formed in 'The Game of Rat and Dragon' (1955) require a *mutual* compatibility between individuals of both species, not just the human partner's generalised liking for cats as an entity. Furthermore, Smith's underpeople articulate their revolution as one that must transform social relations of production in order to end their exploitation, insisting 'We are not ending time ... We are just altering the material conditions of Man's situation for the present historical period'.[8] Part of this material situation is the history of humanity's uneven social relations with animals, which has been one between subject and object, but which must be transformed into one between two – albeit not identical – subjects.

Marx defines labour-power as 'the aggregate of those mental and physical capabilities existing in the physical form, the living personality, of a human being, capabilities which he sets in motion whenever he produces a use-value of any kind'.[9] In *The Economic and Philosophic Manuscripts of 1844*, he argues that, when the worker is reduced to the status of a commodity,

> what is animal becomes human and what is human becomes animal. Certainly eating, drinking, procreating, etc. are also genuinely human functions. But abstractly taken, separated from the sphere of all other human activity and turned into sole and ultimate ends, they are animal functions.[10]

In his particular historical moment, Marx suggests that eating, drinking and procreating are sufficient for animal being, but that human species-being requires more. Under alienated conditions, 'Life itself appears only as a means to *life*',[11] a brute struggle for survival that he posits as acceptable for animals but alienating for humans. In our historical moment, however, we are far more aware of capacities that animals possess for cognition and for social relations with humans and one another.[12]

Marx condemns capitalism not just because of inequality and exploitation, which as he was well aware exist under other economic systems. Capitalism is unique in that it impoverishes the human psyche and degrades all social relations among people, reducing people from full human being to an existence as a commodity, valued solely as labour-power. Capitalism, Marx argued, alienated humans from their conscious creative activity, transforming a social life activity into mere work done for the capitalist. But he saw the labour of animals as different from that of humans for two reasons: first, animals produce things for their use-value and cannot calculate as would be required to think of exchange-value;[13] second, animals labour out of instinct and not as part of imaginative and conscious creation. Therefore, animals cannot be alienated from the products of their labour in the same way as can humans. This species distinction, at the heart of Marx's consideration of labour, is no longer consistent with the ways in which animals are integrated into the social relations of capitalism.[14] I want to move beyond this anthropocentric conception and consider in similar terms the damage capitalism does to all life – the lives of human subjects alienated from the rest of nature by capitalist social relations[15] and the lives of non-human subjects reduced to commodities in the service of capital. Allowing non-human, sentient beings to be treated as commodities is simultaneously a structure of subjectivity and a social relation produced by capitalist conceptions of value and, as such, perpetuates capitalism.

Marx's concept of species-being differentiates humans from other species. Labour plays a special role in this differentiation since, Marx argues, it is through labour that 'man' transforms the world, realising the vision of his imagination in materiality. Therefore, humanity's specific capacities are intimately connected to our capacity to labour, to choose and control what we make, and to realise not just instinctual promptings but intellectual projects. Thus, Marx concludes, alienating labour alienates us from our own species-being, the essence of what it means to be human.[16] Yet his distinction between the imaginative labour of humans and the instinctual, responsive behaviour of animals has not held up in the decades since. The species-being of non-humans is not identical to humanity's, but nonetheless this species-specific being is, or should be, more than merely functioning as machines for capital accumulation. The differences between our historical situation and his – differences not only related to changes in our understanding of animal being but also to the increasingly mechanised and massive slaughter of animals for food,[17] the creation of animals as laboratory tools, the real subsumption of nature[18] in genetic changes made to other species – require that we reassess our notions of species-being and animal labour. We need to recognise that this changed historical situation is part of capital's intervention into human and animal lives and social relations – that animals 'do *not* "naturally" become private property, no more than humans "naturally" come to sell their labor'.[19] Social relations, like needs, are materially produced and vary with time and place.

If we take seriously animals' capacity for social relations, then reducing their existence to beings-for-capital is a violation of their species-being as much as reducing humans to labour-power is a violation of ours. Marx argues that capitalist labour conditions alienate a person in four ways: from nature, by removing him from the sensuous existence of nature as his home and site of subsistence; from 'himself', by making 'his life activity, his *essential* being, a mere means to his *existence*';[20] from 'his' own body, by making nature exterior to a human life within culture; and from species-being, from the social relations of humans among ourselves. Similarly, Barbara Noske suggests, animals are alienated through their integration into the productive processes of capital: from their product, from their productive activity, from their fellow creatures, and from nature itself.[21] Animals are alienated from their own bodies and offspring, turned into products for human consumption. They are alienated from their own productive activity when it is removed from a full, natural life and situated in the factory conditions of agribusiness, such as the unnaturally large sows kept in farrowing crates, unable to move, so that they do not crush their offspring. Animals raised in agribusiness conditions are alienated from their fellow creatures, overcrowded to maximise profit, and mutilated (for example, the de-beaking of chickens and amputation of pigs' tails) so that their stress reaction to this artificial existence does not damage the profitability of their bodies. Like human labourers, they are alienated from nature itself, physically removed from a context in which they might exist as something other than living machines, and often altered so that they no longer resemble their natural ancestors. Thus, 'animal alienation amounts to alienation from species life'.[22] Cordwainer Smith's representation of the underpeople suggests a similar evaluation in one character's observation: 'People never loved underpeople. They used them, like chairs or doorhandles. Since when did a doorhandle demand the Charter of Ancient Rights?'[23]

Our current techno-scientific social relations with animals in western culture are characterised by 'moral schizophrenia'.[24] We have established affective and familial relationships with some species, while we kill more farm animals in more devastating ways than at any other time in human history. Recent research in animal cognition increasingly notes their capacity for intelligence, language and tool-use, while at the same time there exists a rising industry of knockout-gene mice, genetically engineered with a damaged gene so as to test its function. Growing evidence requires us to recognise that animals, like humans, are social beings. This implies that when animals enter into capitalist structures of exchange their participation is a social relation between species; but, like that between producers and consumers, it is denied or repressed by the commodity form. If we concede that animals are social beings, able to be alienated from their species-being, then we must think of their labour as labour-power, which has consequences for how we think about labour and value in Marxist theory.

Smith's *Norstrilia* (1975) reveals that the entire economy of the Instrumentality is dependent upon a biological secretion of certain sick sheep that confers immortality on humans. The underpeople rebel, constructing their revolution in terms of resistance to the human culture's long history of disavowing human–animal social relations:

> How many cats have served and loved man, and for how long? How many cattle have worked for man, been eaten by man, been milked by men across the ages, and have still followed where men went, even to the stars? And dogs. I do not have to tell you about the love of dogs for men. We call ourselves the Holy Insurgency because we are rebels. We are a government.[25]

Smith's 'The Dead Lady of Clown Town' (1964), which recounts the beginning of the revolution, is set in a period far earlier than most of the other *Instrumentality* stories. It continually reminds the reader of this ancient history, and that 'we must remember that centuries passed before mankind finally came to grips with the problem of the underpeople and decided what "life" was within the limits of the human community'.[26] The revolution itself is rather anticlimactic: it 'lasted six minutes and covered one hundred and twelve meters',[27] ending with the slaughter of most of those involved and the burning of the leader, D'joan, a dog-girl. Smith suggests, however, that revolution cannot be measured in minutes and metres, but needs to be assessed with reference to the long, slow transformation of consciousness that it sparked. He further emphasises that this transformation of social relations is not possible without collective struggle, that 'mankind would [not] ever get around to correcting ancient wrongs unless the underpeople had some of the tools of power – weapons, conspiracy, wealth, and (above all) organization with which to challenge man'.[28]

By connecting his tale of alienated labour to the history of alienated human–animal social relations, Smith suggests that there are many and provocative parallels between capital's exploitation of humans and of animals. The animal body was the first sentient part of nature that was appropriated into property and exploited as a means to human ends, rather than being an end in itself. Animals occupy a particularly fraught location within the nexus of production, exploitation and alienated social relations. Bob Torres posits a number of links between commodity fetishism and the exploitation of animals as commodities. The capitalist drive to extract surplus value affects animals on two levels – in their lives as commodities and in their lives as labour-power. The forces of capital modify the bodies of domestic animals in various, often incredibly damaging ways, such as the forced maturation of broiler chickens which results in 'young birds who are often unable to walk, flap their wings, or even stand up',[29] in order to make them better producers. The logic by which capital organised the work process in order to extract maximum surplus value is analogous to the way that the commodification of animals has been organised in the factory-farming system to extract maximum profit. In both cases, species life is not relevant beyond that which is necessary to reproduce the human as labour-power or the animal as commodity. Recounting his education in a college of agricultural science, Torres notes, 'I was taught to view cows as producers.... We learned about how much (or how little) space one could give a dairy cow, and that increasing the number of cows in a space meant increased profit, within certain limits'.[30] There are clear similarities to Fordist and post-Fordist labour practices, in which work processes are organised so as to maximise the extraction of surplus value and minimise the degree to which any aspect of the worker's life other than his/her existence as labour-power appears in capital's calculations.

Capitalists monopolise the means of production and force wage labourers to work for them in order to survive, which is similar to the processes by which animals were domesticated and restricted to life within capitalist social structures. Both transformations rely on the privatisation of land and other resources necessary for life, use violence to punish or kill off those who continue to occupy land now deemed private property, and restrict the bodily activity of those incorporated into the production system. Rather than seeing such homologies as evidence that capitalism has reduced humans to the status of animals, I would question the logic of a category of being that allows any living creature to be treated as merely a commodity, both because of new understandings of animal cognition, emotion and social life and because the structural existence of such a category perpetuates the logic by which is it acceptable for some beings to have enormous wealth and comfort while others live in degraded and painful conditions. The rise of agribusiness, the transformation of nature into a factory and the reduction of sensuous productive activity to calculated productivity have damaged human and animal life alike. Animals became commodities and humans became labour-power in a mutually entangled set of transformations.

Torres links meat consumption to the structures of commodity fetishism inasmuch as it relies on the consumer's ignorance of the system of production behind that which is consumed; were consumers able to see the social relations (both human and animal) behind the appearance of commodities, he argues, many would at the very least change their consumption habits. Meat production is a specific instance of the larger commodity system: full comprehension of the relations of exploitation and the entire social systems they represent – the human/animal boundary and the capitalist mode of production – would require (that is, both depend upon *and* demand of us) radical change. Marx himself stresses the importance of a non-alienated social relationship with nature, arguing that 'The worker can create nothing without *nature*, without the *sensuous external world*. It is the material on which his labour is realised, in which it is active, from which and by means of which it produces'.[31] The real subsumption of nature prevents any social relation between humans and this sensual world, which is transformed into another factory of production. The agro-industrial model of agriculture, which depleted soil and displaced small, local producers, was primarily aimed at translating wartime nitrogen production into the agro-chemical farming revolution; the export of these methods through the Marshall Plan and 'green revolution' initiatives helped US corporations while decreasing the amount of food for people in the world.[32] Animals, people and the environment all lost for the sake of corporate profit.

The seed of social change that the dog-girl D'joan plants during her short-lived revolution is a vision of a transformed and non-alienated relationship between humans and other life. Her message is about resisting a relationship with all other life that sees value only in the accumulation of capital:

> I bring you life-with. It's more than love. Love's a hard, sad, dirty word, a cold word, an old word. It says too much and it promises too little. I bring you something much bigger than love. If you're alive, you're alive. If you're alive-with, then you know the other life is there too – both of you, any of you, all of you. Don't do anything. Don't grab, don't clench, don't possess. Just be. That's the weapon.[33]

Smith's revolutionary underpeople understand that the way to a better and non-alienated life is the recognition of the other as a subject, not merely an object – what Haraway calls letting 'the question of how animals engage *one another's gaze responsively* tak[e] center stage'.[34] Being 'alive-with' lets humans return to nature, not as conquerors and not merely to 'grab ... clench ... possess', but instead to 'just be' a part of a larger social collective and of an existence that does not put capital accumulation at its centre. The state of alive-with allows species-being to flourish for all species, human and non-human. SF examples such as Smith's provide alternative models of how we might imagine less alienated inter-species social relations; one of the ways of beginning this work in our material reality is by acknowledging animals' contribution to capital accumulation as an alienated social relationship, and seeking to end that alienation as a way to improve animal and human lives.

Capitalism has successfully used racism and sexism to fragment the working class and produce groups of *Homo sapiens* deemed non-human and hence expendable as labour.[35] Permitting the exploitation of non-human creatures whom we are now compelled to acknowledge as sentient and social (even if not sentient and social in precisely the same ways that we are) allows this structure of subjugation to remain available for use against groups of *Homo sapiens*. The treatment of workers from the Global South, either in sweatshops located in the South or as legal or illegal immigrant labour in the North, is only the latest in a long history of such moves. As McNally notes, wages are so low in globalised sweatshop labour that 'many commentators use the language of slavery to describe the conditions' and 'The Anti-Slavery Society estimates that there are 200 million people worldwide who might be described as "slaves" – people performing bonded labour to pay off a variety of debts'.[36] Theorising animals as alienated labour-power requires a rethinking of the concept of value, and of how we understand the labour of animals and those employed under such conditions. In suggesting that animals' contributions to capital accumulation should be recognised as labour-power and as an alienated social relation, I am not arguing that the exploitation of animals is identical to the exploitation of wage labourers or slaves. Instead, my suggestion is that we need to recognise that there are multiple species-beings, and that animals can be alienated from their species-being as much as humans can be from ours. In Smith's *Instrumentality* stories, this conclusion requires the recognition that 'these are people, not underpeople. But they have dog-thoughts, cat-thoughts, goat-thoughts, and robot-ideas in their heads'.[37] A reconceptualised Marxist theory of labour-power could similarly make room for the subjectivity and alienation of animal being without conflating animals' species-being with human species-being.

Affinities between human and animal exploitation and alienation under capitalism point to ways in which the reduction of animals to commodities produces a cultural milieu in which it is correspondingly easier to reduce humans to labour-power and exchange-value. It is not coincidental, for example, that slaughterhouses are among the most dangerous workplaces, and that they frequently employ the most vulnerable workers – immigrants (illegal and otherwise).[38] Changing society to a more collective structure would eliminate this alienation, acknowledging that animals too have mental and physical capacities beyond their utility as beings-for-capital. As Torres points out, under capital, not only do domesticated animals hand themselves and their bodies over for a fixed period of time, but also

> the entirety of their production is oriented toward the needs of their owner, and the goal is maximal profit. The individuality, sentience, and biological

needs of animals involved in this process are entirely and fully subjugated to production and profit.[39]

The property status of animals is a serious obstacle to efforts for animal welfare reform,[40] which has consequently had to turn to legal activism. But the centrality of property to both human and animal suffering in late-capitalism suggests that Marxism, too, might want to address the property status of animals as part of an effort to imagine and create a less alienated life, overcoming human alienation not only from productive activity but also from nature, by resisting its commodification and returning to a relation in which nature is part of the sensuous world of a full human life – a world which also allows for the full species-lives of non-humans.

Notes

1. Cordwainer Smith, 'Under Old Earth', in James A. Mann, ed., *The Rediscovery of Man: The Complete Short Fiction of Cordwainer Smith* (Framingham: NESFA Press, 1999), p. 304.
2. David McNally, *Another World is Possible: Globalization and Anti-Capitalism*, revised and expanded edition (Winnipeg: Arbeiter Ring Publishing, 2006), pp. 122, 123.
3. Marge Piercy, *He, She and It* (New York: Fawcett Crest, 1991), pp. 412, 418.
4. John Berger, 'Why Look at Animals?', in *About Looking* (New York: Pantheon, 1980), p. 11.
5. Cordwainer Smith, 'The Dead Lady of Clown Town', in Mann, *Rediscovery*, p. 224.
6. Cordwainer Smith, 'The Ballad of Lost C'mell', in Mann, *Rediscovery*, p. 403. Smith's 'hominids' are *Homo sapiens* modified to survive in the very un-Earth-like conditions of some colony worlds. They often look less like humans than do the underpeople, but their genetic relationship to human rather than animal 'stock' ensures their higher social status.
7. Smith, 'Dead Lady of Clown Town', p. 224.
8. Cordwainer Smith, *Norstrilia* (New York: Ballantine, 1975), p. 249.
9. Karl Marx, *Capital: A Critique of Political Economy*, Vol. 1, transl. Ben Fowkes (New York: Penguin Books, 1976), p. 270.

10. Karl Marx, *The Economic and Philosophic Manuscripts of 1844* (New York: International Publishers, 1964), p. 111.
11. Ibid., p. 113.
12. Marx argues for the historical variability of needs:

> On the other hand, the number and extent of [humankind's] so-called requirements, as also the manner in which they are satisfied, are themselves products of history, and depend therefore to a great extent on the level of civilization attained by a country; in particular they depend on the conditions in which, and consequently the habits and expectations with which, the class of free workers has been formed. In contrast, therefore, with the case of other commodities, the determination of the value of labour-power contains a historical and moral element'. (*Capital*, p. 275)

The extent and type of our social relations are also a product of history. As we have arrived at a particular conjuncture in which it is increasingly recognised in various ways that animals are sentient beings with whom we share the world, not merely resources for human projects, Marxism needs to account for this changed context in its theories of labour and exploitation. For examples of our increased knowledge of the capacities of non-human animals in the late twentieth and early twenty-first centuries, see Ralph Acampora, *Corporal Compassion: Animal Ethics and Philosophy of the Body* (Philadelphia: University of Pittsburg Press, 2006); Philip Armstrong and Laurence Simmons, eds, *Knowing Animals* (Leiden: Brill, 2007); Lorraine Daston and Gregg Mitman, eds, *Thinking with Animals: New Perspectives on Anthropomorphism* (New York: Columbia University Press, 2005); Jacques Derrida, *The Animal That Therefore I Am*, ed. Marie-Louise Mallet, transl. David Wills (New York: Fordham University Press, 2008); Donna Haraway, *When Species Meet* (Minneapolis: University of Minnesota Press, 2007); William A. Hillix and Duane M. Rumbaug, *Animal Bodies, Human Minds: Ape, Dolphin and Parrot Language Skills* (New York: Kluwer/Plenum, 2004); and Jennifer Wolch and Jody Emel, eds, *Animal Geographies: Place, Politics and Identity in the Nature–Culture Borderlands* (London: Verso, 1998). The discipline of Human–Animal Studies is increasingly central to humanities academic scholarship, with both Temple University Press and Columbia University Press publishing HAS series.

13. Marx argues that there are two conditions for someone to sell labour-power as a commodity: the possessor 'must have it at his disposal, he must be the free proprietor of his own labour-capacity', and the labourer must be 'compelled to offer for sale as a commodity that

very labour-power which exists only in his living body', as he is unable to sell the commodities he has made with his labour-power (*Capital*, pp, 271, 272). Animals are excluded from this definition of freedom, as they are owned and thus not owners of themselves and their capacity for labour. I would argue, however, that it is an aspect of our denied social relations with animals under capital that produces this situation. They are transformed from wild into owned precisely by the social relations of capital which turn nature into property. Thus their status might be thought of as analogous to African-Americans under slavery, who were legally defined as non-free by capitalist legal structures. Furthermore, with the increasing consolidation of global capitalism and its commodification of nature, many animals find themselves in the same status as humans, able to survive only by submitting to a place within the social relations of capitalist production, since there is little if any space left on the globe which would allow them to pursue lives separate from human social systems.

14. Marx suggests that the surplus value objectified as capital is a surplus of exchange-values, and he rules the animal out of the possibility of producing exchange-values because it cannot enter into the calculative social relations of capitalist exchange. However, animals can be alienated from an embodied existence of full, sensuous species life as much as can humans (although I would maintain species specificity: that each species has its own homologous but not identical species-being). While animals cannot consciously enter into capitalism's calculations of exchange, there is evidence to suggest, for example, that in situations of domestication there is an exchange of tameness for certain kinds of sustenance (note the difference between dog breeding and wolf breeding, and dogs' dependence upon humans to care for their young). We need to start thinking of domesticated animals as our partners in the creation of a human–animal culture, one that was as transformed by the move from feudalism to capitalism as were human class relations. Animal participation is clearly different from human participation in the market, but they participate nonetheless, and thus a less species-centric way to think about the economic and its social relations is required.

15. Paul Burkett argues that capital creates a version of nature strictly as a resource for generating exchange-value, and thus fails to see nature as a social relation between humans and their material conditions of existence. This obfuscation 'corresponds to the social separation of the labourers from necessary conditions of their production, that is, to the fundamental class relation of capitalism' (*Marx and Nature: A Red and Green Perspective* (Basingstoke: Palgrave Macmillan,

1999), p. 62). An alienated relationship to nature is therefore an extension of the alienated relations among humans that are produced by capitalism, and yet another instance of its exploitative nature.

16. Species-being in German is *Gattungwesen*, which translates as 'mankind-essence'. However, *wesen* is not an abstract essence in each human being, but rather a solid reality that is an ensemble of social relations. The word is taken from Feuerbach, who used it in *The Essence of Christianity* (1841) to distinguish man from animal (see Dirk Struik's footnote to Marx, *Economic and Philosophic Manuscripts*, p. 111).

17. Philip McMichael argues that the rise in meat consumption (and corresponding rise in slaughter) is 'not an evolutionary process; rather it expresses the power relations of successive food regimes that have promoted forms of animal protein, and over-production, such as artificially-cheapened surplus corn stocks that underwrite "supersizing" in the fast food industry' ('Feeding the World: agriculture, development and ecology', in Leo Panitch and Colin Leys, eds, *Coming to Terms with Nature* (London: Merlin Press, 2006), p. 182).

18. Following Marx's argument about the difference between the formal and the real subsumption of labour, William Boyd, W. Scott Prudham and Rachel Schurman argue that we are living in the moment of transition between the formal and real subsumption of nature under capitalism. In the real subsumption of labour, workers lost all autonomy and control over the work processes, becoming merely cogs in machines. In the real subsumption of nature, capital moves from merely incorporating nature's processes into systems that produce profit to '"improving" nature directly rather than simply making labor more productive' ('Industrial Dynamics and the Problem of Nature', *Society & Natural Resources* 14: 7 (2001), p. 565).

19. Jason Hribal, '"Animals are part of the working class": a challenge to labor history', *Labor History* 44: 4 (2003), p. 436. Marx and Engels argue that

> Language is as old as consciousness, language is practical consciousness that exists also for other men, and for that reason alone it really exists for me personally as well; language, like consciousness, only arises from the need, the necessity, of intercourse with other men. Where there exists a relationship, it exists for me: the animal does not enter into 'relations' with anything, it does not enter into any relation at all. For the animal, its relation to others does not exist as a relation. Consciousness is,

therefore, from the very beginning a social product, and remains so as long as men exist at all.

From *The German Ideology*, available at www.marxists.org/archive/marx/works/1845/german-ideology/ch01.htm (accessed 17 July 2008). Animals' capacity for language use is one of the chief areas in which the formerly accepted human/animal boundary has been challenged and found permeable. One might presume that, given his attentiveness to historical materialism, Marx might rethink this passage had he access to this new data, and thus I feel it is consistent to argue that we have social relations with animals within a Marxist framework despite Marx's own proclamations to the contrary.

20. Marx, *Economic and Philosophic Manuscripts*, p. 183.
21. Barbara Noske, *Beyond Boundaries: Humans and Animals* (Toronto: Black Rose Books, 1997), pp. 19–20.
22. Ibid., p. 20.
23. Smith, 'Dead Lady of Clown Town', p. 244.
24. See Gary Francione, *Introduction to Animal Rights: Your Child or the Dog?* (Philadelphia: Temple University Press, 2000).
25. Smith, *Norstrilia*, pp. 247–8.
26. Smith, 'Dead Lady of Clown Town', p. 276.
27. Ibid., p. 268.
28. Smith, 'Ballad of Lost C'mell', pp. 403–4.
29. Donna Haraway, *When Species Meet*, p. 267.
30. Bob Torres, *Making a Killing: The Political Economy of Animal Rights* (Oakland: AK Press, 2007), p. 18.
31. Marx, *Economic and Philosophic Manuscripts*, p. 109.
32. See McMichael, 'Feeding the World', pp. 176–7.
33. Smith, 'Dead Lady of Clown Town', pp. 256–7.
34. Haraway, *When Species Meet*, p. 22.
35. McNally argues that slavery under British colonialism was different from other forms of slavery because of its link with capitalist social organisation. Feudalism does not 'subject the producers – usually peasants – to systematic supervision, control and regulation of their work process', unlike capitalism, which 'increases the "efficiencies" of exploitation by seizing control of the work process itself and systematically subjecting wage labourers to the most intricate and invasive systems of supervision, direction and management' (*Another World is Possible*, pp. 144–5). The exploitation of animals under capitalist factory farming is likewise qualitatively different from other forms of agricultural exploitation of animals.
36. McNally, *Another World is Possible*, pp. 185, 193.
37. Smith, 'Dead Lady of Clown Town', p. 273.

38. See Torres, *Making a Killing*, p. 45, which draws on the US Bureau of Labor Statistics' 2005 report. Upton Sinclair's *The Jungle* (1906) also points out this homology from the early days of stockyards and slaughterhouses. See also Gail A. Eisnitz, *Slaughterhouse* (New York: Prometheus Books, 2007), which establishes through interviews with current and former slaughterhouse employees that the pressure to work to the pace of the disassembly line is the main contributor to human injury, animal suffering, and the atmosphere of casual brutality towards the animals that characterises most such workplaces.
39. Torres, *Making a Killing*, p. 64.
40. See Gary Francione, *Animals, Property and the Law* (Philadelphia: Temple University Press, 1995).

7

KEN MacLEOD'S PERMANENT REVOLUTION: UTOPIAN POSSIBLE WORLDS, HISTORY AND THE *AUGENBLICK* IN THE *FALL REVOLUTION* QUARTET

Phillip Wegner

And if I speak so often of the incalculable and the undecidable it's not out of a simple predilection for play nor in order to neutralize decision: on the contrary, I believe there is no responsibility, no ethico-political decision, that must not pass through the proofs of the incalculable or the undecidable. Otherwise everything would be reducible to calculation, program, causality, and, at best, 'hypothetical imperative'.

Jacques Derrida[1]

History will not forgive revolutionaries for procrastinating when they could be victorious today (and they certainly will be victorious today), while they risk losing much tomorrow, in fact, they risk losing everything.

V.I. Lenin[2]

This essay is concerned with Scottish SF writer Ken MacLeod's complexly intertwined *Fall Revolution* quartet, consisting of *The Star Fraction* (1995), *The Stone Canal* (1996), *The Cassini Division* (1998) and *The Sky Road* (1999). The quartet represents not only one of the most interesting recent utopian visions, but also an attempt to rethink the contemporary nature of the political act and agency. This series has some important things to tell us about the specific historical situation out of which it emerged, in terms both of SF's history and the larger social and political horizons the genre inhabits.

Prominent on the US editions of these novels is Kim Stanley Robinson's declaration that MacLeod 'is writing revolutionary

SF. A nova has appeared in our sky'. Robinson's enthusiasm for MacLeod points towards a project they share: the reinvention of utopia for our era of globalisation. There are significant formal and thematic parallels between MacLeod's quartet and Robinson's *Mars* trilogy (1992–96). First, both are long and deal with a vast historical period: in MacLeod's case, over 1,400 pages extending from the 1960s through the twenty-fourth century. Both deploy the SF device of life extension: in MacLeod, this includes, as in Robinson, nanotechnology longevity treatments, but also the digital uploading of 'dead' individuals into either cloned or machine bodies, and the transformation of human beings into a new kind of digital 'posthuman' electronic subject, the Fast Folk. Fredric Jameson's comments on these aspects of Robinson might also be applied to MacLeod:

> Sheer length, sheer reading time, is crucial here in order to develop an *analogon* of historical time itself, as its overdeterminations slowly evolve across the longer Martian years, which the device of the longevity treatments prevents from forming into generations.... It is something of a scientific laboratory experiment in its own right, for human collective history knows rhythm and a logic radically distinct from the normal biological life span, and its paradoxes and unknowabilities stem as much from that incommensurability as they do from the other one that opposes biological individuals to larger multiplicities.[3]

In this manner, both works take up the task of attempting a figuration of historical processes themselves.[4]

Second, both also share a distinctive spatial vision. Of Robinson, Jameson writes:

> Unlike the 'monological' utopias of the tradition, which needed to dramatize a single utopian possibility strongly because of its repression from Terran history and political possibility, this more 'polyphonic' one includes the struggle between a whole range of utopian alternatives, about which it deliberately fails to conclude.[5]

MacLeod stages this proliferation of and interaction between utopian possible worlds in various ways. *The Star Fraction* presents a twenty-first-century UK fragmented into innumerable small, autonomous states and urban enclaves, and half of *The Sky Road* is set – in the years following *The Star Fraction*'s 'Fall Revolution' – in a world broken up into numerous small nations and surrounded by autonomous orbital satellite communities (the UN now displays 'the two thousand, three hundred and ninety seven flags of the nations of the Earth and its colonies').[6] Surrounding and pressing upon even these fractured micro-states are the central Asian Sheenisovs – a nomadic 'barbarian' socialist movement – and the Scottish Greens. These formations bear a striking resemblance to Deleuze and Guattari's 'war machine', a nomadic collective that contains within itself mechanisms to ward off the 'apparatus of capture' that is the modern state formation.[7] (In *The Sky Road*, the latter is represented by the electronic and communicational 'net' encircling the globe, which the Sheenisovs' unique technologies enables them to circumvent.) *The Stone Canal* focuses in part on the anarcho-libertarian-capitalist community on the distant planet of New Mars, while *The Cassini Division* explores the interaction between inhabitants of New Mars, the members of the twenty-fourth-century anarcho-socialist Solar Union and the post-human Fast Folk of Jupiter. A similar diversity is evident in MacLeod's manipulation of generic conventions: his use of cyberpunk, techno-thriller, hard SF, space opera, near-future dystopia, first contact and others exemplifies SF's 'generic discontinuity'.[8]

These formal and representational complexities make any simple summary of the quartet a daunting task. Serving as a unifying thread throughout the four volumes are three characters – Jonathan Wilde, David Reid and Myra Godwin – who first encounter each other in the early 1970s as university students inhabiting (as did MacLeod) the radical subcultures of Scotland and Great Britain. The three become influential leaders in the first decades of the twenty-first century: Wilde founds a movement to campaign for space colonisation and becomes a leader of an anarchist commune; Reid converts to free-market libertarianism and becomes a successful entrepreneur; and Godwin rises to the position of president-dictator of the International Scientific and Technical Workers' Republic (ISTWR) located within the borders of Kazakhstan. The first volume (in which these three characters remain largely off-stage) focuses on the events of a revolution, aided by a ghostly artificial intelligence, against a US/UN global hegemony. In the subsequent volumes we learn that splits within the space-dwelling communities result in the formation of an Outwarder faction, who subsequently upload themselves to become the rapidly evolving Fast Folk and launch a devastating attack on humanity. Reid and his followers migrate through a wormhole to found the world of New Mars; accompanying them is the uploaded consciousness of Wilde, who, after his body is cloned, leads a challenge to Reid before travelling back through the wormhole. Meanwhile, the remnants of humanity that survive the Fast Folk attack form an interplanetary utopian Solar Union, and begin a longstanding détente against the posthumans. This struggle comes to a climax in the twenty-fourth century with the extermination of the Fast Folk when they apparently attempt to mount another assault. The final volume focuses, in alternating chapters, on Godwin's rise to power and a centuries-hence utopian alternate history (in which humanity is about to begin once again the journey to outer space) that results from her decisions during a moment of global crisis.

Summation of the quartet is rendered even more difficult because this story unfolds through a distinctly non-linear plot structure. In *The Stone Canal* and *The Sky Road*, alternating chapters narrate histories separated by centuries. A number of the last events, chronologically, are recounted in volume three, some of the earliest in volume four; and most readers understand the far future of *The Sky Road* as an alternate history to that told in *The Cassini Division*. The quartet thus disrupts conventional progressivist notions of historical linearity and destabilises any simple privileging of one of these possible worlds over the others as the culmination of a deterministic historical process.

Finally, much of the plot consists of first-person representations of various worlds, with narrator-protagonists who are both interested in their worlds and limited in their outlook. A good deal of the 'action' takes the form of political discussions and strategising over what represents the best possible way of being in the world.[9] This emphasis on the (re)politicisation of everyday life tells us something about the historical situation in which MacLeod was writing, and signals a kinship with the pedagogical labours of Bertolt Brecht: like Brecht, MacLeod's fiction

> is not concerned with drawing a 'moral' exactly … [but] with leaving that process open, and allowing the audience to have its own opinion and to frame its own moral, all the while attempting to suggest strongly – nay, even insist – that it cannot not do so.[10]

This invocation of Brecht brings us to the question of the dialectical relationship between modernism and SF, a relationship not unlike that of the interwoven temporalities and spaces in the quartet. On the one hand, SF, emerging as a particularly original representational technology in the late nineteenth century with H.G. Wells, is always already as modernist as, say, film.[11] The formal specificity of SF as a modernist practice is most effectively grasped in Darko Suvin's definition of it as 'the literature of cognitive estrangement', of which Jameson notes,

> Suvin's originality as a theorist of both science fiction and utopias all at once, is (among other things) not merely to have linked the two generically; but also to have conjoined the SF and utopian critical tradition with the Brechtian one, centering on estrangement (the so-called V-effect); and to have insisted not merely on the function of SF and Utopia to 'estrange', to produce a V-effect for the reader from a normal 'everyday' common-sense reality, but also to do so 'cognitively' (a no less Brechtian component of the definition). The reassertion of the cognitive means … a refusal to allow the (obvious) aesthetic and artistic status of the SF or utopian work to neutralize its realistic and referential implications.[12]

Moreover, Jameson argues that SF emerges when and where it does to fill the void left by the waning of one of the most significant realist genres, the historical novel:

> We are therefore entitled to complete Lukács' account of the historical novel with the counter-panel of its opposite number, the emergence of the new genre of SF as a form which now registers some nascent sense of

the future, and does so in the space on which a sense of the past had once been inscribed.[13]

Through its 'realist' representation of the future, SF engages in its form of (modernist) estrangement or defamiliarisation:

> For the apparent realism, or representationality, of SF has concealed another, far more complex temporal structure: not to give us 'images' of the future – whatever such images might mean for a reader who will necessarily predecease their 'materialization' – but rather to defamiliarize and restructure our own experience of our own *present*, and to do so in specific ways distinct from all other forms of defamiliarization.[14]

In short, Jameson shows how SF is a wholly unique form of what we might call 'realist (cognitive) modernism (estrangement)'. Whereas high modernism estranges through violations of formal expectations, SF estranges through its realistic content, whose referent is 'absent'.[15]

However, when we turn to SF's specific history, we discover a more delimited modernist 'period' within it; or more precisely, a number of different 'modernist' moments. Jameson argues that film has two histories – of the silent and sound eras – and that each of the two 'evolutionary species' that results passes through similar developmental stages: from an early 'realism' (D.W. Griffith for silent, classical Hollywood for sound), a moment in which occurs 'the conquest of a kind of cultural, ideological, and narrative literacy by a new class or group'; through a 'modernist' period of formal experimentation (of 'Eisenstein and Stroheim', and of the 'great *auteurs*'); and finally, although only in sound film, into a full-blown 'postmodernism'.[16] Something similar occurs in the history of SF: following its realist emergence (Wells, E.M. Forster, Alexander Bogdanov), the first modernist moment (Yevgeny Zamyatin, Alexei Tolstoy, Aldous Huxley, Karel Čapek, Olaf Stapledon) is interrupted in the late 1920s by the Soviet crackdown on literary and artistic experimentation and the emergence in the US of pulp magazine SF. The genre subsequently passes through a second realist stage (the so-called Golden Age) before opening up in the late 1950s into its great modernist period, which extends through the New Wave into the mid 1970s. This is followed by postmodern SF, signalled most dramatically by the appearance of cyberpunk in the 1980s and its subsequent rejoinder in the 'critical dystopias'[17] of Robinson, Marge Piercy and Octavia Butler. The 1990s, for reasons I will elaborate, witnesses another turn of the wheel, as new and established SF and fantasy writers (Robinson, MacLeod, Butler, China Miéville, Philip Pullman, Joe Haldeman) all react against the earlier postmodern SF, especially cyberpunk, and 'repeat' SF's earlier modernist phases.[18] This science-fictional post-postmodernism runs parallel to similar developments in cultural and social theory in the 1990s (Jameson, Jacques Derrida, Slavoj Žižek, Michael Hardt, Antonio Negri, Alain Badiou, Giorgio Agamben, Gayatri Spivak, Kojin Karatani and Judith Butler, among others) that in various ways returned to themes (the universal, truth, ontology, totality, utopia) that were anathema to postmodernism.

One consequence of the quartet's modernist form is that it shifts attention away from the representation of other worlds to the processes by which they come into being: the moment of political decision and forms of agency through which they emerge. As one character exclaims,

> You know more than you know. I have to tell you to wake up! Be on your guard! Small decisions can decide great events, as I know too well. Without a socialist revolution, in the next historical period at that, a catastrophe threatens the whole culture of mankind. The battles may be determined, but not their outcome: victory requires a different ... determination.[19]

MacLeod's vision thus resonates with Georg Lukács's modernist theorisation of the *Augenblick*, the 'moment' to intervene in a situation:

> What is a 'moment' (*Augenblick*)? A situation whose duration may be longer or shorter, but which is distinguished from the process that leads up to it in that it forces together the essential tendencies of that process, and demands that a *decision* be taken over the *future direction of the process*. That is to say the tendencies reach a sort of zenith, and depending on how the situation concerned is handled, the process takes on a different direction

after the 'moment'. Development does not occur, then, as a continuous intensification, in which development is favorable to the proletariat, and the day after tomorrow the situation *must* be even more favorable than it is tomorrow, and so on. It means rather that at a *particular* point, the situation demands that a decision be taken and the day after tomorrow might be too late to make that decision.[20]

In the *Augenblick*, 'the decision, and with it the fate of the proletarian revolution (and therefore of humanity), depends on the subjective element'.[21] The *Augenblick* is a situation in which a

certain particular demand possesses ... a global detonating power ... The art of [the] *Augenblick* – the moment when, briefly, there is an opening for an *act* to intervene in a situation – is the art of seizing the right moment, of aggravating the conflict *before* the system can accommodate itself to our demand.... the Lukácsian *Augenblick* is unexpectedly close to what, today, Alain Badiou endeavours to formulate as the Event: an intervention that cannot be accounted for in terms of its pre-existing 'objective conditions'.[22]

Aimed at restoring the radical subjective dimension to Marxist theory (and taking as its target Second International–style determinism), Lukács nevertheless argues that his theorisation of the *Augenblick* is to be distinguished from the voluntarism of 'a Luxemburgist theory of spontaneity' that turns 'the concrete truth of particular and concrete historical "moments" into the abstract falsehood of a permanently decisive influenceability of the process. Such a "left" theory of moments ignores precisely the instant of dialectical change, the concrete, revolutionary essence of the "moment"'.[23] It is thus the ability both to recognise and to intervene in the moment that defines the 'art of insurrection', and the concrete historical embodiment of this '*conscious, subjective* moment of the revolutionary process' is not the abstract masses but a 'class-conscious vanguard'.[24] In this way,

Lukács advocates the dialectical unity/mediation of theory and practice, in which even the most contemplative stance is eminently 'practical' (in the sense of being embedded in the totality of social (re)production and thus expressing a certain 'practical' sense of how to survive in this totality), and, on the other hand, even the most 'practical' stance implies a certain 'theoretical' framework; it actualizes a set of ideological propositions.[25]

An example of the *Augenblick* is Lukács's composition of *History and Class Consciousness* (1919–22), 'one of the few authentic events in the history of Marxism':[26] a vanguardist (i.e. modernist) intervention that actualises a set of ideological propositions and thereby changes the coordinates of its situation, and whose own conditions of possibility come to a close shortly thereafter. But these conditions would be 'repeated' – in the 1960s, as signalled by the global revival of *History and Class Consciousness* following its 1967 republication, and again in the 1990s, with the discovery and publication of Lukács's *A Defense of History and Class Consciousness*.

For Žižek, this formulation of the *Augenblick* makes Lukács the 'philosopher of Leninism'. At one point, Wilde notes that his group 'had learned the left's one sound lesson, Leninism',[27] and examples of these repetitions of Lenin, this capacity to seize the moment of the *Augenblick* and practise the rare art of insurrection, abound in the quartet. *The Star Fraction* ends with the AI that played a crucial role in original events of the series, stating: 'When their existence endangered that of humanity, with Space Defense hours away from an irrevocable decision, I made a choice'.[28] In *The Stone Canal*, when Wilde is offered in the mid 1990s an opportunity to form a corporate-funded autonomous 'grassroots organization campaigning *for* industrial development, instead of against', he reflects:

> The big thrill wasn't that they were offering me power – they were offering me a bit more influence, that was all. No, what made the hairs on my neck prickle was that they thought I might – any decade now – *have* power; that I might represent something that it was a smart move to get on the right side of well in advance; that somewhere down the line might be my Finland Station.[29]

Accepting their offer leads to the founding of the Space Movement, which dramatically shapes all of subsequent history. Later in the novel, when he is a senior figure in a London anarchist commune (as he also appears in *The Star Fraction*), his decision not to sell their 'nation's' nuclear capacity to Germany reorders the globe. He declares: 'I had reached my Finland Station'.[30]

The most controversial seizure of the moment occurs in *The Cassini Division*, when Ellen May Ngwethu uses the opportunity of a computer virus attack by Jupiter's Fast Folk to unleash an asteroid bombardment that exterminates them. MacLeod here offers the opportunity to reflect on one of radicalism's intractable problems – the legitimacy of political violence – but thwarts any easy attempt to render a final judgement upon the morality of this action. Ellen is adamant that her action is necessary and justified if humanity is to survive – it is precisely this inflexibility that enables her to act in the *Augenblick*; but there is also a good deal of evidence that her past experiences have created in her a deep and intractable bias against the Fast Folk. In their pre-Singularity human lives, as the Outwarder faction of the Space Movement, they were responsible for the murder of her parents and many of her friends; and she lives in a terribly immediate way the aftershocks of the Fast Folk's first viral assault, centuries earlier, on the Earth and its colonies that led to a massive loss of life and a Dark Century of warfare and conflict: 'After the conflict, I didn't just have an ideological dislike, and aesthetic distaste, for the Outwarders. Hatred was flash-burned into my brain'.[31] Characters with very different extended life experiences argue against her action, and the novel concludes with a debate over its legitimacy:

> 'Original sin?' interrupts the bishop. 'I'm surprised at you!'
>
> The two Calvinist clergymen smirk politely. Reid shakes his head.
>
> 'They showed it by their actions,' he says. 'By what they did to our ships.'
>
> 'Ah, but was that enough to condemn an entire ... species?' the Reformed Humanist asks. 'I suspect Ellen May Ngwethu and her crew acted precipitately, but with a degree of premeditation, a refusal to consider alternatives, which in itself –'
>
> 'We live in a tough world,' says the rabbi. 'As my people have traditionally put it, life is short and shit happens.'[32]

Intriguingly, however, the real concern might lie elsewhere: as one character puts it, 'but it's so final! Everything will change'.[33] Arguments against the morality of radical or revolutionary action often betray a deeper anxiety produced by the undecidability of change: when we act in the 'moment' we know things will change, but whether for the better or worse cannot be known in advance. However, as both the quartet and my epigraph from Derrida stress, it is only in embracing that undecidability or incalculability that a free and, in Badiou's terms, the only truly 'human' act can occur.[34]

The finest example of seizing the *Augenblick* is found in the closing pages of *The Sky Road* (and of the quartet). Myra Godwin, fearing the dissolution of her 'nation' in the face of the Sheenisov onslaught, seeks military aid. Her efforts are unsuccessfully directed to the Eastern US,[35] and then to a UK mired in a struggle to defend its integrity against the Greens operating with near-impunity within its borders. Her actions alert US and UN forces to the ISTWR's banned cache of nuclear weapons, inherited from the Vatican, hidden among the clutter of space stations, weapons platforms, communication satellites and junk orbiting the planet.[36] When she refuses to relinquish these weapons of mass destruction, they begin to level the nation's major cities and, even more sinisterly, direct their fire at the refugee groups streaming out of them. When her own caravan comes under attack, Myra decides to detonate the orbital weapons, thereby unleashing the 'ablation cascade', an event that 'means the end of satellite guidance, global positioning, comsats, the nets, everything! It'll be like the world going blind!'.[37] It is precisely this 'unexpected and undreamt' event that creates the preconditions for the emergence of the post-national 'utopian' world present in the alternating chapters.

In the final pages of Myra's narrative we are presented with this striking scene:

> Riding into the first dawn of the new world, Myra knew the little camcopter dancing a couple of meters in front of her might well be relaying the last television news most of its watchers would ever see.

Behind her, in a slow struggle that ended with the ambulances and litters of the injured and dying, the Kazakh migration spread to the horizon. The sun was rising behind them, silhouetting their scattered, tattered banners. There was only one audience, now, that was worth speaking to: the inheritors.

'Nothing is written,' she said. 'The future is ours to shape. When you take the cities, spare the scientists and engineers. Whatever they may have done in the past you need them for the future. Let's make it a better one.'[38]

The quartet's final image – a statue of Myra, located in a Scottish community hundreds of years hence, 'riding, at the head of her own swift cavalry ... and, floating bravely above her head and above her army, the black flag on which nothing is written'[39] – resonates with one that occurred in our world only a few years before MacLeod turned to writing SF:

The most sublime image that emerged in the political upheavals of the last years – and the term 'sublime' is to be conceived here in the strictest Kantian sense – was undoubtedly the unique picture from the time of the violent overthrow of Ceausescu in Romania: the rebels waving the national flag with the red star, the Communist symbol, cut out, so that instead of the symbol standing for the organizing principle of the national life, there was nothing but a hole in its center. It is difficult to imagine a more salient index of the 'open' character of a historical situation 'in its becoming', as Kierkegaard would have put it, of that intermediate phase when the former Master-Signifier, although it has already lost the hegemonical power, has not yet been replaced by the new one.... what really matters is that the masses who poured into the streets of Bucharest 'experienced' the situation as 'open', that they participated in the unique intermediate state of passage from one discourse (social link) to another, when, for a brief, passing moment, the hole in the big Other, the symbolic order, became visible.[40]

With this figuration of the 'hole in the big Other', we arrive at the true utopian content of MacLeod's rich and complex narrative: dismantling any notion of rigid historical determinism and fully opening up the closure of prehistory, MacLeod's utopia cannot be identified with any of the variety of possible worlds mapped in this work (although, as in Robinson, we might read this very ensemble itself as a figuration of a utopian space beyond the bordered totality of the nation-state). Rather, the work's utopia is that of the future as permanent revolution, a temporal locale wherein we are once again endowed with the power, and responsibility, to act as political subjects.

All of this also speaks to the historical context out of which MacLeod's, Robinson's and Žižek's utopian imaginaries emerge. This period – located between what I describe as the 'two deaths' of the beginning of the end of the Cold War, with the 'fall' of the Berlin Wall on 9 November 1989, and the end of the beginning of the terrible new historical situation of the global 'war on terror', with the destruction of the World Trade Center on 11 September 2001 – forms a strange transitional space between an ending (of the Cold War) and a beginning (of our post-9/11 world).[41] This place between two deaths, the location between a Real Event (the unexpected and unplanned end of the Cold War) and its Symbolic repetition (the 9/11 attacks), is strictly speaking 'non-historical', precisely because it is open to a number of possible 'symbolizations/historicizations'. Such an 'empty place' is experienced in its lived reality as 'a place of sublime beauty as well as terrifying monsters'.[42] It feels like a moment of 'terrifying monsters', of hauntings by a living dead past and the 'compulsion to repeat', yet is simultaneously experienced as a moment of 'sublime beauty', of the openness and instability that Žižek invokes in the passage cited above, of experimentation and opportunity, of conflict and insecurity – a place, in other words, wherein history might move in a number of very different directions.

The 1990s witnessed a host of new developments – the rise of a debate over globalisation; the rapid expansion of the new communication and information technologies of the internet and the World Wide Web; the explosive emergence, especially in the second half of the period, of a new counter-globalisation 'movement of movements'; as well as some of the theoretical and cultural developments I alluded to above. All of these indicate the degree to which the 1990s represent a unique period of struggle, one enabled by the Event of the collapse of the Soviet bloc, and waged over the significance of this Event. For the Event of the first death – the end of the Cold War – in effect ended for the global cultural and political left the legacy of the twentieth century, and opened up the space for new kinds of political and cultural experimentation. Crucially in this decade, no outcome was determined outside this struggle: that is, there was no way to know a priori what the repetition of the Event might be. Indeed, it will be the identification of the second death that becomes during the 1990s the very prize struggled over.

It is this sense of the 1990s as a situation of sublime openness and renewed struggle that is so effectively figured in the quartet. Indeed, the disorienting effects of the fall of the Eastern bloc are registered in the central chapter of *The Stone Canal*, set in the 1990s:

> 'I haven't changed my ideas, long-term – but I know a defeat when I see one. Getting over the end of the Second World will take generations, and it won't be our generations. The last time I hung out with the left was during the Gulf War. The kids don't know shit, and the older guys –' he grinned suddenly like the Dave I knew better '– that is, the ones older than us, they look like men who've been told they have cancer.'[43]

But the rest of the novel (and of the quartet) demonstrates that this situation should be understood as an opportunity – another *Augenblick* – not only for reimagining radical politics, but also for transforming the world.

At the same time, a rather different view emerged, which held that the US was the 'victor' in the Cold War, and thus had the obligation to 'lead' the world – a view that promised to have dire consequences for the rest of the globe, as the first Gulf War less than two years later indicated. Unsurprisingly, this issue is also of central concern to MacLeod. Louis Marin argues that any utopia is constituted through a careful neutralisation of elements of the specific historical context from which it emerges which then enables the productive figurative operations of the text to go to work.[44] In the quartet, the focus of its neutralising machinery turns out to be nothing less than the US itself, imagined less as a discreet national community than as a figure for what can now be understood as an emerging form of global sovereignty that would replace that of the Cold War: that of Empire:

> After the world war there was a world government. It was officially known as the United Nations, unofficially as the US/UN, and colloquially as the Yanks. It kept the peace, from space, or so it claimed. What it actually did was prevent innumerable tiny wars from becoming big wars. But in order to maintain its power, it needed little wars, and they never stopped. We had war without end, to prevent war to the end.[45]

One of the key mechanisms by which Empire secures hegemony is rigid enforcement of a global monopoly on state violence, especially in the form of nuclear weapons. In the Fall Revolution, this monopoly is ingeniously dissolved, as various micro-states rent out their nuclear capacity:

> They exported nuclear deterrence. Not the weapons themselves – that, perish the thought, would have been illegal – but the salutary effect of possessing them.... for the first time, nuclear deterrence was available to anyone willing to pay for it, and the cost was reasonable enough for every homeland to have one.[46]

Nuclear proliferation becomes *the basis of*, rather than a barrier to, the movement towards utopia (defined as the maximal proliferation of utopian worlds in a situation of permanent revolution). Unable to impose its vision of global order, the monarchical (in Hardt and Negri's Spinozan terminology) US and its various aristocratic vassals dissolve away, enabling the final movement from the long dark era of prehistory into the chaos and drama of history itself:

> We know as well as you do that a power such as the US must become cannot administer the world. Police it, at a very high level, yes. But as some powers move up from the nation, others devolve to the local community. We have the opportunity to encourage autonomy and diversity. Let us take it, and spare our country years of agony.[47]

In this way, MacLeod, like Hardt and Negri, sees that the very conditions that enable the establishment of Empire are also those that make its defeat an equally real possibility. The outcome is not guaranteed, making history, once again, a field of struggle.

The question remains: Is it still possible to imagine this kind of change and struggle in the post-9/11 world?[48] If our answer is in the negative, then there may be one final and vital lesson to be taken from MacLeod. In the last pages of *The Star Fraction* we get this snippet of dialogue: 'What we thought was the revolution ... was only a moment in the fall';[49] in MacLeod's introduction to the US edition, he notes that this 'remark has a theory of history behind it'.[50] Such a theory holds that historical temporalities unfold on scales to which our cognitive organs are not normally attuned, and that the consequences of our decisions and actions may not be registered in the immediate moment, or even in our all-too-human lifespan. But those consequences are there, albeit often in forms we cannot imagine or expect, and hence our responsibilities remain to seize the *Augenblick*: to act as if utopia stands poised at every moment to make its tiger's leap into history.

Notes

1. Jacques Derrida, *Points ... Interviews, 1974–1994*, ed. Elisabeth Weber (Stanford: Stanford University Press, 1995), p. 273.
2. V.I. Lenin, *Collected Works, Vol. 26* (Moscow: Progress Publishers, 1972), pp. 234–5.
3. Fredric Jameson, *Archaeologies of the Future: The Desire Called Utopia and Other Science Fictions* (London: Verso, 2005), p. 396.
4. 'History is the trade secret of science fiction, and theories of history are its invisible engine' (Ken MacLeod, preface to *The Star Fraction* (New York: Tor, 2001), p. 11).
5. Jameson, *Archaeologies*, p. 410. This proliferation within a single text of utopian possible worlds and the staging of the clash between them is not original to Robinson; something similar occurs in Yevgeny Zamyatin's *We* (1921) and Ursula Le Guin's *The Dispossessed* (1974). See Phillip Wegner, *Imaginary Communities: Utopia, the Nation, and the Spatial Histories of Modernity* (Berkeley: University of California Press, 2002).
6. Ken MacLeod, *The Sky Road* (New York: Tor, 2001), p. 257. That there is something particularly Scottish about this interest in devolutionary and decentralising processes is also suggested by

Tom Nairn, *Faces of Nationalism: Janus Revisited* (London: Verso, 1997).

7. See Gilles Deleuze and Félix Guattari, *A Thousand Plateaus: Capitalism and Schizophrenia*, transl. Brian Massumi (Minneapolis: University of Minnesota Press, 1987).

8. Jameson, *Archaeologies*, pp. 254–66.

9. MacLeod used 'the real Fourth International (seedbed of most of the sects of the British far Left) as a model of revolutionary politics' (Ken MacLeod, 'Politics and Science Fiction', in Edward James and Farah Mendlesohn, eds, *The Cambridge Companion to Science Fiction* (Cambridge: Cambridge University Press, 2003), p. 239).

10. Fredric Jameson, *Brecht and Method* (London: Verso, 1998), pp. 106–7.

11. If one dates SF to Mary Shelley, then one might accept Tony Pinkney's suggestion that romanticism was already a proto-modernism. 'Editor's Introduction: Modernism and Cultural Theory', in Raymond Williams, *The Politics of Modernism: Against the New Conformists* (London: Verso, 1989), pp. 1–29. Cf. Michael Löwy and Robert Sayres, *Romanticism Against the Tide of Modernity*, transl. Catherine Porter (Durham: Duke University Press, 2001).

12. Darko Suvin, *Metamorphoses of Science Fiction: On the Poetics and History of a Literary Genre* (New Haven: Yale University Press, 1979), p. 12; Jameson, *Archaeologies*, p. 410.

13. Jameson, *Archaeologies*, pp. 285–6.

14. Ibid., p. 286.

15. See Marc Angenot, 'The Absent Paradigm: An Introduction to the Semiotics of Science Fiction', *Science Fiction Studies* 6: 1 (March 1979), pp. 9–19.

16. Fredric Jameson, *Signatures of the Visible* (London: Verso, 1990), p. 156.

17. See Tom Moylan, *Scraps of the Untainted Sky: Science Fiction, Utopia, Dystopia* (Boulder: Westview, 2001).

18. The concept of 'repeating' is taken from Slavoj Žižek, who called for a repetition of Lenin's modernist project of social and cultural transformation:

> As a result, *repeating* Lenin does not mean a *return* to Lenin – to repeat Lenin is to accept that 'Lenin is dead', that his particular solution failed, even failed monstrously, but that there was a utopian spark in it worth saving. Repeating Lenin means that we have to distinguish between what Lenin actually did and the field of possibilities he opened up, the tension in Lenin between what he actually did and another dimension: what was 'in Lenin more

than Lenin himself'. To repeat Lenin is to repeat not what Lenin *did* but what he *failed to do,* his missed opportunities.

Slavoj Žižek, 'Afterword: Lenin's Choice', in Žižek, ed., *Revolution at the Gates: Selected Writings of Lenin from 1917* (London: Verso, 2002), p. 310. Cf. Sebastien Budgen, Stathis Kouvelakis and Slavoj Žižek, eds, *Lenin Reloaded: Toward a Politics of Truth* (Durham: Duke University Press, 2007). I discuss Joe Haldeman and Octavia Butler's 1990s SF in Phillip Wegner, *Life Between Two Deaths, 1989–2001: US Culture in the Long Nineties* (Durham: Duke University Press, 2009).

19. MacLeod, *Star Fraction,* p. 51.
20. Georg Lukács, *A Defense of History and Class Consciousness: Tailism and the Dialectic,* transl. Esther Leslie (London: Verso, 2000), p. 55.
21. Ibid., p. 58.
22. Slavoj Žižek, 'Postface: Georg Lukács as the Philosopher of Leninism', in Lukács, *Defense of History and Class Consciousness,* p. 164.
23. Lukács, *Defense of History and Class Consciousness,* p. 59.
24. Ibid., p. 57.
25. Žižek, 'Postface: Georg Lukács as the Philosopher of Leninism', p. 172.
26. Ibid., p. 151.
27. Ken MacLeod, *The Stone Canal* (New York: Tor, 2001), p. 145.
28. MacLeod, *Star Fraction,* p. 320.
29. MacLeod, *Stone Canal,* pp. 113–14, 116–17.
30. Ibid., p. 184.
31. Ken MacLeod, *The Cassini Division* (New York: Tor, 2000), p. 162.
32. Ibid., p. 304.
33. Ibid., p. 133.
34. Alain Badiou, *Ethics: An Essay on the Understanding of Radical Evil,* transl. Peter Hallward (London: Verso, 2001), p. 49.
35. In another common trope of recent SF, the US has broken up into two nations, one on each coast, separated by a loose grouping of religious-fundamentalist, white-supremacist and indigenous peoples' enclaves. On this trope, see Phillip Wegner, 'The Last Bomb: Historicizing History in Terry Bisson's *Fire on the Mountain* and Gibson and Sterling's *The Difference Engine*', *Comparatist* 23 (1999); and 'Learning to Live in History: Alternate Historicities and the 1990s in *The Years of Rice and Salt*', in William J. Burling, ed., *Kim Stanley Robinson Maps the Unimaginable: Critical Essays* (Jefferson: MacFarland, 2009).
36. Space-junk is the model for Rem Koolhaas's junkspace: 'what remains after modernization has run its course, or, more precisely,

what coagulates while modernization is in progress, its fallout' (Rem Koolhaas, 'Junkspace', in Chuihua Judy Chung, Jeffrey Inaba, Rem Koolhaas and Sze Tsung Leong, eds, *Project on the City 2* (Köln: Taschen, 2001), p. 408).

37. MacLeod, *Sky Road*, p. 394.
38. Ibid., p. 401.
39. Ibid., p. 406.
40. Slavoj Žižek, *Tarrying with the Negative: Kant, Hegel, and the Critique of Ideology* (Durham: Duke University Press, 1993), p. 1.
41. See Wegner, *Life Between Two Deaths*.
42. Slavoj Žižek, *The Sublime Object of Ideology* (New York: Verso, 1989), p. 135.
43. MacLeod, *Stone Canal*, p. 119.
44. See Louis Marin, *Utopics: The Semiological Play of Textual Spaces*, transl. Robert A. Vollrath (Atlantic Highlands: Humanities Press International, 1984).
45. MacLeod, *Stone Canal*, p. 207. See Michael Hardt and Antonio Negri, *Empire* (Cambridge: Harvard University Press, 2000), and *Multitude: War and Democracy in the Age of Empire* (Cambridge: Harvard University Press, 2004).
46. MacLeod, *Stone Canal*, pp. 156–7.
47. Ibid., p. 192.
48. MacLeod acknowledges 9/11 as the sign of the closure of a particularly open historical period:

> Douglas Adams encapsulated the scientific attitude as 'Any idea is there to be attacked.' A like iconoclasm in political and social matters is its extension and precondition. This view is not only recent, but rare. Its global hegemony seemed assured after the Fall of the Wall; less so, after the Fall of the Towers.

MacLeod, 'Politics and Science Fiction', p. 231.
49. MacLeod, *Star Fraction*, pp. 314.
50. Ibid., p. 11.

Part III

Back to the Future

8

'MADONNA IN MOON ROCKET WITH BREECHES': WEIMAR SF FILM CRITICISM DURING THE STABILISATION PERIOD[1]

Iris Luppa

To discover the extent and impact of Marxist film criticism during the years of the Weimar Republic (1919–33) it is not enough simply to refer to the early work of established left-leaning Weimar film theorists Rudolf Arnheim, Béla Balázs and Siegfried Kracauer, nor would it suffice merely to add Walter Benjamin's writing on the link between film and modernity or the media-theoretical essays of Bertolt Brecht dating from the so-called stabilisation period (1924–29). In fact, many reviews and other examples of film criticism from implicit and explicit materialist perspectives can be found in the Republic's daily press and weekly magazines. Articles by writers who were socialists or communists, such as Axel Eggebrecht, Heinz Lüdecke and Alfred Durus, writing for a proletarian audience in the spirit of the 'Proletkult' (proletarian culture) programme, could be found in such communist publications as *Die Rote Fahne*, *Die Arbeiter Illustrierte Zeitung* and *Kulturwille*.[2] There were also many left-leaning liberal writers who equally contributed to the frequently overtly political discourses on film, reflecting the Republic's extreme political polarisation – writers such as Willy Haas, Herbert Ihering, Andor Kraszna-Kraus and Kurt Pinthus, who contributed daily editorials, film reviews and wider film-theoretical and cultural debates in the daily *Film-Kurier*, *Berliner Börsen-Courier*, and magazines like *Weltbühne* and *Tage-Buch*.

Marxist writing on film took many forms: from advocating the greater distribution and screening of Soviet montage films and exposing the bourgeois ideology prevalent in films produced by Germany's capitalist film industry – especially the Hugenberg-owned Ufa (Universum-Film AG) studios – to engaging with the social function of film as a tool for education and political agitation. As early as 1922, Béla Balázs, writing in *Die Rote Fahne*, argued that 'for the most part', bourgeois films

> are already conscious tools for propaganda employed by the counter revolutionary capitalism ... not to mention the hundreds of films written as blatant propaganda against communist Russia. There's only one thing to do: to make use of the huge agitational power of film for our own objectives ... we have to have our own film factories producing our own films.[3]

Sabine Hake draws attention to debates among communist critics who argued that films with a revolutionary content called for new forms of representation and stylistic innovation, and those who felt that existing modes with a high degree of identification would serve best to politicise the audience, as film would only find its true form in a post-revolutionary society.[4]

This essay examines leftist responses to SF in Weimar cinema, and asks why and to what extent the genre was of concern to Marxist critics. It then discusses the left's critical response to two highly influential SF films by Fritz Lang – *Metropolis* (1927) and *Frau im Mond* (1929) – demonstrating the scope as well as the limitations of these approaches to the genre, including their focus on narrative elements at the expense of visual analysis and a refusal to engage with mass popular culture.

Marxist Perspectives on Weimar SF and the Capitalist Film Industry in 1920s Germany

Axel Eggebrecht's 'Technology, labour and science of the future: possibilities of a future film', published in *Kulturwille* (1927), provides a good example of a dialectic-materialist approach to the genre. He argues that the capitalist film industry is part of a wider 'amusement industry' (akin to what Adorno later terms 'culture industry'), capable only of producing 'crafted' mass commodities. Nonetheless, Eggebrecht regards film as the 'greatest art form of the 20th century', which, he argues, 'because it is the legitimate child of industrial late capitalism ... now has to express the entire emptiness of this epoch'.[5] This view is characteristic of, on the one hand, the left's growing awareness of film's potential in reaching large audiences with a view to politicising the working-class spectatorship and, on the other, a recognition that the film industry in its current state was inextricably linked to the capitalist mode of production and capitalist ideology. Eggebrecht notes that, whereas young proletarian dramatic artists were able to break through the 'capitalist grip of the commercial stage theatres', the same was impossible in the film industry, where projects demanded far bigger budgets, and that even if capital for the production of a proletarian film *was* made available, distribution regulations and censorship would prevent them from reaching the masses:

> With this insight we have already answered the question to what extent the film of today can be a prophet, create a utopia, show us the future: it cannot. The class that wholly dominates it doesn't like giving a prognosis of the future ... [this class] feels too insecure about its own status to give the future a serious thought.[6]

This comment clearly illustrates Marxist film criticism's emphasis on the prevailing link between the mode of production and the dominant bourgeois ideology in film. Eggebrecht's view of capitalism as an economic system in its final stages, unable to produce a vision of the future because of the inevitability of social change in the form of proletarian revolution, shows the focus on political agitation in communist writing on film.

Eggebrecht's critique is characteristic of wider Marxist debates on film, but he also draws attention to the generic specificity of the SF film, arguing that film's ability to represent reality as well as spectacular fantastical images makes it the medium 'most capable of showing us a future that does not as yet exist'.[7] He predicts that film, used to suppress the proletariat at this stage, will eventually help to liberate it. For now, he argues, SF films can only paint a 'despairing' image of the future, because any vision of the future is inextricably linked to political ways of seeing: 'There can be no utopia without [political] conviction, optimism, or goals':

> However, the producers of today's films have no other goal than to make money.... Film's capitalist structure keeps it from fulfilling its most important obligations. Not until our brighter future itself approaches can [film] be the instrument of this future. Any theoretical recognition of its possibilities cannot alter that fact.[8]

Significantly, although Eggebrecht concedes that capitalism is still the dominant mode of production in all industries, including film, he repeatedly refers to the 'demise' of the era and of a (capitalist) class 'insecure' about 'its own status'. In contrast, in Weimar's rapidly industrialised society the proletariat, currently suppressed by a (democratic) system that guarantees ownership of capital, is readying itself to take over what Eggebrecht calls 'the machines'. SF's capacity to show audiences glimpses of a utopian post-capitalist future is suppressed by the film industry.

The question of the future, and of how it is represented on screen, is one of the key issues for Marxist film critics, for whom the historical development towards a post-capitalist society is part of a rational process, not a dystopian fantasy. Any anxiety about the future is part of a wider insecurity of the bourgeoisie faced with an increasingly class-conscious proletariat. SF in Weimar cinema thus becomes a site of conflict between rational and irrational positions on a textual and meta-textual level. The following analyses of *Metropolis* and *Frau im Mond*[9] will take the critical reception of both films as a starting point to elucidate the thematic and stylistic similarities and differences in their methods and meanings with reference to aspects of the Weimar context. The aim of this comparative approach is to trace the critics' examination of the films' ideological function while also – in addition to their narrative-based reviews – taking Lang's scrupulous handling of film rhetoric into account.

Metropolis

Since its premiere in Berlin in January 1927, critics have found the wealth of discourses, themes and art-historical references in Fritz Lang's *Metropolis* a fertile ground for discussion. In an extensive review of *Metropolis*, Willy Haas, one of Weimar's most prominent critics writing for the *Film-Kurier*, summarises the content of *Metropolis* as follows:

> A little Christianity, with the idea of the 'mediator', of religious services in the catacombs, of the holy mother of humankind Maria ... a little socialism, with the thoroughly modern cult of the machine, the proletariat enslaved and robbed of their souls, and the perfect 'accumulation of capital', to put it in entirely Marxist terms ... a little Nietzscheanism, with the worship of the superman.[10]

Above all, contemporary critics pointed out the lack of a clear perspective about the future in Lang's film. Willy Haas notes, 'Everything is mixed together so carefully in such a way that the script manages neatly to evade any suggestion of an uncompromising idea and no "tendency" – Heaven forbid – is able to develop'.[11] Several other critics interpreted the film's lack of any clear 'tendencies' in explicit political terms, aware that Lang's 'future film' presented a forceful comment on *contemporary* Weimar society's ideas and fears of the future.[12] For example, Herbert Ihering pointedly describes *Metropolis* as 'an ideological film without an ideology', able to accommodate a 'technical city of the future and the romanticism of the shady bower', which reduces 'factual' themes into 'atrocious kitsch'.[13] For him, it can only produce empty gestures, devoid of political meaning: 'Effects not because ideologies urge towards explosions, but because the film wants its effects'.[14]

Eggebrecht's review of *Metropolis* is one of the most explicitly Marxist readings of the film. Interestingly, he writes his review as if in an imagined future, introducing it as a 'preview' of a film-historical study written and published in the year 2003:

> It was the fashion of the first phase between the great class wars of the 20th century, which we now refer to as the middle European mediocrity: the upper classes ordered their intellectual advisers to wrestle with the creation of a world view, which already no longer existed. Exhausted, insecure, full of a secret anxiety about the impending explosions of social tensions, these

superstitious minds found refuge in the symbolism of the middle ages and in a desperate–snobbish admiration of machines, whose dull rhythm their tired souls couldn't comprehend, which is why they found them adorable in a romantic–atavistic fashion ... In those times lived Fritz Lang.[15]

Eggebrecht thus defines the 1920s as a time of great social tensions on the brink of 'explosion'. Although the years 1924–29 were not as unstable politically and economically as the immediate post-war years, the Republic's parliament was largely unable to govern, partly due to the lack of compromise between pro- and anti-democratic parties in the Reichstag. Ineffective coalitions confirmed the flaws of a parliamentary democratic system to communists and emerging fascist groupings; in this context, Eggebrecht's review illustrates the standpoint of a writer for whom radical political change is not a utopia but a prospect of the near future. His comment about 'impending explosions of social tensions' once more points to his historical-materialist understanding that the increasing conflict between proletariat and bourgeoisie marks the final stage before revolutionary change will bring about a classless society. From his imaginary viewpoint in 2003, this social revolution has already occurred, hence his agitational opening remark on Weimar Germany as a mere 'phase' between class wars.

In his review, Eggebrecht calls *Metropolis* 'a gigantic labyrinth of half-truths and misunderstandings, truly a mirror and reflection of its times', and repeatedly refers to Lang and von Harbou as part of a class of intellectuals out of touch with the issues they wish to represent: 'Lang sought to unite and reconcile all the currents and convictions of the mind in this Über-Chicago of our supposed future'.[16] Eggebrecht's decision to write about the film from an imagined future position creates an interesting slippage between the present as 'past' and a future that is, supposedly, *almost* here. Both the film and the writing on the film thus signal a shared consciousness of society 'on the brink' of change; yet, whereas Lang's film can only present the future as a capitalist Über-Chicago, Eggebrecht's review presents a post-capitalist viewpoint.

Frau im Mond

In his October 1929 review of *Frau im Mond* in the weekly Berlin culture magazine *Die Weltbühne*, Rudolf Arnheim's scathing opening remarks sum up his view of Lang's latest picture:

> Fritz Lang films are parvenus, trashy novels that have come into money. The fact that one of the Nick Carter rags, which appear in this film as extras, only cost ten pfennigs, although *By Rocket to the Moon* cost millions, is really the only difference between the two products.[17]

In a similar vein, Herbert Ihering comments in the *Berliner Börsen-Courier* on the day after the premiere: 'Again, and again, we observe [Lang] fail when it comes to the topic, the script, the text'.[18] Heinz Pol, writing for the *Vossische Zeitung*, accuses Lang of treating his chosen subject-matter without the gravity it merits: 'The modern idea of the rocket vehicle, the rocket plane, as well as certain notions of what might well be possible in future, surely to be taken seriously, have not been popularised, but intolerably vulgarised'.[19] Hans Sahl's review in *Der Montag Morgen*, caustically entitled 'Shady bower inside the moon rocket', refers to the outcome of Fritz Lang and Thea von Harbou's collaboration as 'technologically advanced Jugend Stil fantasies, facades without content, Blue Stocking inside the moon rocket'.[20]

Although the majority of critics readily acknowledged Lang's achievement in terms of accurately portraying modern rocket technology through the use of expert camera work and trick technology, this aspect of *Frau im Mond* was overshadowed by what the critics in the aforementioned reviews perceived as its excessive sentimentality, the proverbial 'shady bower' inside the moon rocket. The critics located much of the film's 'kitsch' in the script, based on a novel by Thea von Harbou originally serialised in the magazine *Die Woche* in 1928.

Ufa, the studio responsible for financing and marketing the film,[21] enlisted Hermann Oberth, a lay astronomer and author of a popular scientific study on space travel entitled *Die Rakete zu den Planetenräumen/By Rocket into Planetary Space* (1923), to work as technical advisor, and Willy Ley, an author of aggressively nationalistic SF novels, to act as scientific advisor on the project.[22] In the run-up to the premiere, *Frau im Mond*, as a silent film in the period of transition to sound cinema, was extensively marketed in order to draw in audiences (who were developing a taste for 'talkies'), and particular emphasis was given to the film's serious 'scientific' credentials and the accuracy of its representation of modern technologies.

Drawing on scientific knowledge and existing technologies is of course characteristic of SF, but the insistence on scientific accuracy (up until the landing on the moon, from which point onwards the film's narrative develops in a purely fantastical direction) creates what critics perceived as a wholly dissatisfying and seemingly unbridgeable gap between the film's modern technological aspects and its nostalgic, sentimental aspiration, with the latter 'vulgarising' the serious intention of the former.

Friede Velten (Gerda Maurus) becomes the site where the conflict between the film's rational (technical) and the irrational (sentimental) aspects is played out, as the following example will illustrate. The first half of the film deals with the decision by entrepreneur Wolf Helius (Willy Fritsch) to travel to the moon based on the scientific plans by Georg Manfeldt (Klaus Pohl), a disgraced professor of astronomy. A group of businessmen and women, represented by their middleman Walt Turner (Fritz Rasp), are equally interested in Manfeldt's theory of gold reserves on the opposite side of the moon and, after commissioning the theft of the plans, use blackmail to coerce Helius into cooperating with them. Beleaguered Helius is further troubled by his secret feelings for Friede, an astronomy student engaged to his chief engineer and loyal friend, Hans Windegger (Gustav von Wangenheim). In the scene in question, set in the office in Helius's flat, Friede announces that she intends to join the moon expedition. Although Helius's flat is situated in a modern city building and is ostensibly furnished in the restrained, practical chic of the Bauhaus, the sober look of the interior is interspersed with objects rooted in a more esoteric style. Particularly noticeable is an expressionist painting on the wall of the office which depicts the universe in a spiralling mass of waves, circles and bright colours. Standing in front of the painting, Friede affirms her decision to join Helius on the trip. Ignoring his objections, she lifts her open-palmed hands to shoulder height, slightly tilts back her head, and raises her eyes towards the ceiling in a trance-like state. The posture gives her a saintly quality, and her elegant but simple white dress, adorned with a sprig of flowers over her chest, adds to the ethereal quality of the character.

This pose is remarkably reminiscent of *Metropolis*'s Maria (Brigitte Helm), preaching to the workers in the catacombs. Both characters embody a spiritual counterpoint to more materialistic characters, such as Joh Frederson (Alfred Abel) in *Metropolis* and the group of capitalists, aptly named 'Five Brains and Chequebooks', in *Frau im Mond*. When one of the Brains and Chequebooks, keen to get the expedition underway, exclaims, 'Why lose more time? I for one want the moon's riches of gold, should they actually prove to exist, to fall into the hands of businessmen and not visionaries and idealists', the implication is that Friede represents the kinds of ideals to which the 'chequebook' objects – such as loyalty, courage, and belief in the importance of the expedition for humanity, rather than financial imperatives.

Both Maria and Friede, in their display of pathos and emotional subjectivity, embody the ethical idealism, humanism and mystical religiosity typical of expressionist heroes, and yet they differ in the crucial aspect of their characters' relationship to technology. Andreas Huyssen describes *Metropolis* as a 'syncretist mixture of expressionism and *Neue Sachlichkeit*, and, more significantly, a syncretist mixture of the two diametrically opposed views of technology we can ascribe to these two movements'.[23] Although Huyssen influentially argued that Maria, in her 'machine vamp' manifestation, plays a crucial role in resolving this 'seemingly irreconcilable contradiction',[24] other critical perspectives have since emerged. For instance, R.L. Rutsky argues that the film is less concerned with resolving the conflict between 'modernism's fears of and fascination with technology' than with a desire to synthesise a 'rationalist, functionalist notion of technology and a notion that emphasizes the irrational, chaotic, and even destructive aspects of technology, that sees it as a dynamic, shocking, almost libidinal force'.[25] Nonetheless, the synthesis between these two opposed perspectives on technology remains unconvincing, and the film's ending is generally considered a problematic compromise between various narrative themes and ideological perspectives.

Judging by the critical reception of *Frau im Mond*, one could assume that the film presents an equally uneasy compromise between different ideologies as does *Metropolis*. Yet the Weimar critics cited above focus in their accusation of the 'shady bower inside the moon rocket' mostly on the film's narrative elements, neglecting to pay attention to its visual rhetoric. A closer look at the film's organisation of its mise-en-scène paints a rather different picture than that of the slightly grotesque 'Madonna in moon rocket with breeches'. Indeed, the focus on Friede as the site in which opposed views about technology are combined in paradoxical compromise reveals the ideological implications of this conciliation between – it seems – the 'hands, heart and the brain', which, I shall argue, leftist critics failed to consider in their dismissal of the film as nothing more than a 'trashy novel' appealing to a mass audience.

Rocket Launch and Moon Rising

The launch sequence, which opens the second half of the film, is significant in that it brings the contradictions identified by the various critics cited above to a dramatic climax. It depicts the final moments before the rocket launch. Friede climbs a rope-ladder to the top of the rocket, which Helius has also christened 'Friede' (peace). Reaching the top, she enthusiastically waves at a group of mechanics below. The film cuts to the space outside the hangar, where a radio broadcaster commentates on the event. An intertitle reads: '...at this moment bells will ring – the sirens of all the factories, trains and ships around the world will wail to honour the pioneers of space navigation...'. The following shot shows a large crowd of spectators in attendance at the site. Listening to the broadcast, the men in the crowd respectfully take off their hats. A montage of shots depicts the transportation of the rocket to its launch site in a water basin, followed by a panoramic shot of the location, which shows workshop halls, cars and people amid woods and gently sloping hills. On the distant horizon, the moon rises.

Having swapped her white flowing dress for a jacket and breeches, and the passive, dreamlike state she occupied in Helius's office for a powerful display of vigorous activity, Friede's ascent of the rocket and her waving to the people below becomes a graphic embodiment of the strength and beauty of both the woman and the machine. She is empowered by the rocket, and her optimism reflects the film's opening title, 'There is no Never, only a Not Yet'. The rural setting of the launch provides a curiously pastoral background, and the link between technology and nature is enhanced by the fact that take-off is scheduled at moonrise. The moon, traditionally linked with femininity and natural flow (both tides and menstrual cycles), strengthens the link between modern technology and femininity already brought into play. A range of narrational choices thus emphasise the union between the two 'Friedes' – the woman and the machine, installing a soul into the cold steel construct, and the radio broadcast, which compels the men to take off their hats (as one would in a church) infuses the scientific mission with ostensibly religious and nationalist overtones.

The combination of these various elements can be related to what Jeffrey Herf has identified as 'reactionary modernism' – namely a loosely organised system of perceptions and beliefs which 'incorporated modern technology into the cultural system of modern German nationalism, without diminishing the latter's romantic and antirational aspects'.[26] According to Herf, reactionary modernist thinkers 'turned the romantic anticapitalism of the German Right away from backward-looking pastoralism, pointing instead to the outlines of a beautiful new order replacing the formless chaos due to capitalism in a united, technologically advanced nation'.[27]

Another moment linking Friede to the rocket occurs after the moon landing. In this scene, she prevents Walt Turner from entering the cockpit (with the intention of taking off and leaving the rest of the crew behind) by wedging her left arm between the door and the door handle and stretching her right arm up to grip one of the loops suspended from the ceiling in order to pull the door towards her. With her arms thus stretched wide apart, she presents a crucifixion image not dissimilar to the scene in *Metropolis* in which Freder is suspended on the dials of a machine. Yet, whereas Freder is symbolically sacrificed on the machine, Friede sacrifices herself to defend the rocket (in the end, Helius and Friede give up their places in the rocket so that the other passengers, Friede's fiancé and the young stowaway Gustav (Gustl Stark-Gstettenbaur), can safely return to Earth).

To dismiss these themes and visual motifs as sentimental kitsch is to ignore, or at the very least denigrate, their impact on the audience. Despite being a silent film in an era in which sound films were becoming the extremely popular norm, *Frau im Mond* was the most successful film in Germany in 1929 – a fact widely ignored by the critics writing on it.[28] In fact, Weimar critic Fritz Olimsky notes in his review that 'At the end of the film, the premiere audience roared with enthusiasm whilst the premiere hacks [*Premierenunken*] went to the literature cafés and tore it apart'.[29] Sabine Hake identifies the 'unwillingness to address the question of mass entertainment and mass media'[30] as one of the key shortcomings of leftist film criticism.

'Nick Carter Rags': *Frau im Mond*'s Engagement with its Own Rhetoric

A film's relationship with its own material was often overlooked in the reviews by left-wing writers at the time. In *Frau im Mond*, although several elements in the film's narrative express reactionary modernist tendencies, there are other elements in the film's systems of narration which arguably work to qualify or counter them. Early sequences contain a variety of generic elements rooted in the serial thriller genre of the early 1920s. In the urban environment of the modern city, we witness the spectacularly staged theft of Manfeldt's manuscripts (in which Helius is drugged by a fake flower girl) and a speedy car chase through the streets of Berlin. The fast-flowing action and frequent crosscutting between simultaneously unfolding events is very similar to techniques employed in Lang's thrillers – *Dr Mabuse, der Spieler* (1922), *Spione* (1928), *M* (1931), *Das Testament des Dr Mabuse* (1933) – to maximise spectacle and excitement. At one point we observe the young boy Gustav reading a comic, the cover of which shows a spaceship approaching the planet Saturn. The comics reappear later in the film, when Gustav is discovered onboard the moon rocket. Proudly announcing that he has been studying astronomy all his life, he produces from his rucksack a number of comics featuring the hero Mingo, dubbed 'The Nick Carter of the Skies'.[31] They are passed around among the adults, who laugh at such titles as 'Moon Vampires', 'The Mystery of the Deadly Moon Rays' and 'Battling with Moon Calves'. As in the earlier sequence, the cover of each comic is pointedly depicted in close-up. Although the adults are amused by Gustav's claim to have studied the 'moon problem', these moments point towards a key cultural phenomenon of the Weimar republic, namely the growth of the mass media.

The existence of this kind of cosmopolitan and liberal mass culture differs greatly from the spiritual, obedient and self-sacrificing values embodied by Friede. Thea von Harbou's original novel, although serialised in a popular magazine, makes no reference to the comics to which the film repeatedly draws attention. This difference demonstrates the extent to which the film qualifies its own sentimental 'shady bower' rhetoric by embracing elements drawn from popular culture, juxtaposing the novel's anachronistic characters (such as Friede) with emerging popular culture heroes reflecting a modern social consciousness (such as Mingo).

Yet, significantly, the response by critics as influential as Rudolf Arnheim was to dismiss *both* the film and the Nick Carter 'rags' as merely cheap 'ten pfennig' popular mass entertainment. As Sabine Hake observes, 'Fixated as they were on the conditions of production, most leftist film critics failed to grasp the potentially subversive quality of visual pleasure', but when 'critics did pay attention to audience psychology, they invariably became more aware of the correspondences between the spheres of production and reproduction'.[32] She gives the example of Walter Pahl, who suggested that the cinema 'is the emotional substitute, indeed, one could almost say the side product of the capitalist–industrial work conditions'.[33] Pahl's observation about the quasi-compensatory character of cinema presages Richard Dyer's influential argument, developed decades later in 'Entertainment and Utopia' (1977), that bourgeois cinema does indeed respond to 'real needs *created by society*'.[34]

David Durst draws attention to the opposed and opposing social, political and cultural wants and needs in Weimar society:

> Nowhere in Western Europe ... was this unstable and alternating amalgam of residual, dominant, and emergent socioeconomic forces and cultural formations more prevalent, nowhere was the contradiction between advanced capital development and older political beliefs so acute than in modern Germany, this 'classical land of non-simultaneity' as Bloch termed it.[35]

For Weimar Marxist and leftist liberal critics with their rational, materialist, quintessentially *forward*-looking perspective to 'overlook' what Carl Schorske terms the 'suspension between the once-was and the not-yet'[36] meant to ignore the *backward*-looking, irrational, sentimental, nostalgic and romantic cravings of a mass audience going to the movies for reasons more complex than mere escapism. In his illuminating review of *Frau im Mond*, Herbert Ihering insists on the need for a 'common ground' of reason as a basis for understanding and communication, which he – crucially – argues, 'is a ground which can be easily won anywhere these days, where the kinds of people able to cope with the challenges [*Abenteuer*] of technology, can be found'.[37] This suggests the possibility of a 'common ground' *not* steeped in a society's yearning for a universal bucolic past, but in anticipation of a possible future, its various manifestations already tangible in a modern city like 1920s Berlin.

Frau im Mond locates the existence of such a society in the perceptible growth of mass communication and entertainment catering for an urban audience with a newfound desire for, and access to, knowledge and political emancipation as traditional (pre-war) hierarchies were attacked and began to dissolve. The film signals the growth of and demand for these popular media through its emphasis on the comic books, and through the ever-increasing presence of newsreel cameramen and radio broadcasts during the launch sequence (from the above-mentioned shots of the radio commentator and the audience gathered on site, to a trick photography shot – a collage of countless disembodied heads and intertitles pulsing, wave-like, across the screen – rendering visible the very transmission of the broadcast to a hitherto invisible global audience). Admiring rather than afraid of the rocket, the spectators who enthusiastically applaud the 'pioneers of space travel' evidently exist not only in the world of the film but, arguably, inside (and outside) the cinema.

Given the centrality afforded the rocket-ship in such spectacular sequences, it is unsurprising that many critics saw this representation of modern technology as a glimpse of utopia sullied by the late-romanticist twaddle of the shady bower. But such glimpses are perhaps not so much centred on the rocket – a vehicle as much open to subjugation by reactionary modernism's pre-fascist thought as to offering a glimpse of a future different from (and for materialists invariably *better* than) the present – as on the film's serial thriller elements and the visual foregrounding of Gustav's comics. For Ernst Bloch, as Mary N. Layoun notes,

> there is no easy dismissal of low or popular culture, of the unorthodox, of the politically incorrect, of the false. And so the text – whether a daydream, a fascist propaganda sheet, a fairy tale, an advertisement, or an expressionist painting – can function (for its audience and/or its producer) as a figure of desire for something beyond itself, a something else that looks not back to a past but forward (the '*Vor*' of *Vorschein*) to a not yet quite foreseeable future.[38]

In the film, the modern media articulate the desire for the passing of old hierarchies and for full human communication without rank or privilege. However, in Bloch's terms, while utopia 'exists, to a considerable, degree, in the dimension of futurity', it is not 'in the future as the latter is imagined by mere chronological forecasting, or in the mechanistic and philistine notions of bourgeois "progress," but rather as the future is the object of *hope*, of our deepest and most radical longings'.[39] As Vincent Geoghegan writes,

> What is most desired is missing in the often uncontrollable present but can be present in a controllable, if, in varying degrees, mythic, past. Harmony, warmth, and belonging can live in the supposed golden days of long ago.... The future ... is not a return to the past but draws sustenance from this past. Memory is the means in the present to ground the future in the past.[40]

In this context, *Frau im Mond*'s shady bower does not vulgarise the possibility of a future utopia but expresses it – intertwining it with the futurity proposed by the rocket, and mediating it into the present moment through the instruments of a mass media and a popular culture that the film's makers did not control but which they could utilise, reflect upon and critique.

Notes

1. My title derives from Heinz Pol's quip, 'Madonna in der Mondrakete, mit Breeches, versteht sich', in his review 'Die *Frau im Mond*: Der neue Lang-Film', *Vossische Zeitung* 489 (16 October 1929), reprinted in Gero Gandert, ed., *Der Film der Weimarer Republik: 1929* (Berlin: Walter de Gruyter, 1997), p. 203. My translation.
2. Sabine Hake, *The Cinema's Third Machine: Writing on Film in Germany 1907–1933* (Lincoln: University of Nebraska Press, 1993), p. 192.
3. Cited in Toni Stooss, 'Erobert den Film! Oder "Prometheus" gegen "Ufa" & Co', in Neue Gesellschaft für Bildende Kunst, eds, *Erobert den Film!* (Berlin: NGBK, 1977), p. 16. My translation. First steps towards a strong proletarian film culture were taken by publicist Willy Münzenberg in his pamphlet *Let's Conquer Film* (1925), and in his effort to increase the import of Russian films. In 1925, Münzenberg founded Prometheus Film, which eventually produced its own revolutionary proletarian films, *Mother Krause's Journey to Happiness* (Jutzi, 1929) and *Kuhle Wampe* (Dudow and Brecht, 1932).
4. Hake, *Cinema's Third Machine*, p. 31.
5. Axel Eggebrecht, 'Technik, Arbeit und Wissenschaft der Zukunft: Möglichkeiten eines Zukunftsfilms', *Kulturwille* 6 (1927). Archive

Stiftung Deutsche Kinemathek, Berlin. My translation. Although never fully translated into English, a summary of its main points and a translation of the final paragraph can be found in Wolfgang Jacobsen, Werner Sudendorf, Martin Koerber and Yvonne Rehhahn, *Metropolis: Ein filmisches Laboratorium der modernen Architektur/ A cinematic Laboratory for Modern Architecture* (Berlin: Axel Menges, 2000).

6. Eggebrecht, 'Technik, Arbeit und Wissenschaft', p. 124.

7. Ibid., p. 124.

8. Ibid., p. 124.

9. The latter title alludes to German romantic Wilhelm Hauff's novella, *Der Mann im Mond* (1825), which parodied the sentimental fiction of Heinrich Clauren. In a 1973 interview, Lang comments: 'I had made a film called *Woman in the Moon*, contrary to the Man in the Moon, hey' (Barry Keith Grant, *Fritz Lang: Interviews* (Jackson: University of Mississippi Press, 2003), p. 171). In the US, the film is also known as *By Rocket to the Moon*.

10. Michael Minden and Holger Bachmann, eds, *Fritz Lang's Metropolis: Cinematic Visions of Technology and Fear* (Woodbridge: Camden House, 2000), p. 85. The *Film-Kurier* was a daily paper founded in 1919. Initially conceived as an industry paper, it became the country's most widely read film daily by the mid 1920s, mostly due to the high quality of its film reviews and discussions. Karl Prümm writes about Willy Haas, the paper's chief editor: 'Film criticism for Haas was an act of revolutionary writing, which returned to prelapsarian beginnings, where object and critical discourse were one and the same thing. This hope gave his texts their dynamics, which were always more than mere commentaries' (Wolfgang Jacobsen, Karl Prümm and Benno Wenz, eds, *Willy Haas: Der Kritiker als Mitproduzent. Texte zum Film 1920–1933* (Berlin: Hentrich, 1991), p. 12. My translation).

11. Minden and Bachmann, *Fritz Lang*, p. 85.

12. Geoff King and Tanya Krzywinska note that the 'speculative mode of science fiction has always included the potential to ask politically-informed questions about our own society' (*Science Fiction Cinema* (London: Wallflower, 2000), p. 22).

13. Minden and Bachmann, *Fritz Lang*, p. 87.

14. Ibid., p. 87.

15. Axel Eggebrecht, '*Metropolis*', *Die Weltbühne* 3 (18 January 1927), p. 115. Archive Stiftung Deutsche Kinemathek, Berlin. My translation.

16. Ibid., p. 115. My translation.

17. Brenda Benthien, ed. and transl., *Rudolf Arnheim: Film Essays and Criticism* (Madison: University of Wisconsin Press, 1997), p. 152.

18. Herbert Ihering, '*Frau im Mond*', *Berliner Börsen-Courier* 484 (16 October 1929), reprinted in Gandert, *Der Film der Weimarer Republik*, p. 201.

19. Pol, 'Die *Frau im Mond*', p. 203.

20. Hans Sahl 'Die Gartenlaube in der Mondrakete: *Frau im Mond*', *Der Montag Morgen* 42 (21 October 1929), reprinted in Gandert, *Der Film der Weimarer Republik*, p. 56. In German, the term 'Gartenlaube' ('arbour' or 'shady bower') carries the influential figurative meaning of sentimental twaddle, rooted in its evocation of the German late-romantic epoch of 'Biedermeier' (1850–75), a literary and artistic style characterised by a conservative or apolitical stance and a focus on impressionist moments, during the time of politically conservative 'Restoration' in Germany. 'Gartenlaube' thus heavily evokes the notion of the philistine petit bourgeois (characterised in generic Spitzweg paintings), who is ignorant of arts and culture and who adapts to, rather than rebels against, his own political subjugation. It is interesting to note that the term appears in several reviews of *Metropolis* and *Frau im Mond*, as a kind of shorthand for what reviewers perceived as sentimental nonsense in both films.

21. For detailed accounts of the film's production see Rainer Eisfeld, '*Frau im Mond*: Technische Vision und psychologisches Zeitbild' in Thea von Harbou, *Frau im Mond* (Munich: Heyne, 1989), Guntram Geser, *Fritz Lang – Metropolis und Die Frau im Mond: Zukunftsfilm und Zukunftstechnik in der Stabilisierungszeit der Weimarer Republik* (Meitlingen: Corian, 1996) and Klaus Kreimeier, *Die UFA Story* (Munich: Hanser, 1992).

22. Geser, *Fritz Lang*, p. 96. Geser includes a comprehensive summary (pp. 94–107) of SF literature during the Weimar period.

23. Andreas Huyssen, 'The Vamp and the Machine: Fritz Lang's *Metropolis*', in *After the Great Divide: Modernism, Mass Culture, Postmodernism* (Indianapolis: Indiana University Press, 1986), p. 68.

24. Ibid., p. 68.

25. R.L. Rutsky, 'The Mediation of Technology and Gender: *Metropolis*, Nazism, Modernism', in Minden and Bachmann, *Fritz Lang*, p. 217.

26. Jeffrey Herf, *Reactionary Modernism: Technology, Culture and Politics in Weimar and the Third Reich* (Cambridge: Cambridge University Press, 1984), p. 2.

27. Ibid., p. 2.

28. In a survey in the *Film-Kurier*, *Frau im Mond* was voted the most successful film of 1929, relegating Arnold Franck's popular mountain

film, *The White Hell of Pitz Palu* (1929), to second place. See *Film-Kurier* (31 May 1930), reprinted in the document section of Gerd Albrecht, ed., *Retrospektive Fritz Lang. Dokumentation. Teil 1: Die Zeit und die Filme bis zum Jahre 1933 in Deutschland* (Bad Ems: Verband der Deutschen Filmclubs, 1964), p. 6j/3.

29. Fritz Olimsky, '*Frau im Mond*', *Berliner Börsen-Zeitung* 484 (16 October 1929), reprinted in Gandert, *Der Film der Weimarer Republik*, p. 202.

30. Hake, *Cinema's Third Machine*, p. 200.

31. Nick Carter was an immensely popular fictional detective, who debuted in the *New York Weekly* dime novel in 1886, had his own dime novel series, *The Nick Carter Library*, from 1896, and appeared in thousands of stories in a variety of Street & Smith publications in the US. Many Nick Carter stories were reprinted overseas, and he also appeared in a number of films from 1908 onwards, and in Europe as well as the US. In the 1940s and 1950s he had radio and comic book series in the US, and was subsequently reinvented as a Bond-like spy for a series of over 250 novels between 1964 and 1990.

32. Hake, *Cinema's Third Machine*, p. 200.

33. Quoted in Hake, *Cinema's Third Machine*, p. 201.

34. Richard Dyer, *Only Entertainment* (London: Routledge, 2002), p. 26; emphasis in original.

35. David C. Durst, *Weimar Modernism* (London: Lexington, 2004), p. xxiv.

36. Quoted in Durst, *Weimar Modernism*, p. xxiv.

37. Ihering, '*Frau im Mond*', p. 202.

38. Mary N. Layoun, 'A Small Reflection on a Dream Thrice Removed of Hope from a Refugee Camp', in Jamie Owen Daniel and Tom Moylan, *Not Yet: Reconsidering Ernst Bloch* (London and New York: Verso, 1997), p. 226.

39. Carl Freedman, *Critical Theory and Science Fiction* (Hanover: Wesleyan University Press, 2000), p. 64.

40. Vincent Geoghegan, 'Remembering the Future', in Daniel and Moylan, *Not Yet*, pp. 17, 31.

9

THE URBAN QUESTION IN NEW WAVE SF

Rob Latham

In William Gibson's 'The Gernsback Continuum' (1981), the narrator, a photographer commissioned to illustrate a coffee-table tome, *The Airstream Futuropolis: The Tomorrow That Never Was*, finds himself haunted by the 'semiotic ghost[s]' of American modernism, hallucinatory shimmers of neon and chrome, shark-fins and lucite. These phantasms cohere in a vision straight out of classic SF, an 'idealized city that drew on *Metropolis* and *Things to Come*, but squared everything, soaring up through an architect's perfect clouds to zeppelin docks and mad neon spires'. An incarnation of one of the 'spray-paint pulp utopias' featured on the covers of Hugo Gernsback's *Amazing Stories* in the 1920s, this retro paradise shimmers briefly in the Nevada desert before evaporating, leaving the narrator with a vague sense that 'the Future had come to America first, but had finally passed it by'.[1]

Gibson makes no bones about the political implications of this vanished future, depicting the denizens of his utopian city as creepy blonde Aryans,

> smug, happy, and utterly content with themselves and their world.... I imagined them thronging the plazas of white marble, orderly and alert, their bright eyes shining with enthusiasm for their floodlit avenues and silver cars.... It had all the sinister fruitiness of Hitler Youth propaganda.[2]

Yet pulp-era SF, while now often viewed as naïve or even reactionary, was in fact 'linked to central elements of progressive thought',[3] such as the 'enlightened technocracy' movement of the 1920s, whose populist advocacy of science education shaped the avid didacticism of Gernback's magazines, and the Popular Front activities of the Young Communist League of the 1930s, which influenced the SF fan group the Futurians (which included Isaac Asimov, Frederik Pohl and C.M. Kornbluth). It was only during the post-World War II period, with the growing consolidation of a hegemonic American technocracy, that the imagery and values of pulp SF came to be seen as a politically dubious, if not dangerous, assemblage of 'showy proto-fascist trappings'.[4] Rather than providing a pop apology for corporate technoscience, pulp SF celebrated the genius of individual scientists and engineers, whose inspired tinkerings 'went well beyond the limited purview of industrial capitalism, stretching those limits into unmanageable realms of social invention'.[5]

Of course, the target of Gibson's satire is as much the modernist architectural movement as it is pulp SF. Indeed, his story could as readily be titled 'The Corbusier Continuum', its delirious projection of an 'illuminated city'[6] being a sarcastic take on the Swiss visionary's 'Ville radieuse', a classless utopia of towering skyscrapers and immaculate public parks. Le Corbusier's utopian manifestos began appearing in the 1920s, inspired in part by the burgeoning New York skyline, as was Fritz Lang's cinematic vision in *Metropolis* (1927). Many of the basic features of his idealised 'city of tomorrow'[7] had been anticipated in Gernsback's own futuristic romance, *Ralph 124C 41+* (1911–12), wherein New York City circa AD 2660 is a centrally planned complex of soaring high-rises, traversed vertically by electro-magnetic elevators and horizontally by aerocabs, powered by massive solar generators, and graced by 'municipal playgrounds' for leisure and recreation.[8] During the 1920s and 1930s, such visions of the modern city had potentially progressive implications, inspiring the Soviet constructivists and other left-wing avant-gardes, whose ambitious goal was conurbations designed for the use and gratification of all.[9] Despite occasional warnings such as Yevgeny Zamyatin's *We* (1924), which decried an autocratic future dominated by glass-walled monoliths, it was only later that such monumentalist schemes would inevitably come to convey a 'sinister totalitarian dignity, like the stadiums Albert Speer built for Hitler'.[10]

Yet even if one discounts the overblown accusations of fascism, it nonetheless remains the case that an abiding ambivalence towards cities, especially centrally planned urban utopias, was evident in futuristic literature well prior to the post-war period. The idealised metropolis, technologically advanced and purged of social conflict, in Edward Bellamy's *Looking Backward* (1888), was counterbalanced by the depiction of future New York in Ignatius Donnelly's *Caesar's Column* (1890), a city governed by a plutocratic elite at the expense of an impoverished, restless proletariat. The growing perception that the modern city was not assuaging, but rather exacerbating, social divisions, and that the outcome might be an eruption of revolutionary violence, led to the rise, at the turn of the century, of the Garden City movement, which sought, through holistic reform, to create collectively owned municipalities governed for the common good. However, the necessity of compromise with capitalist interests – such as landlords, who balked at the notion of abolishing ground rents – tended to dilute its collectivist basis, leaving merely the innovation of centralised urban planning, which generated a host of new-town blueprints and other suburban schemes well into the twentieth century.[11]

The ambivalence towards the industrial city evident in nineteenth-century utopian writing also marks the history of left-wing theoretical engagements with urbanism. Classic Marxist theory has little to say about cities as such, apart from Engels' exposé of *The Condition of the Working Class in England* (1844), with its stark rendering of the ills of urban poverty, and his essay on 'The Housing Question' (1872), which analysed the role of real estate speculation in breeding crowded slums. Marx himself, aside from sporadic observations about the role of metropolitan agglomeration in promoting proletarian class consciousness, offered no overarching theory of urbanisation, and often seemed deeply suspicious of the cosmopolitan ethos of inveterate urban demimondes, as in his portrait of the hangers-on at the court of Louis Bonaparte:

decayed roués with dubious means of subsistence and of dubious origin, alongside ruined and adventurous offshoots of the bourgeoisie ... vagabonds, discharged soldiers, discharged jailbirds, escaped galley slaves, swindlers, mountebanks, *lazzaroni*, pickpockets, tricksters, gamblers, *maquereaux* [pimps], brothel keepers, porters, literati, organ grinders, ragpickers, knife grinders, tinkers, beggars – in short, the whole indefinite, disintegrated mass, thrown hither and thither, which the French call *la bohème*.[12]

Yet such scathing visions of bohemian decadence must be balanced against Marx's own clear fondness for 'the cultural infrastructure of cities' – for example, his longtime refuge, the British Museum – and their welcoming embrace of 'maverick spirits and dissidents' like himself.[13] And Marx's occasional praise for how the industrial concentration of urban population was systematically overcoming rustic seclusion – 'the idiocy of rural life'[14] – left little doubt where his real sympathies lay.

It was not until Walter Benjamin's celebration of the *flâneur* in the 1930s, however, that a serious Marxist defence of cosmopolitan existence would be articulated. For Benjamin, the nineteenth-century strollers of the Parisian boulevards and the shopping arcades emerged as urban heroes, renegade dreamers wandering amid the alienated phantasms of capitalist modernity. Yet the *flâneur* remains a decidedly ambivalent creature, beguiled by urban fashion while sensing all too plainly the hollow 'enthronement of merchandise' it represents.[15] Hardly an agent of revolutionary change, this anonymous drifter is a 'threshold' figure, seeking refuge in the crowd yet never fully of it, an amalgam of naïveté and cynicism who perceives finally the emptiness of the 'cult of commodities' surrounding him.[16] The *flâneur*'s half-hearted cosmopolitanism prefigures the programme of urban cultural combat articulated by the French situationists in the 1960s; while undoubtedly more militant in its postures and strategies, the latter too concedes the ineradicable alienation of private experience in the face of a commodified cityscape swiftly receding behind a veil of total reification – 'a pseudo-world apart', a 'fallacious paradise'.[17] Ethico-political alliances with working-class groups remain as ambiguous, in the situationists' society of the spectacle, as the *flâneur*'s vague alignment with the crowd:

> situationist writing carried over some of the *flâneur*'s cavalier attitudes; page upon page passionately denounced alienation and extolled revolution, but the reader was only directed toward a deeper understanding of the ghetto-dwellers' real lives with an anonymous wave of the hand.[18]

In short, the analysis and defence of urban experience has, for left-wing theorists, been fraught with pitfalls and contradictions from the outset. It was not until the rise of Marxist geography in the early 1970s, with the early work of Manuel Castells and David Harvey,[19] that successful attempts were made to wed a detailed critique of urban structure with a tentative embrace of cosmopolitan practices. This development coincided with an SF movement – the so-called 'New Wave' – devoted, at least in part, to revisiting and reconceiving representations of the city inherited from the pulps.[20] In the balance of this essay, I will read these two bodies of material against one another, to see how cutting-edge urban theory and avant-garde speculative fiction conspired, during the 1970s, to offer a multi-pronged – and potent – diagnosis of the looming crisis of the modern city.

For the city was definitely in crisis, as evidenced by the plight of New York, which was compelled, in 1975, to seek a federal bailout to avoid imminent bankruptcy and the suspension of services.[21] This emergency was spurred by contingent historical factors, such as a spike in energy costs prompted by the OPEC oil embargo and the resulting stagflation, but they merely accelerated a recessionary process already well underway, highlighting and intensifying the effects of deep-seated structural contradictions in metropolitan organisation. In particular, the city government's role in orchestrating 'collective consumption' was swiftly reaching a point of diminishing returns. According to Castells, collective consumption is the 'consumption of commodities whose production is not assured by capital, not because of some intrinsic quality, but because of the specific and general interests of capital'; such commodities – for example, mass transportation, public education, social services of various kinds – are 'necessary to the reproduction of labour power and/or to the reproduction of social relations', but their overhead has traditionally been absorbed by the state and funded by taxes, municipal bonds and other public financing measures.[22] These services are essential to capital because they reproduce and sustain the urban working classes while also shielding private profit from the attendant costs and risks. But the growing scope of public-sector services during the post-war period, combined with the economic shocks of the 1970s, exposed – and shattered – the fragile social compact underlying this arrangement.

As public services began to contract or fail, and as retrenchments were made in the system of collective consumption at the expense of the working class, the 'displaced class struggle'[23] latent in the built environment became more pointed and pronounced. Tensions over services emerged as flashpoints of economic and political combat, and the spatial inequalities of city life – for instance, the process of 'ghetto formation' that inevitably results from the patterns of capitalist land use[24] – provided fodder for collective demands for a more equitable distribution of civic space and resources.[25] While Harvey's early writings remained optimistic about the potential for genuine reform – for the consolidation of new modes of socio-economic reciprocity at the community level, reinvigorating even while displacing the frayed networks of traditional kinship and ethnicity – the actual historical outcome of the urban crisis of the 1970s was a series of privatisation strategies and so-called 'welfare reforms' that either converted municipal services into profit-making operations or else de-funded and devolved them onto overstrained local support systems. This neo-liberalist transformation is still ongoing, but it is fair to say that the repercussions have not obviously been progressive.[26]

I turn now to the question of how New Wave SF responded to this crisis of urban structure and city life. It is necessary to begin with the socio-political orientation of the New Wave, since it is commonly held that the movement was solidly on the left, in contrast to the presumed rightward slant of pulp SF. This is true to a certain extent, yet as we have seen, any attempt to characterise the pulp tradition as monolithically conservative is difficult to sustain in light of groups like the Futurians, who were in some ways more radical than their 1960s successors. What is fair to say is that New Wave writers were generally antipathetic towards technocratic institutions and values, embracing broadly countercultural alternatives; yet as with the counterculture itself, this posture often resolved into questions of personal philosophy rather than political commitments per se. This 'life-style SF', as Brian Aldiss calls it, placed 'the emphasis on experimental modes of living more in accord with contemporary pressures'.[27] To the extent that these pressures, during the 1960s and 1970s, had political ramifications, in the sense of entailing an ideological agenda, the New Wave was certainly on the left, but in the often hazy and amorphous way of most contemporaneous dissident movements.

Having said this, to dismiss the New Wave as *merely* a series of lifestyle postures – as Thomas Disch has recently done, describing it as little more than 'the Zeitgeist demanded of SF in the Age of Aquarius … a celebration of the [youth] audience's daydreams, of Inner Space and future fashions … sex, drugs, and rock 'n' roll'[28] – is considerably to understate its militancy in context. Leaving aside the sheer churlishness of Disch's judgement, it is interesting to observe that its author is someone whose own work was at the forefront of New Wave innovation, both formal and political. Disch's novels of the 1960s, such as *The Genocides* (1965) and *Camp Concentration* (1968), were flashpoints of controversy within the field, staking out positions on social issues such as ecological destruction and out-of-control militarism calculated to provoke and infuriate conservative readers.[29] Disch was also the author of one of the most searching urban dystopias of the period, *334* (1972), whose caustic depiction of the socio-political crisis of the modern city set a new standard for SF's engagement with 'the urban question'.

334 collects six interlinked stories focusing on the residents of a subsidised housing block in New York city, located at 334 East Eleventh Street, at the start of the third decade of the twenty-first century. It is a satirical projection of a looming near future in which Castells' collective consumption has reached unsustainable levels, spawning a vast bureaucracy, MODICUM, which (as its name implies) dictates a bare minimum of subsistence for all city dwellers. MODICUM, initiated in the 'pre-Squeeze affluent 1980s'[30] in order to deal with the dovetailing crises of urban congestion and declining living standards, started out as a modest welfare programme, but soon morphed into a pervasive, paternalistic regime administering not only housing allotments but an invidious system of social credits that determines an individual's fitness for education, employment and even child-bearing. Self-serving calculations designed to game this system – for example, improving one's credit score through spurious good works or securing comfortable accommodations by exaggerating or manipulating one's dependants – have replaced traditional civic virtue, whose maintenance has been consigned to a well-meaning though woefully harassed cadre of social workers, one of whom comes to suspect 'that the great machineries of the welfare service might actually do more harm than good'.[31]

As this overview suggests, the novel's attitudes towards contemporary urban transformation are ambivalent – a blend of progressive critique and reactionary disgruntlement. Like the Marxist geographers, Disch plainly deplores the anti-democratic centralism of the city planners responsible for the glass-and-brick nightmares his characters inhabit, whose drab enormity evokes the wastelands of London's worst Council Estates or Chicago's Cabrini Green. Echoing Castells' critique of the 'deteriorated way of life' imposed by the Parisian *grand ensembles*,[32] and in the process lampooning the utopian monumentalism of Le Corbusier and pulp-era SF, Disch's eponymous building, architecturally 'on a par with the pyramids' in its grim uniformity,[33] houses 3,000 tenants in 812 apartments on 21 floors, not counting the homeless 'temps' who shelter on landings and staircases. Its elevators have long since ceased to function, isolating the elderly and infirm in their cheerless eyries, visited only by MODICUM agents and slumming sociology students. Disch's sympathies are clearly with the struggling inhabitants of this dreary urban maze, whose hard-scrabble lives – prey to myriad 'causeless incurable terrors'[34] – are sketched with a meticulousness and intensity quite unusual in the genre. Indeed, given its profound absorption in the mundane rituals of working-class experience, *334* might be called naturalist SF.

Just as classic naturalist writing embodied a forceful critique of capitalist society,[35] so *334* offers a cutting commentary on the economic imperatives undergirding the MODICUM regime and the social ideologies supporting it. As in Harvey's work, with its focus on the 'structured coherence' linking public and private sectors of the urban economy,[36] the connections between the welfare bureaucracy and the general consumer system of this future society are carefully detailed; black markets and other informal modes of exchange are tolerated adjuncts to the rationed services and regulated expenditure overseen by 'the federal income-and-purchase computers'.[37] The characters' 'cheap synthetic diet'[38] is supplemented by narcotic palliatives marketed by Pfizer and available in popular drinks and chewing gum. Meanwhile, television proffers images of unfettered consumption accessible only to the lucky suburbanites who have escaped the inner city, yet still beguiling to the urban underclass that faithfully consumes its messages. Though the high tide of post-war affluence has receded from these urban backwaters, the stranded survivors nonetheless remain deeply nostalgic for its fantasised bounty. Several characters find a catchy jingle from a new Ford commercial dancing at odd moments through their heads, although none of them own or could afford a car. Similarly, their fondest daydreams are rife with images of long-lost consumerist utopias: 'What is heaven?' one ponders. 'Heaven is a supermarket.... Full of everything you could ever ask for'.[39] In fact, the Metropolitan Museum – before being bombed by a self-styled urban guerrilla – even stages an installation recreating a classic A&P store, replete with aisle upon aisle of alluring commodities, all of it 'fake ... no matter how realistic it might look, all just imitations'.[40]

On the other hand, despite the convergence of the novel's social-critical animus with the insights of Marxist geography, its scrutiny of this 'crummy subsidized slum'[41] sometimes suggests less a concern for its socio-economic status ('slum') and more an outrage at its aesthetic impoverishment ('crummy') and moral dependency ('subsidized'). This lurking conservative streak sits rather uneasily with 334's more progressive assessments. The bombing of the Met is a case in point: ultimately an act of pure vandalism, it is driven not by radical ideology but by a senseless nihilism inspired by the absolute decadence of the urban surround. 'The city cried out to be bombed', one character muses. 'The amazing fact is that no one ever thought to do it before'.[42] The leftist revolutionaries depicted in the story are comical figures, alienated dropouts huddling in clandestine cells and maundering on about 'why the Revolution, though so long delayed, was the next inevitable step'.[43] This is a future that has foreclosed political options, permitting only, as an alternative to the vacuousness of consumption, meaningless acts of random violence – such as the arbitrary murder of an anonymous stranger plotted by a band of high school kids.[44] In this society of the spectacle, 'it was all consumership, everything they might have done, and they were tired, who isn't, of being passive'; even sex has lost its appeal, the teenagers bored by the clinically explicit 'hygiene demonstrat[ions]' sponsored by the local school board while the adults are driven to ever more extreme depravities to fuel their jaded appetites, as in a gruesome subplot involving a necrophile cult procuring unclaimed corpses from a hospital morgue.[45]

In short, 334 lapses at times into indignant moralising, seeming more concerned with imagined ethical and aesthetic deprivations than with palpable economic inequities. The ostensible demise of artistic sensibility emerges as a particular flashpoint for Disch's fury, leading to some uncharitable depictions of working-class life: on the one hand, he indicts the capitalist culture industries for the ongoing commodification of popular experience; on the other, his characters willingly conspire in this debasement and revel in the resulting philistinism. One old man, pathologically addicted to soap operas, makes a religious ritual of his daily viewing, dutifully 'renewing himself at the source'.[46] Another bleakly ironic scene involves a primetime special (co-sponsored by the omnipresent Pfizer) dramatising the life of Walt Whitman, whose sonorous paean to the common life of the city in 'Crossing

Brooklyn Ferry' (1856) inspires only disdain and confusion in his contemporary spectators: 'A dirty old man slobbering after teenagers', one character concludes, while another pipes up, '"I think it's wonderful ... I think it's very artistic. The colors!" It was the utmost she could manage'.[47] This is a society, we are given to infer, rapidly descending into barbarism, a verdict cemented by the oddest of the subplots, featuring a disaffected MODICUM agent who, through pharmaceutical mediation, enjoys a dream existence as a fourth-century matron stoically enduring the collapse of Roman civilisation at the hands of uncultured hordes. Only the nascent christians show any optimism in the face of this epochal disaster, expecting any minute 'to see the City of God shoot up like an urban renewal project'.[48]

As this metaphor suggests, *334* is sceptical about the possibility of redeeming the modern city from its world-historical crisis. The disillusioned social worker's attitudes become emblematic of the novel's own bad faith: superficially committed to missionary reform, she is actually a pagan fatalist plodding wearily through the last days of an imploding empire. Her liberal sympathies, fed by routine frustrations, leave her 'wriggl[ing] in the meshes of an indefinite guilt', and she almost welcomes an outburst of nihilist violence – as when she races onto the roof to witness the fiery destruction of the Met, avidly 'offering herself to these barbarians', the alterity of whose experience remains opaque to her until the very end.[49] That the bomber's hijacked plane eventually crashes 'into a MODICUM project at the end of Christopher Street',[50] butchering hapless bystanders, points up the essential emptiness of her gesture of pseudo-rebellion. While she is quite obviously being mocked here, the novel also apparently endorses aspects of her contradictory, self-defeating rage, taking refuge in a Spenglerian pessimism regarding the prospect of social transformation and consigning its characters to 'the cold facts of a winter existence'.[51] As Castells observed, even the most well-meaning critiques of public housing projects can readily 'feed all the reactionary ideologies about the dehumanization of the city',[52] and frankly, Disch's social judgements sometimes descend from the Olympian gloom of *The Decline of the West* to the mordant griping of the Moynihan Report, blaming the victims of the welfare state for their own presumed inadequacies (crass tastes, habitual idleness, 'federal contract babies').[53]

Yet if *334* is ultimately less an unswerving arraignment of capitalism than a problematic critique of that 'great octopus, Bureaucracy'[54] – complete with all the pitfalls one might expect in such an enterprise, including a tendency to focus on societal symptoms rather than the economic disease – it is also, unquestionably, the most compelling treatment of urban crisis in the New Wave canon, precisely because of the suggestiveness of its underlying contradictions. Indeed, these contradictions deserve to be read dialectically, as proof of the unavoidably divided nature of social experience under capitalism. In particular, the MODICUM system illustrates the abiding tension between capital's wealth-generating capacity and its perennially unequal distribution of resources: it is an example of what Harvey calls an institution 'geared to the maintenance of scarcity'.[55] Thus, the social 'barbarism' the novel worries over is actually an inescapable product of the imperatives of capitalist 'civilization' itself, and the 334 building is a monument to this paradox: a triumph of civic engineering designed to satisfy fundamental needs, it is also a physical and moral wasteland dismally warehousing a redundant population. 'Human dignity is more than a zipcode number', observes one character, 'or so they say'.[56]

As befits its dialectical complexity, *334* encompasses the two main trends characterising the New Wave urban dystopia: evocations of sweeping technocratic monumentalism, such as Felix Gottschalk's *Growing Up in Tier 3000* (1975) or Robert Silverberg's *The World Inside* (1971), and of irremediable decadence and breakdown, such as Charles Platt's *Twilight of the City* (1977) or Samuel R. Delany's *Dhalgren* (1975).[57] Silverberg, for example, depicts vast megalopoli (called 'urbmons', for urban monads) in a hypertrophic, over-regimented future where capitalism has cemented its absolute mastery over the built environment.[58] Platt, by contrast, shows the waning of capital's grasp as cities catastrophically contract and fail, forcing citizens into beleaguered enclaves squabbling over diminishing resources and the shattered remnants of public authority. In *Dhalgren*, the collapse is already complete, with the world-weary city of Bellona offering a romantically ruined shelter for a kaleidoscopic array of bohemian subcultures. Each of these novels has its specific strengths – with Delany's being a sterling example of how the politics of the New Wave intersected with the ethos of the youth counterculture – but only *334* grasps the full force of capitalist urbanism, in which development and decay, progress and poverty are not contradictions but mutually constitutive realities.

Of course, even *334* could not predict the forthcoming neoliberal regime, which would respond to the historical crisis of the modern city by radically revising the socio-economic terrain. It was not until the advent of cyberpunk in the 1980s that the contours of the new urban landscape, with its innovative collusions between private power and public space, began to come into sharper focus. William Gibson's *Virtual Light* (1993), for example, offers a hard-bitten take on regnant neoliberalism, with its privatised police forces patrolling affluent gated communities while the underclass flounders amid the wreckage of a shredded welfare state. As Roger Burrows points out, cyberpunk SF was in explicit and ongoing conversation with Marxist geography, Gibson's fiction being linked with Mike Davis' potent meditations on the postmodern cityscape in 'a highly recursive relationship' of cognitive mapping.[59] *Blade Runner* (Scott, 1982) likely supplied a powerful impetus for this linkage, providing for contemporary viewers an image of the city as influential as Lang's *Metropolis* had been six decades before.[60] But it was the urban dystopias of the 1970s, with their trenchant delineation of the spatial connections between capitalist economy and everyday metropolitan life, that set the tone for subsequent treatments. In this regard, Harvey provides a fitting summary of the essential insight of New Wave SF: 'The built environment requires collective management and control, and it is therefore almost certain to be a primary field of struggle between capital and labor over what is good for accumulation and what is good for people'.[61]

Notes

1. William Gibson, 'The Gernsback Continuum', in *Burning Chrome* (New York: Arbor House, 1986), pp. 34, 36, 30, 37. Gibson's fictional *Airstream Futuropolis* spawned a host of real-world imitators, including Joseph J. Corn and Brian Horrigan's *Yesterday's Tomorrows: Past Visions of the American Future* (Baltimore: Johns Hopkins University Press, 1984), Eric and Jonathan Dregni's *Follies of Science: 20th Century Visions of Our Fantastic Future* (Denver: Speck Press, 2006), and Daniel H. Wilson and Richard Horne's *Where's My Jetpack?: A Guide to the Amazing Science Fiction Future That Never Arrived* (New York: Bloomsbury, 2007). For an analysis of this phenomenon, see Elizabeth Guffey, *Retro: The Culture of Revival* (London: Reaktion, 2006).
2. Gibson, 'Gernsback Continuum', p. 38.
3. Andrew Ross, *Strange Weather: Culture, Science and Technology in the Age of Limits* (New York: Verso, 1991), p. 102.
4. Ibid., p. 118.
5. Ibid., p. 131.
6. Gibson, 'Gernsback Continuum', p. 38.
7. The English translation of Le Corbusier's *Urbanisme* (1925) was called *The City of To-Morrow*.
8. See Hugo Gernsback, *Ralph 124C 41+* (Lincoln: University of Nebraska Press, 2000), pp. 93–102.
9. For a critique of the failure of Soviet constructivism, see Manfredo Tafuri, *The Sphere and the Labyrinth: Avant-Gardes and Architecture from Piranesi to the 1970s*, transl. Pellegrino d'Acierno and Robert Connolly (Cambridge: MIT, 1990), pp. 149–70.
10. Gibson, 'Gernsback Continuum', p. 31.
11. The foundational text of the Garden City movement was Ebenezer Howard's *To-Morrow: A Peaceful Path to Real Reform* (1898). On the conflict between his collectivist vision and capitalist realities, see Stanley Buder, *Visionaries and Planners: The Garden City Movement and the Modern Community* (New York: Oxford University Press, 1990). For comparative discussions of Howard and Le Corbusier, see Robert Fishman, *Urban Utopias in the Twentieth Century: Ebenezer Howard, Frank Lloyd Wright, Le Corbusier* (Cambridge: MIT Press, 1982), and David Pinder, *Visions of the City: Utopianism, Power and Politics in Twentieth-Century Urbanism* (Edinburgh: Edinburgh University Press, 2005).
12. Karl Marx, *The 18th Brumaire of Louis Bonaparte* (New York: International, 1963), p. 75.
13. Andy Merrifield, *Metromarxism: A Marxist Tale of the City* (New York: Routledge, 2002), p. 23.

14. Karl Marx and Frederick Engels, *Manifesto of the Communist Party*, in David Fernbach, ed., *The Revolutions of 1848: Karl Marx, Political Writings, Volume I* (New York: Vintage, 1974), p. 71.
15. Walter Benjamin, 'Paris, Capital of the Nineteenth Century', in *Reflections: Essays, Aphorisms, Autobiographical Writings*, transl. Edmund Jephcott (New York: Schocken, 1986), p. 152.
16. Ibid., pp. 156, 153.
17. Guy Debord, *Society of the Spectacle* (Detroit: Black & Red, 1983), paragraphs 2, 20.
18. Simon Sadler, *The Situationist City* (Cambridge: MIT Press, 1998), p. 56.
19. An important inspiration for this new trend in Marxist theory was Henri Lefebvre. On his influence on Castells and Harvey, see Ira Katznelson, *Marxism and the City* (Oxford: Clarendon, 1993), pp. 92–140. For a critique of Marxist geography, see Kian Tajbakhsh, *The Promise of the City: Space, Identity, and Politics in Contemporary Social Thought* (Berkeley: University of California Press, 2001).
20. The convergence between Marxist geography and the New Wave was quite direct in the case of Harvey, who published an essay on 'The Languages of Science' in *New Worlds* in 1967 while a geography lecturer at the University of Bristol.
21. See Roger E. Alcalay and David Mermelstein, eds, *The Fiscal Crisis of American Cities: Essays on the Political Economy of Urban America with Special Reference to New York* (New York: Vintage, 1977), and William K. Tabb, *The Long Default: New York City and the Urban Fiscal Crisis* (New York: Monthly Review, 1982).
22. Manuel Castells, *The Urban Question: A Marxist Approach*, transl. Alan Sheridan (Cambridge: MIT, 1977), pp. 460–1.
23. David Harvey, 'The Urban Process Under Capitalism: A Framework for Analysis', *The Urbanization of Capital: Studies in the History and Theory of Capitalist Urbanization* (Baltimore: Johns Hopkins University Press, 1985), p. 27.
24. David Harvey, *Social Justice and the City* (Baltimore: Johns Hopkins University Press, 1973), pp. 134–5. Harvey's discussion of ghetto formation builds directly upon Engels' 'The Housing Question'.
25. On tenants' activism in the context of debates over housing priorities (focusing on Paris in the 1960s), see Manuel Castells, 'Urban Renewal and Social Conflict', in *City, Class and Power*, transl. Elizabeth Lebas (New York: St Martin's, 1978), pp. 93–125.
26. See David Harvey, *A Brief History of Neoliberalism* (New York: Oxford University Press, 2005), and Jason Hackworth, *The Neoliberal City: Governance, Ideology, and Development in American Urbanism* (Ithaca: Cornell University Press, 2006).

27. Brian W. Aldiss with David Wingrove, *Trillion Year Spree: The History of Science Fiction* (New York: Avon, 1988), p. 291.
28. Thomas M. Disch, *The Dreams Our Stuff Is Made Of: How Science Fiction Conquered the World* (New York: Free Press, 1998), pp. 110–11.
29. On *Camp Concentration*'s critique of militarism, see Thomas L. Wymer, 'Naturalism, Aestheticism and Beyond: Tradition and Innovation in the Work of Thomas M. Disch', in Thomas D. Clareson and Thomas L. Wymer, eds, *Voices for the Future, Volume Three* (Bowling Green: Bowling Green University Popular Press, 1984), pp. 186–219. On *The Genocides* as a condemnation of 'ecological imperialism', see Rob Latham, 'Biotic Invasions: Ecological Imperialism in New Wave Science Fiction', *Yearbook of English Studies* 37: 2 (2007), pp. 103–19.
30. Thomas M. Disch, *334* (New York: Avon, 1974), p. 15.
31. Ibid., p. 107.
32. Manuel Castells, *The City and the Grassroots: A Cross-Cultural Theory of Urban Social Movements* (Berkeley: University of California Press, 1983), p. 76.
33. Disch, *334*, p. 15.
34. Ibid., p. 127.
35. See Walter Benn Michaels, *The Gold Standard and the Logic of Naturalism* (Berkeley: University of California Press, 1988).
36. Harvey, *Urbanization of Capital*, pp. 139–44.
37. Disch, *334*, p. 48.
38. Ibid., p. 95.
39. Ibid., p. 243.
40. Ibid., p. 171.
41. Ibid., p. 17.
42. Ibid., p. 112.
43. Ibid., p. 176.
44. This subplot animates *334*'s most famous section, 'Angouleme', minutely deconstructed in Samuel R. Delany, *The American Shore* (Elizabethtown: Dragon Press, 1978).
45. Disch, *334*, pp. 157, 124.
46. Ibid., p. 61.
47. Ibid., p. 190.
48. Ibid., p. 109.
49. Ibid., p. 113.
50. Ibid., p. 116.
51. Ibid., p. 98. Spengler's *The Decline of the West* (1918) is directly quoted here in the context of the MODICUM agent's mournful pondering of the fate of empires. For an analysis of decadent cities

in SF, see Tom Henighan, 'The Cyclopean City: A Fantasy Image of Decadence', in *Extrapolation* 35: 1 (Spring 1994), pp. 68–76.

52. Castells, *Urban Question*, p. 162.

53. Disch, *334*, p. 205. The Moynihan Report – New York Senator Daniel Patrick Moynihan's *The Negro Family: The Case for National Action* – was released in 1965, two years before Disch began publishing the stories eventually gathered into *334*. Its central thesis – that the African-American family suffered from a 'tangle of pathology', exacerbated by urban poverty but still largely self-inflicted – was hugely controversial at the time. See Lee Rainwater and William L. Yancey, eds, *The Moynihan Report and the Politics of Controversy* (Cambridge: MIT, 1967). Its underlying views continue to feed into debates about racial politics and social justice. See S. Craig Watkins, *Representing: Hip Hop Culture and the Production of Black Cinema* (Chicago: University of Chicago Press, 1998), pp. 218–26. *334*'s initial episode – 'The Death of Socrates', originally published as 'Problems of Creativeness' in *The Magazine of Fantasy and Science Fiction* in 1967 – is the one most deeply engaged with racial issues, reproaching MODICUM's social credits system as a new eugenics programme that revives the worst excesses of scientific racism, but also showing how this system can nonetheless be gamed by ambitious blacks who, exploiting the so-called 'Jim Crow Compromise' (Disch, *334*, p. 21), amass bonus points through dubious self-improvement strategies. The complex racial politics of *334* are beyond the scope of this essay; suffice to say that I believe Disch manages to inoculate himself against a possible imputation of racism by broadening his critique of the putative 'tangle of pathology' into a corrosive assessment – at once progressive and reactionary – of urban working-class culture as a whole. The Hansens, the family that dominates the novel, are predominantly white but no less socio-economically dysfunctional for that. In other words, for Disch, social pathology is primarily a result of the experience of poverty and its potential amelioration by the state, rather than a legacy of racial segregation and its historical remedies, and thus his book responds to a longer tradition of poverty programmes in the US than the Moynihan Report engages. On that tradition, see Alice O'Connor, *Poverty Knowledge: Social Science, Social Policy, and the Poor in Twentieth-Century America* (Princeton: Princeton University Press, 2001).

54. Disch, *334*, p. 253.

55. Harvey, *Social Justice*, p. 139.

56. Disch, *334*, p. 117.

57. On representations of the city in SF more generally, see Eric S. Rabkin, 'The Unconscious City', in George E. Slusser and Eric S.

Rabkin, eds, *Hard Science Fiction* (Carbondale: Southern Illinois University Press, 1986), pp. 24–44; Robert Sheckley, *Futuropolis: Impossible Cities of Science Fiction and Fantasy* (New York: A&W Visual Library, 1978); and Gary K. Wolfe, *The Known and the Unknown: The Iconography of Science Fiction* (Kent: Kent State University Press, 1979), pp. 86–124. Cf. Richard Lehan, *The City in Literature: An Intellectual and Cultural History* (Berkeley: University of California Press, 1998), which links early utopian and proto-SF visions with mainstream literary depictions.

58. Silverberg extrapolates the theories of Italian architect Paolo Soleri, in particular his vision of giant city-sized structures called arcologies (see www.arcosanti.org/theory/arcology/main.html). On Silverberg's novel, see Thomas P. Dunn and Richard D. Erlich. 'The Mechanical Hive: Urbmon 116 as the Villain–Hero of Silverberg's *The World Inside*', *Extrapolation* 21: 4 (Winter 1980), pp. 338–47.

59. Roger Burrows, 'Virtual Culture, Urban Social Polarisation and Social Science Fiction', in Brian D. Loader, ed., *Politics, Technology and Global Restructuring* (New York: Routledge, 1997), p. 39.

60. On *Blade Runner* in relation to a cinematic tradition of urban dystopias, see the essays in the 'City Spaces' section of Annette Kuhn, ed., *Alien Zone II: The Spaces of Science Fiction Cinema* (New York: Verso, 1999), pp. 75–143.

61. David Harvey, *Consciousness and the Urban Experience: Studies in the History and Theory of Capitalist Urbanization* (Baltimore: Johns Hopkins University Press, 1985), p. 47.

10

TOWARDS A REVOLUTIONARY SCIENCE FICTION: ALTHUSSER'S CRITIQUE OF HISTORICITY

Darren Jorgensen

Amid the tumult of May 1968, on the new Nanterre campus in Paris, intellectuals were pelted with rotten food, shouted down during lectures and subjected to student nudity. The problem that protestors had with academics was simply that – in the words of a slogan scrawled on blackboards – their 'structures don't march in the streets'. The 1960s brought the question of praxis to the fore, as the streets and campuses of Paris and the US were filled with the bodies of dissent. Yet these protests did not succeed in overthrowing the French state, or even ending the American war in Vietnam. Instead, they brought about the institutionalisation of a New Left in western universities. The failures of the 1960s uprisings were the condition by which Marxist intellectuals found themselves employed by the state capitalism that they wanted to overthrow. SF studies was a part of this New Left in North American universities, boosted by a new generation of literary scholars who wanted to interrogate the ideologies of bourgeois and patriarchal literatures. The popular genre of SF not only presented an alternative to the high modern literature that had until then been institutionally canonised, but perhaps also even offered a critical, historically engaged mode of cultural production.

The most influential Marxist of this generation of American literary scholars was Fredric Jameson, who privileged SF by arguing that it '*is in its very nature a symbolic meditation on history itself,* comparable in its emergence as a new genre to the birth of the historical novel around the time of the French revolution'.[1] In this essay and others from the early 1970s, Jameson argues not only for the historical interpretation of SF, but also for the idea that SF is an historically self-conscious genre. Yet historicism was not the only version of Marxism at work in the 1960s and 1970s, and this understanding of the genre was conceived in an ongoing debate with the anti-historicist, scientific Marxism that took its inspiration from the writings of Louis Althusser. The institutionalisation of the former strand of Marxism in western universities came at the price of the latter, which challenges the logic of historicism and remains a viable critical practice. This essay will turn to Althusser in order to propose another road for a Marxist thinking of SF.

In his early essays on SF, Jameson takes as his departure the notion that the genre is best understood historically because it exhibits a self-consciousness about history. However, his assumption that SF is more historical than other genres contains a contradiction: if history determines genre, no one genre should be more historical than any other. Jameson defers to history as the ground of his analysis while discursively constructing this history, relying on texts to construct that which is also a material horizon for the production of meaning. As John Frow puts it, this 'is surely a case of having one's referent and eating it too'.[2] This contradiction can also be found in Darko Suvin's influential Marxist theorisation of SF that proclaims the historical quality of the genre in its ability to illuminate its 'author's empirical environment'.[3] Again, this historicist circularity wants to claim agency for a genre that speaks of its own conditions of production. The argument returns to the normative judgements that literary studies has traditionally made about the value of some texts over others, so that, for instance, Suvin can conclude that 'all subsequent significant SF can be said to have sprung from Wells's *Time Machine*', a novel that exhibits those historically reflexive features of the genre that Suvin has already defined.[4] In two special issues of *Science Fiction Studies* published in 1975, Suvin canonised the work of Philip K. Dick and Ursula K. Le Guin on the same grounds. In his capacity as co-founding editor of this North American journal, Suvin claimed that

> Both of these leading American SF writers of the last 15 years write out of and react against historically the same human – psychological and socio-political – situation: the experience of the terrible pressures of alienation, isolation, and fragmentation pervading the neo-capitalist society of the world of the mid-20th century.[5]

In doing so, Suvin set the tone for a raft of interpretations of Dick in particular as a privileged commentator upon history – a position afforded by the historical self-consciousness assumed for SF.

Jameson's essays in these special issues help to illuminate some of the consequences of historicism for the thinking of SF. They put to work the historicist methodology that Jameson first outlined in 'Metacommentary' (1971), and developed most extensively a decade later in *The Political Unconscious* (1981),[6] arguing for the dialectical supremacy of a metacommentary that preserves the received, common-sense meaning of a text, but also subjects it to a greater, Hegelian inversion of this meaning within a historical totality. For example, Jameson's essay on Dick's *Dr Bloodmoney, or How We Got Along After the Bomb* (1965), turns the novel's modernist tendencies into a meditation upon the atomic bomb.[7] What is at first understood to be experimentation within genre fiction – playing with generic limits for literary effect – becomes a consideration of the fragmentations of history itself. Thus the meaning of literary modernism is both preserved and succeeded by a metacommentary that is interested in the historical conditions that produce it. In this essay, Jameson demonstrates his methodology while arguing against competing theories of literary study, one of which is Althusser's scientific version of Marxism. As an American scholar of French studies, Jameson was well aware of the debates raging over the work of Althusser in France and the UK. Although Jameson would not stage a comprehensive argument against Althusser until *The Political Unconsious*, he rehearses it in this essay. Adapting the semiotic square of A.J. Greimas and F. Rastier,[8] Jameson turns its contraries into Hegelian contradictions, shifting from a structuralist method of reading to a dialectical one.[9]

Yet it is not this methodological shift that most betrays the shadow of Althusser in the essay on Dick. Instead, it is the subject of the contradictions themselves. The first, between theory and praxis, underpins Althusser's deconstruction of historicism in his argument for a scientific Marxism that is better able to produce revolutionary consciousness. For Althusser, historicism is neither scientific nor revolutionary because it is ideologically fixated, trapped by its own discovery of historical content in subjects that it had already determined to be historical.[10] The second contradiction that Jameson identifies in *Dr Bloodmoney* is between science and language. This encodes the disputes that follow from Althusser's dismissal of Marx's earlier, humanistic writings and his reading of *Capital* as proposing an objective science that is consequent upon capitalism, but independent of it.[11]

Jameson takes his contention that Dick favours language over science even further in his contribution to the *Science Fiction Studies* special issue on Le Guin, arguing that science is synonymous with capitalism itself.[12] His reading of Le Guin's *The Left Hand of Darkness* (1969) imagines a science extricated from capitalism, but can only do so by turning to a novel that features a human species with a completely different biological system – the Gethenians, who lack sexual desire for most of the year. While their world is stable, with none of the psychic pathologies that torment our own society, it has also not undergone an industrial revolution, so Gethenian science develops at a medieval pace. Consequently, Jameson is able to identify the desire for science with the desire of capitalism, conflating one with the other. This is not the science that Althusser advocates, which has developed alongside capitalism but is not a part of it, and which remains, in spite of capitalism, an objective and free mode of experimentation.

But Jameson uses Althusser's own terminology to read Dick's *Dr Bloodmoney*. Althusser's theorisation of ideology is his most enduring contribution to Marxist literary studies, and Jameson uses it to demonstrate that, between science and language, Dick's novel concludes from a position that supports language and the artist. This is a common enough judgement in subsequent studies of Dick, which frequently point to his humanism, but Jameson's argument is trapped in the circularity that haunts his historicist definition of SF as a historically conscious genre. To say that Dick's novel is a 'defense on the part of the artist, and an idealistic overemphasis on language and art in the place of political action'[13] is of little consequence when Dick is, after all, a producer of language and art. Indeed, such a conclusion remains bound by the mutual recognition structures that produce ideology, entailing an interpretation that sets out *'to recognise itself* in an artificial problem manufactured to serve it both as a theoretical mirror and as a practical justification'.[14] Ideology functions in the service of whatever competing discourse enlists it; but, according to Althusser, the functionality goes two ways, producing both the object of criticism and the criticism itself. This is what Althusser means when he argues that ideology has a conditional autonomy, since its actual message, whatever side it takes amid competing political ideas, is dependent upon this reflective, repetitive structure. Here lies the fundamental difference between Jameson and Althusser: while Jameson claims everything is ideological,[15] Althusser identifies a science that eludes ideology, and in doing so challenges the premise of mediation that makes Marxist historiography possible. Ultimately the content of ideological production is not as significant for Althusser as the fact of ideological production itself.

For some Marxist commentators who were part of the activism and revolutionary politics of the 1960s, Jameson's work reflects a communism in desperate straits. His attempt to bring together contradictory discourses was the equivalent of a popular front in critical theory[16] that compromised the revolutionary modes of thought that were committed to an immediate and undiluted overthrow of capitalism. In James Iffland's terms, the problem with Jameson's Marxism is that it comes to be 'recognized as something else', something that is not revolutionary Marxism.[17] The principal site of revolutionary struggle, the class war and its praxis, is subsumed by matters of aesthetics. As Cornel West argues, Jameson's adoption of formalist strategies was just 'breathing life' back into old, bourgeois texts.[18] West condemns Jameson's attraction to the aesthetics of capitalism, even though Jameson wants to subsume this attraction to a greater, historical logic. As actual, lived communism recedes into the past, it is tempting to read this shift from revolution to art as part of a retreat from real-world politics.[19] Like the ambivalence of art itself towards politics, Jameson's metacommentary forges no new paths for revolutionary action.[20] It 'either rests upon no specifiable historical forces potentially capable of actualizing it or upon the notion that every conceivable historical force embodies it', and Marxism comes to have 'little or no political consequences', no praxis to accompany its theory.[21] As Althusser recognised, ideological analysis alone is not enough to produce revolution.

It is from the inadequacies of this historicist approach that we can turn to alternative methodologies for thinking about SF. The most concise critique that Althusser makes of historiography is its tendency to assume a transparent mediation between the structure of capitalism and the superstructure of culture, as if one would imply the other[22] – as if the institutions responsible for managing genre, such as the university, are not a part of the historical logic of expression, in which structural contradictions are represented by cultural reproduction. Historicism repeats the ideologies of these institutions by not reflecting upon them. Thus we must turn to examples of the relationship between texts and the world that negotiate such institutions differently.

My first example is anecdotal. In an interview, Henri Lefebvre mentions, years after the event, that he discussed a translation of Clifford Simak's *City* (1952) with the situationists.[23] This SF novel imagines a machine-maintained world in which life has been freed by technology to explore its potentiality. The irony of the novel, and part of Lefebvre's interest in it, lies in the fact that it is not human life that achieves utopia. Humans, unable to cope with a world without work, have died out, and intelligent dogs have inherited the Earth. The novel is a revolutionary one because, unlike Dick, Simak imagines a world that lies beyond the sentimentality of humanism, a world that has been thoroughly transformed at the level of the species. Its dialectic takes place between a species and the technology that enables its members to run their lives, in an exploration of post-revolutionary life. The novel was an inspiration for Lefebvre's work on the everyday, as well as for the anti-intellectual situationists themselves. Like Simak, the situationists imagined a world without the contradictions brought about by labour, and acted and published texts with a view to breaking out of these contradictions.[24] Thus SF has a relation to revolutionary praxis, even if the terms of this relationship are obscure. There is no causal relation between situationist praxis and *City*, and yet the two resonate with each other. *City*'s description of a posthuman utopia run by machines and the actions of the situationists both realise a world without work. Thus the situationists allow us to read *City* literally, rather than metaphorically, as a realisation of that liberated consciousness that lies beyond capitalism. In playing a part in the situationist milieu, in informing the situationist experiments for re-imagining the city, Simak's *City* was part of a different continuum by which to think through the relationship of revolution to SF. This is a relationship of reciprocal exchange between text and revolution, as a novel informs a revolution that, in turn, enables a reading of the novel as revolutionary possibility. It is to such lived relations that SF scholars might turn for encouragement.

Such readings of SF novels on the level of the actual have been little explored by the left, but have long been adapted by right-wing novelists and governments. For example, SF author Gregory Benford was once employed to imagine a monument to signal the deadly dangers of a nuclear waste dump for at least 10,000 years; more infamously, a group of SF writers including Larry Niven, Jerry Pournelle and Greg Bear formed the Citizen Advisory Panel on National Space Policy, whose 1984 report, *Mutual Assured Survival* (1984), argued for the militarisation of space, and persuaded President Reagan to develop the Strategic Defense Initiative – the 'Star Wars' programme.[25] These writers effortlessly shifted from the fictional to the actual. Could left-wing SF writers also be taken seriously, and consulted on the direction of the world? One imagines Kim Stanley Robinson, author of *Red Mars* (1996), advising on the upcoming American Mars mission, or Greg Egan, author of *Quarantine* (1992), employed to plan out a New Hong Kong in remote Northern Australia. To do so, however, requires a shift in leftist thinking from understanding SF as a coded expression of history to seeing it as an actualisation of history.

My second example suggests a very different relation between text and revolution. It comes from Lefebvre's student, Daniel Cohn-Bendit. In *Obsolete Communism: The Left-Wing Alternative* (1968), he is scathing in his criticism of the French Communist Party's obstruction of the May 1968 uprising by refusing to support street action, extend strikes or assist in workplace occupations. The tragic outcome was a police hunt through the streets of Paris, with students who did not find shelter in sympathetic homes being severely beaten. Cohn-Bendit's bitterness over this develops into a critique of party-based Marxism on the ground, from the point of view of a revolutionary situation. He turns to Leon Trotsky to illustrate the way that, even in the first years of the Russian revolution, communists put the interests of the party over those of the workers themselves. When a counter-revolutionary uprising in Petrograd in 1921 demanded that the local Soviet committees be sacked and replaced with new Soviets, the party ordered that the rebels be attacked, with Trotsky ordering soldiers 'to shoot the Kronstadt "rebels" down like partridges'.[26] Presuming to lead rather than follow the masses, the party sought to control and subvert a revolution that was taking place from below. In this, they exceeded the function of militant revolutionaries, who should, according to Cohn-Bendit, not so much direct or even educate the masses as 'express their common aspirations'[27] and clarify the nature of the struggle back to the revolution.[28] Cohn-Bendit, who represented the student movement during the first two weeks in May, is careful to define himself as an accidental spokesperson for the movement, as nothing more than 'a plagiarist when it comes to the preaching of revolutionary theory and practice'.[29] He disavows the idea that theory has an active role in revolution, describing it instead as the echo of a greater, lived discourse.[30] The revolutionary text, or the text as revolutionary, gestures to this excess of possibilities that lie outside of it, rather than to the interiority of its own expressive agency. Cohn-Bendit tied his book to these possibilities, declaring that the proceeds from its sale would be used to finance more Molotov cocktails, thus offsetting its place in the world of commercial publishing with its material role in revolution[31] and bringing into question the material and institutional relations of contemporary Marxist theory to revolution.

For literary theorist Pierre Macherey, a student of Althusser's, the difference between historicism and revolutionary criticism lies in the difference between representation and figuration. While ideology springs from the former, a novel is always more than its ideological content, slipping into figurations that do not always express ideology. This bulk of literary material in a novel makes up a string of differential images, and constitutes the identity of fiction that is also a non-identity because it remains insensible to thought. The writer recognises ideology as an obstacle to the real project of fiction, and so 'the book begins to walk alone, to move in an unforeseen direction' so as to elude ideology.[32] Interpretation misses this crucial play of fiction that assumes a life of its own. Instead, figuration thinks the fact of this life, turning criticism into an exchange between fictions and the world they inhabit, in a series of shared images. This is a philosophy of literature because it turns to the conditions by which fiction is produced as fiction, to that necessity by which it becomes itself. It is a Marxist philosophy of literature because it is materialist, not differentiating between fiction and the world. Macherey chose Jules Verne to illustrate his position because Verne was immersed in the possibilities of his time, in a writing project that wanted to travel to the far reaches of the planet, to the centre of the Earth, to the moon. His exploration of the reaches of the actual constitutes a writing that is bound to the world, as well as positioning the author as a scientist who investigates possibilities.

Althusser himself models an intellectual practice that is revolutionary, although today the memory of his work is obscured by biographical detail. To call for a return to Althusser is to counter a generation for whom this communist intellectual definitively lost battles that were both personal and political. It is necessary to distinguish the younger, scientific Althusser from an older man who was traumatised by domestic and political events, just as Althusser himself differentiated between a younger and an older, scientific Marx.[33] In the 1960s, Althusser was the very model of the organic intellectual, his commitment to the French Communist Party determining his modes and subjects of analysis. He set out to redress what he saw as dogmatic adaptations of Hegel that had described historical reason within Marx's thought. His writing sought to foster a sense of the present as an historical opportunity, to create in his reader a sort of revolutionary consciousness. Yet Althusser did not partake in the revolution of his time and place, famously watching May 1968 from his window, as his declared commitment to a communist revolution was in the last instance determined by his commitment to the party. In both theory and practice, he did not want to reproduce the circularities of historicism, circularities that the May 1968 movement was condemned to reproduce. He drew on the lessons of the Russian revolution to argue that a successful revolution is not determined by history, but is in fact overdetermined, as its multiple causes tip into a revolutionary consciousness that, crucially, is also not determined by these causes.[34] Althusser describes a consciousness of the historical moment that exceeds its own conditions. He turns this argument to the contemporary situation, to any contemporary situation, by asking: What historical moment is not overdetermined? In what situations are the contradictions of capitalism not more or less in evidence? To be committed to actualising revolution is to see these contradictions everywhere, to realise that there is no better moment for revolutionary action than the present. Revolutionary consciousness is not an historical consciousness, but this historical action of revolution. In arguing against the significance of historicism within Marxism, Althusser turns a consciousness of history into a consciousness that is critical of this historical consciousness. Historicism is for Althusser an ideology because it reproduces itself, rather than overdetermining its own conditions of production in order to create revolution. He sought to demonstrate that the consciousness of history is not the consciousness of revolution by creating a critique that is proximate to revolutionary action. It is not historical consciousness, but the excess of this consciousness that is the condition for a revolution's actualisation. Althusser wanted to think past the strictures of ideology, to traverse the mirror structures of ideological production so as to arrive at this revolutionary consciousness. The play of ideology is, after all, merely the play of the superstructure, and what is more important is the ultimately determining structure of capitalism.

Although May 1968 is generally counted among Althusser's personal and political failures, Louis Marin's *Utopiques* (1973) contends that the events had a very Althusserian quality of exceeding historical causality. However, he argues, this was also the reason for the revolution's failure, because revolutionaries found themselves beyond their own understanding of what they were doing. Marin considers revolution to be beyond representation, and a fundamental problem for the intellectual whose task is to represent it. This is the same problem that Althusser set himself in trying to address revolution itself, rather than its history. Marin writes of May 1968:

> For a few weeks historical time was suspended, all institutions and laws were again challenged in and by discourse, and networks of communication were opened among those immersed in one way or another in the experience. May 1968 was not only a liberating explosion and an extratemporal moment of overthrow; it was also the seizure of every opportunity to speak. Subjects and objects were exchanged so that suddenly discourse seemed to conjure up its referent. It appeared to make manifest, through its verbal expression and by its images, desires. Both roaming in reality and fixated in words, these desires could not have been accomplished by discourse itself. Rather, it brought those who spoke to such a point of excess that they could do nothing but misjudge the discourse that animated them. They consequently found themselves beyond themselves, beyond what they thought or believed.[35]

Marin describes the 'clarity of perception' that came with the event, a clarity that dissolved the abstract and uneven relations between representation and desire.[36] These are 'breakaway experiences' during which anything can happen.[37] They are beyond ordinary experience, beyond judgement, incomparable to anything else. They constitute, in Althusser's terms, the consciousness of revolution itself, the resolution of alienation in capitalism with a spontaneity lived in the present moment. Yet in Marin's description, this lived revolution is incommensurable with itself. The revolution goes beyond itself, or at least beyond the most basic mechanisms of representation. It encounters its own non-identity, in a shift of the meaning of revolution as it is constituted in non-revolutionary moments of being. It brings into being that which cannot be recognised outside itself, that which is a part of history, but is more fundamentally not a part of this history. Revolution is, within itself, an absolute difference.

The problem with this encounter with absolute difference was that it led only to a repetition of what had come before, to a return of what Jacques Lacan called the discourse of the Master. In his May 1968 seminar, on the radicalised Nanterre campus itself, Lacan predicted that this Master would return to occupy the place of power because this law is embedded structurally in language.[38] The noisy interruptions audible on the recording of this seminar testify to student discontent with his prognostications, but the consequences for the student revolutionaries proved to be far more dire than Lacan described: a new Master did not replace the old, but rather the old retained power, foreclosing the promise of a new way of living and creating the illusion of an infallible system of state and economic power. This failure to effect change in 1968 has marked the conceptualisation of revolution for Western Marxism ever since, and it is to this failure that SF studies owes its place in university institutions. The New Left gained intellectual credibility in the west at the cost of revolutionary change. It is not surprising, then, that the methodologies of this New Left reproduce a thinking of failure.

In 2006, the critical theory journal *Symploke* devoted a special issue to 'increasing levels of intellectual discouragement', yet such discouragement was already written into the historicist project that has achieved such institutional success since the 1960s.[39] In one contribution, David R. Shumway argues that today's intellectuals define themselves by inactivity, by their irrelevance to actual events.[40] This has been the case for Marxist intellectuals as well, whose particular discouragement lies in revolutions that failed to actualise in the west, and yet upon which Marxist critique is based. For Western Marxists, this revolution might just as well be SF, belonging as it does to the imagination of some speculative future. Yet, as we have seen, Althusser's critique of historicism points to a consciousness of the revolutionary possibilities of reading that exceeds this historicist ideology.

It is necessary, then, to turn away from a historicism which is all too caught up in a simple model of expressivity to produce revolutionary consciousness. Althusser's anti-humanist and anti-historicist study of Marx can help us to overcome the presumptions of the expressivity that has long informed bourgeois studies of literature, and to rethink SF. In *Reading Capital* (1970), Althusser turns to the institutional conditions for literary studies and to the question of value in professional scholarship that has developed alongside capitalism.[41] The relative autonomy of literary studies is caught up with this systemic determination of value, a determination that is implied in the ideological reifications of capitalism. Marxism's own interventions into literary studies are also situated amid these ideological reifications, as they decode the ideological representations that determine the significance of a novel, or theorise the generic system that determines the valuation of literature. An Althusserian method proposes instead to investigate the experimental conditions by which such representations come about. It wants to reproduce the consciousness by which the absolute difference of a novel's experience is created, a consciousness that makes a novel contemporary with the reader's own consciousness. For this Althusserian approach, SF is not so much a Suvinian cognitive estrangement as an identification with revolutionary possibility, producing the consciousness of the absolute difference that creates it.

It is possible, then, to think about SF not in the bourgeois terms of the novel, but as an experimental science. The object of study is not the ideological reproduction of SF, but a philosophical self-reflection upon these conditions of ideological reproduction. To read is to discover the absolute difference a novel has from its own ideological form, to the degree that it overcomes its own implication in bourgeois structures of generic reproduction.

Consequently, Le Guin's *The Left Hand of Darkness*, which imagines a human species without a sex drive, can be taken as a concrete, scientific suggestion to engineer a human society that is not warped by libidinal investments. In looking to the limits of a world of ideological reproduction, Le Guin engineers the shock and disgust of actual difference, and its possibility in the science of genetics. Reading Le Guin as a proposition of actual difference brings the experience of reading closer to us, without the distorting effects of interpretation and ideas of mediation. Althusser's critique of ideology creates opportunities for discovering the experimental science that SF has in common with revolutionary consciousness. For Althusser, such science is the self-consciousness of capitalism, and enables a thinking of the conditions by which capitalism produces ideology. In Le Guin's novel, for instance, the figuration of a world without sex reveals the ideology of a sexed world. This is revolutionary because, as that which eludes ideology, this world without sex does not repeat that which has gone before, but inhabits the contemporary moment of creation. In this, Althusser looks to the absolute difference that escapes historical repetition, that creates the consciousness that is of itself revolutionary. SF is, as a genre, a structure of ideological reproduction, but it also fosters a critical and revolutionary consciousness of absolute difference.

With gratitude to Ian Buchanan, Fredric Jameson and Patrick Quick, whose generosity of mind enabled this essay.

Notes

1. Fredric Jameson, 'In Retrospect', *Science Fiction Studies* 1: 1 (Fall 1974), p. 275; emphasis in original.
2. John Frow, *Marxism and Literary History* (Oxford: Basil Blackwell, 1986), p. 38.
3. Darko Suvin, *Metamorphoses of Science Fiction: On the Poetics and History of a Literary Genre* (New Haven: Yale University Press, 1979), p. 8.
4. Ibid., p. 221.
5. Darko Suvin, 'The Science Fiction of Ursula K. Le Guin', *Science Fiction Studies* 2: 3 (November 1975), p. 203.

6. See Fredric Jameson, 'Metacommentary', *PMLA* 86: 1 (January 1971), pp. 9–18; and *The Political Unconscious: Narrative as a Socially Symbolic Act* (Ithaca: Cornell University Press, 1981).

7. See Fredric Jameson, 'After Armageddon: Character Systems in *Dr Bloodmoney*', *Science Fiction Studies* 2: 1 (March 1975), pp. 31–42. Reprinted in Jameson, *Archaeologies of the Future: The Desire Called Utopia and Other Science Fictions* (London: Verso, 2005), pp. 349–62.

8. See A.J. Greimas and F. Rastier, 'The Interaction of Semiotic Constraints', *Yale French Studies* 41 (1968), pp. 86–105.

9. *The Political Unconscious* develops this argument by turning Althusser's philosophical distinctions between types of causality into a dialectical argument, arguing that Althusser's Marxist science is historicist after all.

10. See Louis Althusser and Étienne Balibar, *Reading Capital*, transl. Ben Brewster (London: New Left Books, 1970), pp. 119–44.

11. See Louis Althusser, *For Marx*, transl. Ben Brewster (Harmondsworth: Penguin, 1969); and Althusser and Balibar, *Reading Capital*.

12. Fredric Jameson, 'World Reduction in Le Guin: The Emergence of Utopian Narrative', *Science Fiction Studies* 2: 3 (November 1975), p. 228. Reprinted in Jameson, *Archaeologies*, pp. 267–80.

13. Jameson, 'After Armageddon', p. 42.

14. Althusser and Balibar, *Reading Capital*, p. 52; emphasis in original.

15. See Fredric Jameson, 'Ideology and Symbolic Action', *Critical Inquiry* 5: 2 (Winter 1978), pp. 417–22.

16. James Kavanagh, 'The Jameson Effect', *New Orleans Review* 11: 1 (1984), p. 25.

17. James Iffland, 'The Political Unconscious of Jameson's *The Political Unconscious*', *New Orleans Review* 11: 1 (1984), p. 27.

18. Cornel West, 'Fredric Jameson's Marxist Hermeneutics', *Boundary* 2 11: 1–2 (1982–83), p. 194.

19. See Perry Anderson, *Considerations on Western Marxism* (London: New Left Books, 1976), p. 76.

20. This is, as I have suggested, reflected in the canonisation of Dick and Le Guin, novelists who narrate a retreat from changes to capitalism, rather than its wholesale transformation. Dick's characters attempt to rediscover their own humanity in worlds that have become less human after an apocalypse (*Dr Bloodmoney* (1965)), dehumanised by a machinic, fascist or commercial culture (*Solar Lottery* (1955), *The Man in the High Castle* (1965), *Ubik* (1969)) or have made pacts with inhuman androids or the dead who exert authority over the living (*The Simulacra* (1964), *Counter-Clock World* (1967)).

As Daniel Fondaneche argues, when cheap translations of Dick circulated in France in the 1970s, he struck 'French readers as a revolutionary, as a prophet. But as a prophet of bygone times: those of the "revolution" of May 1968'. ('Dick, the Libertarian Prophet', transl. Daniele Chatelain and George Slusser, *Science Fiction Studies* 15: 2 (July 1988), p. 149.) Dick's portrayals of the fragmentations of the psyche in mid-twentieth-century capitalism are exemplary. However, although his fiction does contain revolutionary glimpses of a changed world, it is ultimately interested in characters' attempts to deal with the world as it is. This is clearly comparable to the experiences of those 1960s revolutionaries who experimented with freedom in forms of protest and revolt, broke with long-established systems of power, and glimpsed the possibility of a different kind of future – yet then returned to their old mode of living. Le Guin's response to the 1960s can be found in *The Dispossessed* (1974), in which the anarchist philosophy of liberation upon which the utopian moon of Anarres was established becomes just another regime of restrictive power. Le Guin's narrative outlines not only the joy of living in this utopia, but also its limits, which drive the protagonist away from the barren moon on which his ancestors, fleeing from the planet around which it orbits, founded their ideal society. Scarcity becomes the penance served upon a revolution for some, rather than for all, and the novel's self-critical qualities do not address revolution so much as its failure. This is not to say that attention to Dick and Le Guin is misguided, but that this contradiction between conservative narrative content and critical imperatives is a generative mechanism for SF scholarship, an abstract machine that demands its own reproduction. This machine is located in institutions that cry witness to May 1968, and is yet invariably removed from a situation that might reproduce anything of the event itself. The universities are a site at which the trauma of failed revolution registers, as their very form – after the 1960s – reproduces this failure.

21. West, 'Fredric Jameson's Marxist Hermeneutics', p. 195.
22. See Althusser and Balibar, *Reading Capital*, pp. 130–1.
23. Kristin Ross, 'Lefebvre on the Situationists: An Interview', transl. Kristin Ross, *October* 79 (1997), p. 75.
24. See Situationist International, 'On the Poverty of Student Life', transl. unknown (1966). Available at http://library.nothingness.org/articles/SI/en/display/4 (accessed 7 July 2008).
25. See Gregory Benford, *Deep Time: How Humanity Communicates Across Millennia* (London: HarperCollins, 2000); and Stephen Dedman, '"Murder in the Air": The Quest for the Death Ray', *Extrapolation* (forthcoming, 2009).

26. Daniel Cohn-Bendit and Gabriel Cohn-Bendit, *Obsolete Communism: The Left-Wing Alternative*, transl. Arnold Pomerans (London: Penguin, 1968), p. 237.

27. Ibid., p. 250.

28. Ibid., p. 251.

29. Ibid., pp. 18–19.

30. See ibid., p. 12.

31. See ibid., p. 11. The sad irony, of course, is that Cohn-Bendit's interest in mobilising violence against capitalism turned into support for capitalist violence. His subsequent career in German and European politics saw him support military interventions in both Bosnia and Afghanistan.

32. Pierre Macherey, *A Theory of Literary Production*, transl. Geoffrey Wall (London: Routledge & Kegan Paul, 1978), p. 217.

33. See Althusser, *For Marx*; and Althusser and Balibar, *Reading Capital*.

34. See Althusser, *For Marx*.

35. Louis Marin, *Utopics: Spatial Play*, transl. Robert A. Vollrath (Atlantic Highlands: Humanities Press International, 1984), p. 3.

36. Hans Koning, *1968: A Personal Report* (London: Unwin Hyman, 1987), p. 13.

37. James Miller, *Democracy is in the Streets: From Port Huron to the Siege of Chicago* (Cambridge: Harvard University Press, 1994), p. 317.

38. See Jacques Lacan, *The Seminar XVII, The Other Side of Psychoanalysis*, ed. Jacques-Alain Miller, transl. Russell Grigg (New York: W.W. Norton, 2006).

39. Jeffrey R. Di Leo, 'Editor's Note', *Symploke* 14: 1–2 (2006), p. 5.

40. David R. Shumway, 'Marxism without Revolution: Towards a History of Discouragement', *Symploke* 14: 1–2 (2006), p. 31.

41. See Althusser and Balibar, *Reading Capital*, pp. 125–6.

11

UTOPIA AND SCIENCE FICTION REVISITED

Andrew Milner

For Kathy Wench, my teenage sweetheart and first love, who grew up to be Kathryn Turnier and died of pancreatic cancer on Christmas Day 2007; and for Marion and Marc, who must learn to imagine life without her.

Raymond Williams was almost certainly the single most important intellectual spokesman for the early British New Left of the 1950s and 1960s. He was a key figure in the development of British cultural studies and the founder of cultural materialism, which although often likened to American new historicism was, he insisted, 'a Marxist theory ... indeed ... part of what I at least see as the central thinking of Marxism'.[1] He was variously – and inaccurately – likened to a British Lukács,[2] a British Bloch,[3] and even, according to *The Times*, 'the British Sartre'. He also had an enduring interest in SF, participating as an editorial consultant for *Science Fiction Studies* and writing an SF novel, *The Volunteers* (1978). His 1978 essay on 'Utopia and Science Fiction', first published in *Science Fiction Studies*, is one of the classic theoretical statements on the relationship between SF, utopia and dystopia. Like Darko Suvin's *Metamorphoses of Science Fiction* (1979), Tom Moylan's *Demand the Impossible* (1986) and Fredric Jameson's *Archaeologies of the Future* (2005), it stressed the close kinship between the genres but, unlike them, it nonetheless insisted on their conceptual separateness. For Williams, they were different albeit cognate genres. This essay will use the categories of Williams' cultural materialism – especially 'selective tradition' and 'structure of feeling' – to interrogate not only Suvin's (and to some extent Jameson's) understanding of the relationship between utopia and SF, but also Williams' own. It will ask and attempt to answer three very general questions about SF: What was it? What wasn't it? When was it?

What was SF?

The first question is one of definition, of course, and academics love definition: it is a quite fundamental part of what they do. And it is difficult to imagine a more archetypically academic definition than Suvin's: 'a literary genre whose necessary and sufficient conditions are the presence and interaction of estrangement and cognition'; distinguished by 'the narrative dominance or hegemony of a fictional "novum" ... validated by cognitive logic'.[4] The testable, even examinable, questions come relatively easily: Where is the estrangement in this novel? What exactly is its novum? Is it strangely new? Is it hegemonic? Is it validated by cognitive logic? It is also a nicely elitist definition, insofar as it is confined to literature (excluding film and television), but nicely contrarian insofar as it seeks to expand the canon to include something as inherently disreputable as SF. It is simultaneously theoretically rich and respectably radical, deriving from Russian Formalism by way of Brecht and from Bloch out of Gramsci. It is, in short, just what the Doctor of Philosophy ordered.

But academics are not the only ones attracted to this kind of exercise: the history of SF is littered with definitions by writers, fans, editors and critics. John Clute and Peter Nicholls list no fewer than eleven main candidates;[5] less traditionally magisterial but more inclusive, Wikipedia.org currently lists 27. The most famous is probably Hugo Gernsback's on the range and scope of his new magazine *Amazing Stories*: 'the Jules Verne, H.G. Wells and Edgar Allan Poe type of story – a charming romance intermingled with scientific fact and prophetic vision'.[6] But Brian Aldiss' 1986 redefinition surely runs it close: 'the search for a definition of mankind and his status in the universe which will stand in our advanced but confused state of knowledge (science) ... characteristically cast in the Gothic or post-Gothic mode'.[7] If

Gernsback's opening editorial was essentially prospective in intent, its referents were nonetheless retrospective: Verne, Wells and Poe. Aldiss' reference to the Gothic is similarly retrospective: hence his decision to trace the origins of the species to Mary Shelley. Verne himself credited Poe as an early influence;[8] Wells' *The Island of Doctor Moreau* (1896) is clearly indebted to *Frankenstein* (1818);[9] Verne and Wells emphatically insisted on their differences from each other;[10] and everyone – Zamyatin, Čapek, Huxley, Orwell – insisted on their debt to and differences from Wells.[11] Orwell also defined his work in relation to the 'kind of book' represented by Zamyatin's *We* (1924).[12] And even Shelley explained the novelty of her fiction in retrospective terms, as being concerned with the possible consequences and ethical implications of a hypothetical scientific development, rather than the supernatural phenomena of more conventionally Gothic romance: 'The event on which the interest of the story depends is exempt from the disadvantages of a mere tale of spectres or enchantment'.[13] Only Aldiss would have described his work as 'science fiction': Gernsback's early magazines published 'scientifiction'; Verne wrote *voyages extraordinaires* and *romans scientifiques*; Wells, 'scientific romances'; Poe, 'tales of the grotesque and arabesque'. The repeated intertextual referencing nonetheless suggests the presence, if not of a genre, then at least of a tradition.

The first part of Suvin's *Metamorphoses* is the account of the structure of a genre, the second, of the history of a tradition, running from More's *Utopia* (1516) to Čapek's *War With the Newts* (1936). If there is an obvious logical complementarity between these exercises, there is also, nonetheless, a practically unresolved tension, in this particular instance, between the literary theorist, aiming to define the genre, and the literary historian, attempting to chart its evolution. So Suvin is simultaneously insistent that the 'concept of SF' cannot be deduced 'empirically from the work called thus', but that it is 'inherent in the literary objects'; that it can be reached only through an effort 'to educe and formulate the *differentia specifica* of the SF narration', but that 'the scholar does not invent it out of the whole cloth'.[14] At first sight, this is bewildering: if the concept inheres in the literary objects, then why can't it be deduced from them? The end-product – but also the axiomatic premise – is his famous definition cited above, in which theory clearly triumphs over history, genre over tradition. But what follows is, nonetheless, the history of a tradition, of which 'the significant writers ... were quite aware'.[15]

Which leads me to two propositions – one on genre, the other on tradition, and both deriving ultimately from Williams. Suvin describes genre as 'a socioaesthetic entity with a specific inner life, yet in constant osmosis with other literary genres, science, philosophy, everyday socioeconomic life, and so on'.[16] This nicely combines a formalist sense of generic specificity with a more historicist sense of the possibility of variation over time. But there is something strange, nonetheless, about this use of the term 'entity', which suggests an overly formalist, perhaps even fetishistic, conception of the socio-aesthetic: socio-aesthetic a genre may be, but an entity it surely is not. The problem here lies with Suvin's understanding of genre as overwhelmingly a matter of classification. It is that, of course, but it is also a set of practical conventions, combining a complex mix of prohibitions, recommendations and prescriptions which together constitute a cultural technology for the production and reception of particular kinds of text. Williams argued that 'form', a term he preferred to genre, was primarily a matter not of classification but of social relationship: 'a social process which ... becomes a social product' and 'the common property ... of writers and audiences or readers, before any communicative composition can occur'.[17] Understood thus, as a prospectively productive force within the literary mode of production, genre loses the fetishistic quality it acquires in Suvin. It also becomes clear why genre inheres in literary objects, but cannot be deduced from them: they bear its impress because it pre-exists them as a tool for their manufacture.

An analogous argument may be mounted with respect to tradition. For Suvin, tradition is inherited from the past, developed and modified in the present, then handed on to the future as a gift from the present-become-past. Hence, Wells

collected ... all the main influences of earlier writers – from Lucian and Swift to Kepler, Verne, and Flammarion, from Plato and Mary Shelley, Poe, Bulwer, and the subliterature of planetary and subterranean voyages, future wars, and the like – and transformed them in his own image, whence they entered into the treasury of subsequent SF.[18]

There are other ways of theorising tradition, however, such as Williams' notion of 'selective tradition'. Culture, he observed, exists at three levels: the lived culture of a particular time and place; the recorded culture of deposited texts, artifacts and knowledges; and the selective tradition sustained subsequently. The tradition thus formed is, at one level, 'a general human culture', at another, 'the historical record of a particular society', but at yet another 'a rejection of considerable areas of what was once a living culture'.[19] Selection is a retrospective process, made and remade, not by the past, but in and for a sequence of successive 'presents', as 'a continual selection and re-selection of ancestors'; it is therefore motivated, in part, by contemporary interests and values, by 'many kinds of special interest, including class interest'.[20] He later restated this position in more expressly Gramscian terms: 'It is a version of the past ... intended to connect with and ratify the present. What it offers ... is a sense of *predisposed continuity*'.[21] Williams' argument was directed at the high literary canon and had as its immediate target cultural conservatives like F.R. Leavis. But what holds for Leavis' 'Great Tradition' also holds for Suvin's SF tradition. It too is necessarily selective.

Which returns us to our starting point in that plethora of definitions, since each of these represents an attempt to redefine the tradition selectively by re-selecting its ancestors. This is as true of Suvin as of Gernsback or Aldiss. As Patrick Parrinder rightly observed of Suvin's *Metamorphoses*: '"Cognitive estrangement" may be taken to be a fact about the 1970s, just as T.S. Eliot's "dissociation of sensibility" was a fact about the 1920s'.[22] This is not to suggest that all definitions are equally valid – though logically they are, since all definitions are by definition true – but only that they are all equally socio-aesthetic, and therefore necessarily to some extent weapons in the struggle for the power to define. This selectivity is most apparent wherever a redefinition explicitly prescribes either inclusion or exclusion. In Suvin's case the relevant instances are, respectively, utopia, included by virtue of its bearing on the novum, and fantasy, excluded by virtue of its cognitive inadequacy.

What wasn't SF? Utopia or Fantasy?

Suvin defines a fictive utopia as an 'imaginary community ... in which human relations are organized more perfectly than in the author's community'.[23] Thus understood, he argues, utopia becomes 'the socio-political subgenre of science fiction',[24] that is, social-science-fiction. This non sequitur had the effect of expanding SF, at a stroke, to accommodate not only More and Bacon, Rabelais and Campanella, Saint-Simon and Fénelon, but also Aeschylus and Aristophanes. It was a controversial move, at odds with much contemporary usage among SF writers, fans and critics. It has supporters, nonetheless: Jameson's *Archaeologies of the Future* cites it with approval on at least five occasions.[25] In effect, Suvin and Jameson were each attempting a redefinition of the selective SF tradition aimed at retrospectively englobing the genre of utopia. For both, the attempt is inspired in part by Ernst Bloch's *The Principle of Hope* (1954–59).

Suvin derived the novum, both as term and concept, from Bloch. The term first appears in a brief reference to 'the Front and the Novum' towards the end of Bloch's 'Introduction',[26] but the concepts are not formally elaborated until chapter seventeen. There, Bloch argues that a 'philosophy of comprehended hope' must stand on 'the Front of the world process', that is, on the historically 'foremost segment of Being of animated, utopianly open matter'.[27] The Front, he continues, is necessarily related to newness, the New, the Novum. And, if the Novum is really new, it will be characterised by 'abstract opposition to mechanical repetition' and by a specific repetition of its own, that of 'the still unbecome total goal-content itself, which is suggested and tended, tested and processed out in the progressive newnesses of history'.[28] Historically, the dialectical emergence of this total content – which Bloch terms the Ultimum – will eventually end repetition, if only because it represents the highest newness, which will triumph by means of a total leap out of everything that has ever existed, a leap towards the newness of identity.[29] Short of the Ultimum, however, there remains only the advancing Front and the series of Novums it encounters. These are not necessarily literary or artistic, but art is nonetheless both 'a laboratory and also a feast of implemented possibilities'.[30]

Bloch's intentions in *The Principle of Hope* were primarily political and philosophical, but the book's range is quasi-encyclopaedic nonetheless, quite literally from dreams to theology. It includes an extensive discussion of utopian literature, from Solon to Morris by way of Plato, the Stoics, Augustine, Joachim de Fiore, Campanella, Owen, Proudhon and Bakunin, culminating in an utterly dismissive account of Wells as 'dilletantism and chaff'.[31] Despite Bloch's enthusiasm for the circus, the fairytale and other older popular forms, post-Wellsian SF rates no mention whatsoever. Indeed, Bloch ignores both the German tradition of the *Staatsroman* – the politically utopian novel, literally the (ideal) state novel – which has been analysed as a direct precursor to SF, and the German SF writers published in English translation by Gernsback.[32] The omission is no mere oversight: as late as 1974, Bloch would remain deeply dismissive of the 'purely technological utopias' of 'science fiction'.[33] The novelty of Suvin's argument was to reverse exactly this judgement and to insist, both with and against Bloch, that 'the novum is the necessary condition of SF'.[34]

Suvin's exclusion of fantasy derives from Brecht's insistence on the interrelation of estrangement and cognition in *Short Organum for the Theatre* (1949), in which he argued for his *Verfremdungseffekt*, or *V-Effekt*, 'designed to free socially conditioned phenomena from the stamp of familiarity which protects them against our grasp today'; the purpose of his theatre is thus a knowledge through estrangement akin to Galileo's 'detached eye'.[35] For Suvin, these become the necessary and sufficient conditions for SF: 'the presence and interaction of estrangement and cognition'.[36] There is clear prescriptive intent here: to exclude myth, folktale and fantasy.[37] Indeed, Suvin's insistence on the cognitive functions of SF is accompanied by a profound aversion to fantasy as 'proto-Fascist revulsion against modern civilization, materialist rationalism, and such … organized around an ideology unchecked by any cognition

… its narrative logic … simply overt ideology plus Freudian erotic patterns'.[38] To market SF alongside fantasy, as commercial bookshops do, is thus a 'rampantly socio-pathological phenomenon'.[39] The exclusion of fantasy is perhaps less controversial than the inclusion of utopia: it echoes a long tradition among SF writers, editors and readers, reaching back to Gernsback and John W. Campbell, Jr, and, before them to Wells, Verne and Shelley. And once again Jameson echoes Suvin: 'the scientific pretensions of SF lend the Utopian genre an epistemological gravity that any kinship with generic fantasy is bound to undermine'.[40] Like Suvin, Jameson registers the commercial pressures towards genre-blending between SF and fantasy and, like Suvin, sees fantasy as 'technically reactionary'.[41] The implication seems clear that only Tolkienesque reactionaries would dabble in such stuff.

And yet, the empirical convergence between SF and fantasy does seem to be a 'fact' of contemporary cultural life. The World Science Fiction Society, which for decades made its annual Hugo Awards on near-Suvinian criteria (despite fantasy long being eligible), broke new ground when it awarded its 2001 prize for the best novel to J.K. Rowling's *Harry Potter and the Goblet of Fire* (2000), and that for the best dramatic presentation to *Crouching Tiger, Hidden Dragon* (Lee, 2000). In 2002, the latter award went to *Lord of the Rings: The Fellowship of the Ring* (Jackson, 2001), and in 2003 it was divided into a long-form award, which went to *Lord of the Rings: The Two Towers* (Jackson, 2002), and a short-form award, which went to 'Conversations with Dead People' (2002), an episode of *Buffy the Vampire Slayer* (1997–2003). In 2004, Jackson swept the board, taking the long-form award for *Lord of the Rings: The Return of the King* (2003) and the short-form award for Gollum's Acceptance Speech at the 2004 MTV Movie Awards. SF proper held up better in the novels and in subsequent competition for the best dramatic presentation, except in 2007, when *Pan's Labyrinth* (del Toro, 2006) won the long-form award. There was no significant sentiment, however, at any of the relevant World Science Fiction Conventions, that these fantasy awards represented some kind of category mistake. Nor did *Science Fiction Studies* – co-founded by Suvin in 1973, and for which Jameson served for many years as a consulting editor – balk at including, in its 2003 special issue on the British SF boom, an extensive discussion of the work of China Miéville,[42] which makes similar use of fantasy. But neither del Toro nor Miéville are Tolkienesque reactionaries: the former has directed two quite explicitly anti-fascist Spanish Civil War films (*Pan's Labyrinth* is, in some respects, a sequel to 2001's *The Devil's Backbone*), while the latter is a key figure in contemporary critical legal theory, a co-editor of *Historical Materialism: Research in Critical Marxist Theory* and an active member of the British Socialist Workers Party, as well as the author of the *Bas-Lag* trilogy – *Perdido Street Station* (2000), *The Scar* (2002) and *Iron Council* (2004) – novels as redolent of Marxism as with magic. If Miéville has apparently retracted his famously intemperate description of Tolkien as 'the wen on the arse of fantasy', this is more for reasons of technical accuracy – by definition, a wen can develop only on the face – than political compromise.

My point is not that Suvin and Jameson are 'objectively' mistaken in their definitions of SF, but rather that those definitions are best understood as interventions into the selective tradition, which one will accept only to the extent that one shares their purpose. And, to judge by the Hugo Awards, China Miéville and *Science Fiction Studies*, theirs seems to have been a largely unsuccessful intervention. My own position is less concerned with shaping the selective tradition than with analysing and explaining it, for which I will draw on Williams' sense of SF, utopia and dystopia as cognate rather than identical, and of these forms as means of cultural production. There are four characteristic types of alternative reality, Williams argued: the paradise or hell; the positively or negatively externally altered world; the positive or negative willed transformation; and the positive or negative technological transformation. SF, utopia and dystopia are each centrally concerned with the 'presentation of *otherness*', Williams continues, and thus depend on an element of discontinuity from 'realism'.[43] But the discontinuity is more radical in non-utopian/non-dystopian SF, since the utopian and dystopian modes require for their political efficacy an 'implied connection' with the real: the whole point of utopia or dystopia is to acquire some positive or negative leverage on the present. By contrast, other kinds of SF and fantasy are free to enjoy greater latitude in their relations to the real.

The willed transformation and the technological transformation are therefore the more characteristically utopian or dystopian modes, because transformation – how the world might be changed, whether for better or worse – will normally be more important to utopia than otherness per se. SF can and does deploy all four modes, but in each case draws on '"science", in its variable definitions'.[44] SF may be utopian or dystopian, and utopias and dystopias may be science-fictional, but the genres are nonetheless analytically distinguishable by virtue of the presence or absence of science (and technology). This issue is carefully avoided by Suvin's treatment of science as equivalent to cognition,[45] but remains central for Williams. And rightly so, surely, for it is what most clearly distinguishes the SF selective tradition not only from the 'older and now residual modes' such as the Earthly Paradise, the Blessed Islands, the Land of Cockayne, but also from non-SF utopias.[46] And there *is* science in both del Toro and Miéville, most obviously in the absolutely realistic and unsentimental representations of the dynamics of repression, oppression and exploitation in Fascist Spain and New Crobuzon, which coexist with, complement and counterpoint the other more genuinely fantastic elements. This is something very close to what Franz Roh, and after him the Latin American 'boom' novelists, meant by 'magical realism'.

When was SF?

This takes us to the third question, that of periodisation. Part of the purpose of Suvin's definition was to expand the genre so as to include a substantial part of the literary and philosophical canon. There are thus, according to Suvin, six main instances of SF in the 'Euro-Mediterranean tradition': the Hellenic (Aeschylus, Aristophanes, Plato, Theopompus, Euhemerus, Hecataeus, Iambulus); the Hellenic-cum-Roman (Virgil, Antonius Diogenes, Lucian); the Renaissance-Baroque (More, Rabelais, Bacon, Campanella, Cyrano, Swift); the democratic revolution (Mercier, Saint-Simon, Fourier, Blake, Shelley); the fin-de-siècle (Bellamy,

Morris, Verne, Wells); and the modern (from Wells, Zamyatin and Čapek through Gernsback and Campbell to the present).[47] Where Suvin detects formal continuities, not only between Wells and More, but between both and Aeschylus, Williams stresses the historical discontinuities between the pre-modern and the modern. This is the general significance of his 'long revolution', but also, here, the specific significance of his 'structure of feeling'.

The latter is a key concept in Williams' work, designed to denote

> a structure in the sense that you could perceive it operating in one work after another which weren't otherwise connected – people weren't learning it from each other; yet ... one of feeling much more than of thought – a pattern of impulses, restraints, tones, for which the best evidence was often the actual conventions of literary or dramatic writing.[48]

From *The Long Revolution* on, he had used the term to designate both the immediately experiential and the generationally specific aspects of artistic process. In *Marxism and Literature*, these emphases are conjoined with a stress on cultural pre-emergence, in which the experiential and generationally specific remain at odds with official culture precisely because they are indeed new: 'practical consciousness is what is actually being lived ... not only what it is thought is being lived'.[49] Structures of feeling, he continues,

> can be defined as social experiences *in solution*, as distinct from other social semantic formations which have been *precipitated* and are more evidently and more immediately available ... it is primarily to emergent formations ... that the structure of feeling, *as solution*, relates.[50]

A structure of feeling is thus the element within the more general culture that most actively anticipates subsequent mutations in the general culture itself – in short, the novum encountered by the advancing front. And a crucial element in the emergent structure of feeling of the mid nineteenth century was, as Williams himself stressed on more than one occasion, the new industrial science and its technologies:

> Again and again, even by critics of the society, the excitement of this
> extraordinary release of man's powers was acknowledged and shared ...
> 'These are our poems,' Carlyle said in 1842, looking at one of the new
> locomotives, and this element ... is central to the whole culture.[51]

It is also what most clearly distinguished the new worlds of SF from
the alternative islands of older utopian fiction.

An emergent culture, Williams observed, requires not only distinct
kinds of immediate cultural practice, but also, and crucially, 'new
forms or adaptations of forms'.[52] The nineteenth-century SF novel
was exactly this: a new form radically different from those that
preceded it. And, insofar as it had been an adaptation of any pre-
existing form, this was not so much the utopia as the historical novel.
Both Suvin and Jameson register the affinities between the latter
and SF: when Suvin introduces pluridimensional temporality into
his basic taxonomy of literary forms, he treats SF as the estranged
counterpart of historical realism;[53] and Jameson argues that the
historical novel ceased to be 'functional' more or less contempo-
raneously with the beginning of SF, in the simultaneous historical
moment of Flaubert's *Salammbô* (1862) and Verne's *Five Weeks
in a Balloon* (1863). In an essay first published in 1982, Jameson
wrote that the new SF registered a 'nascent sense of the future ... in
the space on which a sense of the past had ... been inscribed'.[54] This
seems a much more productive starting point for SF history than the
post-Suvinian obsession with More which actually opens Jameson's
Archaeologies, and towards which the 1982 essay, included in it,
also moved. For the typical subject-matter of SF is future history,
euchronia and dyschronia, rather than utopia and dystopia; its
precursors Scott and Dumas, rather than More and Bacon. Verne
was, of course, a protégé of Dumas. And Verne's second SF novel,
written in the same year as *Five Weeks in a Balloon* but rejected
by his editor, Hetzel, as too pessimistic, and therefore unpublished
until 1994, was *Paris in the Twentieth Century*.

With this connection between SF and the historical novel tentatively
established, I would like to proceed to a few concluding remarks on
the history of SF as a form. Williams identified three distinct levels
of form, which he termed respectively 'modes', 'genres' and 'types'.

Here, 'mode' refers to the deepest level of form, as in the distinction between the dramatic, lyrical and narrative modes, which persist historically through quite different social orders; 'genre' refers to relatively persistent instances of each mode, such as the epic and the novel within the narrative mode, which are subject to greater variation between different social orders; and 'type' denotes radical distributions, redistributions and innovations of interest within given modes and genres, still more variable and still more dependent on particular social relations.[55] The examples Williams gave of the latter included bourgeois drama and the realist novel. But it should be clear that, in these terms, SF represents exactly such a radical redistribution and innovation of interest within the novel and short story genres, which occurs, in the first instance, in the nineteenth century. This is clearly a much less literary business than either Suvin or Jameson would have it. Of course, SF texts have rifled through the western cultural legacy in search of inspiration: *Forbidden Planet* (Wilcox, 1956) famously rewrote *The Tempest* with Robby the Robot in the role of Ariel. But SF readers, writers and critics do not claim Shakespeare for their own in anything like the way Gernsback claimed Poe, Verne and Wells; nor that in which Bruce Sterling claimed Shelley's *Frankenstein* as 'a wellspring of science fiction as a genre', albeit only 'humanist' SF.[56] Borrowings from Shakespeare – or from More or Plato – can be important and interesting; but they are borrowings from outside the selective tradition of SF, nonetheless.

The SF selective tradition was conceived in England and France – that is, at the centre of nineteenth-century capitalism, which was also, in Franco Moretti's terms, the core of the nineteenth-century world literary economy.[57] Just as the earlier decades of the century had been dominated, in terms of both sales and translations, by the historical novels of Scott and Dumas, so were the later by the scientific romances of Verne and Wells. Astonishingly, Verne is still in the early twenty-first century the most widely translated of all French novelists, no matter how inadequate many of the translations.[58] The SF selective tradition continued in Britain and France throughout the twentieth and into the twenty-first (through

Huxley, Orwell, Lewis, Wyndham, Hoyle, Clarke, Moorcock, Ballard, Banks, MacLeod and Miéville in Britain; Rosny, Anatole France, Renard, Spitz, Boulle, Merle, Walther, Brussolo, Arnaud and Houellebecq in France). The US has a fitful presence in the early tradition, essentially through Poe and Bellamy, but each of these is arguably more significant for their impact on the Anglo-French core, through Verne and Morris respectively, than on America itself. In the twentieth century the selective tradition's frontiers expanded to include the Weimar Republic (Gail, von Harbou and Lang, von Hanstein), early Soviet Russia (Belyaev, Bogdanov, Bulgakov, Mayakovsky, Platonov, Alexei Tolstoy, Zamyatin) and inter-war Czechoslovakia (Čapek, Troska). Exported to Japan in the post-World War II period (Abe, Hoshi, Komatsu, Murakami), it also flourished in Communist Poland (Fialkowski, Lem, Wisniewski-Snerg) and more significantly in late-Communist Russia (Altov, Bilenkin, Bulychev, Emtsev and Parnov, the Strugatsky brothers, Tarkovsky). During the inter-war period, the genre also flourished in the US, which very rapidly became central and eventually near-hegemonic (Gernsback, Campbell, Asimov, Heinlein and the pulps) – a situation which continued through the New Wave (Delany, Dick, Ellison, Spinrad, Tiptree, Zelazny) and feminism (Le Guin, Russ, Piercy) and on to cyberpunk (Gibson, Sterling) and the new humanism of writers like Kim Stanley Robinson. In the twentieth century, and in America in particular, this type also expanded to embrace other media, notably film and television.

At the risk of over-generalisation, let me suggest that there are three main geo-historical moments in this tradition. Their darker undercurrents not withstanding – one thinks of Nemo and of the Morlocks – Verne and Wells had generally written from within a self-confidently optimistic positivism, often bordering on the utopian. SF in Germany, Russia and *Mitteleuropa* abandoned this liberal futurology, opting either for an explicitly communist utopianism or, perhaps more interestingly, for dystopia, whether communist or capitalist – a theme later re-imported into England by Orwell, that most un-English of English icons. Positivistic SF would be resumed in inter-war America – but in a different register, nonetheless – as an escapist response to the Great Depression rather than the easy celebration of scientific triumphalism. Hence the quasi-Marxian character of Isaac Asimov's early 'Futurianism'.[59] This second epistemic shift is vital, and was a distinctly American achievement. Through it, a marginal sub-form eventually succeeded in generalising itself across the entire field of popular culture, from novel to film to television, so as to become the nearest we may ever have to a postmodern epic. It is a messy beast, of course, as fashionably hybrid as any postmodernist could wish, an 'at once liberating and promiscuous mode', as Williams wrote, which 'has moved beyond the utopian; in a majority of cases ... because it has fallen short of it.' But, as he also observed, 'it is part of the power of science fiction that it is always potentially a mode of authentic shift: a crisis of exposure which produces a crisis of possibility; a reworking, in imagination, of *all* forms and conditions'.[60] A resource of hope, then, at least in part, at least potentially.

Notes

1. Raymond Williams, *Marxism and Literature* (Oxford: Oxford University Press, 1977), pp. 5–6.
2. Terry Eagleton, *Criticism and Ideology: A Study in Marxist Literary Theory* (London: New Left Books, 1976), p. 36.
3. Tony Pinkney, 'Williams and the "Two Faces of Modernism"', in Terry Eagleton, ed., *Raymond Williams: Critical Perspectives* (Cambridge: Polity, 1989), pp. 28–31.
4. Darko Suvin, *Metamorphoses of Science Fiction: On the Poetics and History of a Literary Genre* (New Haven: Yale University Press, 1979), pp. 7–8, 63.
5. John Clute and Peter Nicholls, eds, *The Encyclopedia of Science Fiction* (London: Orbit, 1993), pp. 311–14.
6. Hugo Gernsback, 'A New Sort of Magazine', *Amazing Stories: The Magazine of Scientifiction* 1 (1926), p. 3.
7. Brian Aldiss with David Wingrove, *Trillion Year Spree: The History of Science Fiction* (London: House of Stratus, 2001), p. 4.
8. See Jules Verne, 'Edgar Poe et ses ouevres', in F. Lacassin, ed., *Textes oubliés* (Paris: Union Générale, 1979).
9. See Robert M. Philmus, 'Introducing *Moreau*', in Philmus, ed., *The Island of Doctor Moreau: A Variorum Text* (Athens: University of Georgia Press, 1993).

10. Jules Verne, 'Jules Verne Interviewed, 9 October 1903', in Patrick Parrinder, ed., *H.G. Wells: The Critical Heritage* (London: Routledge, 1997), pp. 101–2; H.G. Wells, 'Preface' to *Seven Famous Novels by H.G. Wells* (New York: Garden City, 1934), p. vii.

11. See Yevgeny Zamyatin, 'H.G. Wells (1922)', in Mira Ginsburg, ed. and transl., *A Soviet Heretic* (Chicago: University of Chicago Press); Karel Čapek, *Letters from England*, transl. Paul Selver (London: Geoffrey Bles, 1925), pp. 180–1; Karel Čapek, 'Appendix: Of the Sexual Life of the Newts', in *War with the Newts*, transl. M. and R. Weatherall (Evanston: Northwestern University Press, 1996); Aldous Huxley, 'To Mrs Kethevan Roberts', 18 May 1931, in Grover Smith, ed., *Letters of Aldous Huxley* (London: Chatto & Windus, 1969), p. 384; George Orwell, *The Road to Wigan Pier* (Harmondsworth: Penguin, 1962), pp. 169–72; George Orwell, 'Wells, Hitler and the World State', in Sonia Orwell and Ian Angus, eds, *Collected Essays, Journalism and Letters: Vol. 2: My Country Right or Left* (Harmondsworth: Penguin, 1970).

12. George Orwell, 'Letter to Gleb Struve', 17 February 1944, in Sonia Orwell and Ian Angus, eds, *Collected Essays, Journalism and Letters: Vol. 3: As I Please* (Harmondsworth: Penguin, 1970), p. 118.

13. Mary Shelley, *Frankenstein, or The Modern Prometheus* (Oxford: Oxford University Press, 1980), p. 13.

14. Suvin, *Metamorphoses*, p. 63.

15. Ibid., p. 12.

16. Ibid., p. 53.

17. Williams, *Marxism and Literature*, pp. 187–8.

18. Suvin, *Metamorphoses*, p. 220.

19. Raymond Williams, *The Long Revolution* (Harmondsworth: Penguin, 1965), p. 68.

20. Ibid., pp. 69, 68.

21. Williams, *Marxism and Literature*, p. 116; emphasis in original.

22. Patrick Parrinder, 'Introduction: Learning from Other Worlds', in Parrinder, ed., *Learning from Other Worlds: Estrangement, Cognition and the Politics of Science Fiction and Utopia* (Liverpool: Liverpool University Press, 2000), p. 10.

23. Suvin, *Metamorphoses*, p. 45.

24. Ibid., p. 61.

25. Fredric Jameson, *Archaeologies of the Future: The Desire Called Utopia and Other Science Fictions* (London: Verso, 2005), pp. xiv, 57, 393, 410, 414–15.

26. Ernst Bloch, *The Principle of Hope*, transl. Neville Plaice, Stephen Plaice and Paul Knight (Cambridge: MIT Press, 1986), p. 18.

27. Ibid., p. 200.
28. Ibid., p. 202.
29. Ibid., pp. 202–3.
30. Ibid., p. 216.
31. Ibid., p. 617.
32. See Martin Schwonke, *Vom Staatsroman zur Science Fiction: Eine Untersuchung über Geschichte und Funktion der naturwissenschaftlich-technischen Utopie* (Stuttgart: Ferdinand Enke, 1957); Linda Jordan, *German Science Fiction in the Science-Fiction Magazines of Hugo Gernsback (1926–1935)* (MA Thesis, Montreal: McGill University, 1986).
33. Arno Münster, ed., *Tagträume vom Aufrechten Gang: Sechs Interviews mit Ernst Bloch* (Frankfurt: Suhrkamp, 1977), p. 71.
34. Suvin, *Metamorphoses*, p. 65.
35. Bertolt Brecht, 'A Short Organum for the Theatre', in John Willett, ed. and transl., *Brecht on Theatre: The Development of an Aesthetic* (London: Methuen, 1974), p. 192
36. Suvin, *Metamorphoses*, pp. 7–8.
37. Ibid., pp. 7–9, 20.
38. Ibid., p. 69.
39. Ibid., p. 9.
40. Jameson, *Archaeologies*, p. 57.
41. Ibid., p. 60.
42. See Joan Gordon, 'Reveling in Genre: An Interview with China Miéville', *Science Fiction Studies* 30: 3, pp. 355–73, and 'Hybridity, Heterotopia, and Mateship in China Miéville's *Perdido Street Station*', *Science Fiction Studies* 30: 3, pp. 456–76.
43. See Raymond Williams, 'Utopia and Science Fiction', in *Problems in Materialism and Culture* (London: New Left Books, 1980), p. 198; emphasis in original.
44. Williams, 'Utopia and Science Fiction', pp. 196–9.
45. Suvin, *Metamorphoses*, p. 13.
46. Williams, 'Utopia and Science Fiction', p. 198.
47. Suvin, *Metamorphoses*, pp. 87, 205.
48. Raymond Williams, *Politics and Letters: Interviews with New Left Review* (London: New Left Books, 1979), p. 159.
49. Williams, *Marxism and Literature*, pp. 130–1.
50. Ibid., pp. 133–4; emphases in original.
51. Williams, *Long Revolution*, p. 88.
52. Williams, *Marxism and Literature*, p. 126.
53. Suvin, *Metamorphoses*, p. 21.
54. Jameson, *Archaeologies*, p. 286.

55. Raymond Williams, *Culture* (Glasgow: Fontana, 1981), pp. 194–6.

56. Bruce Sterling, 'Cyberpunk in the nineties', *Interzone* 38, pp. 39–41.

57. Franco Moretti, *Atlas of the European Novel 1800–1900* (London: Verso, 1998), p. 174.

58. See UNESCO, *Index Translationum* (First Quarter, Paris: UNESCO, 2008).

59. See Damon Knight, *The Futurians* (New York: John Day, 1977).

60. Williams, 'Utopia and Science Fiction', p. 209; emphasis in original.

AFTERWORD

COGNITION AS IDEOLOGY: A DIALECTIC OF SF THEORY

China Miéville

The Negation of Some Negation or Other

Implicit in an early proposed subtitle of this collection – 'Marxism, Science Fiction, Fantasy' – was an argument, even a polemic, with and about something approaching an orthodoxy. In conceiving its remit as Marxist approaches to SF *and* fantasy, the clause implies that it is due to more than coincidence or bad taxonomy that the two sub-genres are shelved near each other: that they are, in fact, at some important and constitutive level, united.

This is neither an uncontroversial contention nor a new debate. Since the publication of his seminal *Metamorphoses of Science Fiction* (1979), the most powerful current in SF scholarship, particularly in Marxist/*Marxisant* traditions, has been that of Darko Suvin, according to which SF and fantasy are and must remain not only radically distinct but hierarchically related. To briefly restate familiar positions, in Suvin's enormously and justly influential, if by now somewhat notorious, approach, SF is characterised by 'cognitive estrangement', in which the alienation from the everyday effected by the non-realist setting – 'an imaginative framework alternative to the author's empirical environment'[1] – is 'cognitively' organised. As one of various Others implied by that model, generic fantasy comes in for a particular savaging, because, though it also 'estranges', it is 'committed to the imposition of anti-cognitive laws', is 'a sub-literature of mystification',[2] 'proto-Fascist', anti-rationalist, anti-modern, 'overt ideology plus Freudian erotic patterns'.[3] Suvin acknowledges that the boundaries between SF and fantasy are often blurred, at the levels of creation, reception and marketing, but this he sees not only as 'rampantly sociopathological',[4] but 'a terrible contamination'.[5]

In the last decade this paradigm has come under increasing question (including by Andrew Milner, in his essay in this volume). Nonetheless, this broadly 'Suvinian' approach remains dominant. In 2000, Suvin himself re-examined the genres and revised his earlier 'blanket rejection' of fantasy to consider it a worthy object of analysis, in an important but frustrating essay, by turns brilliantly perspicacious and abruptly theoretically foreclosed.[6] Admirable fantasy is now acknowledged as at least a possibility, though one less likely than similarly laudable SF – but it is telling that, even here, Suvin's grudging open-mindedness is not predicated on any erosion of the proposed firewall between fantasy and SF,[7] but is an *unfortunate necessity*: the quantitative explosion of fantasy (an expression of social traumas) and ebbing of SF is a situation the critic 'may to a large extent rightly dislike'[8] but is one with which it is her intellectual responsibility to engage.

Arguably the two most important recent Marxist works on SF, both drawing in key (if not uncritical) ways on Suvin, continue to privilege SF over a sharply distinguished fantasy. Fredric Jameson, for whom the utopian function is the fundamental unit of what radicalism SF possesses, describes fantasy, which lacks SF's 'epistemological gravity' as 'technically reactionary'.[9] According to Carl Freedman's *Critical Theory and Science Fiction*, supposedly cognition-less fantasy can offer at best 'irrationalist estrangements'.[10] (The strength of this tradition, and its ideological hold even on those critical of it, may be one reason why – with no intentionality that either editor can recall – fantasy disappeared from this volume's subtitle and the information for contributors.)

Elsewhere, I have argued that this sharp distinction is untenable.[11] Indeed, I believe that the embedded condescension and even despite towards fantasy that this paradigm has bequeathed stands as perhaps the major obstruction to theoretical progress in the field. However, given the importance of so much work indebted to the Suvinian position, as well as its extraordinary paradigmatic resilience – and in the face of all the cheerful consumption-level blurring of that SF/fantasy boundary that Milner points out – this intervention starts not from opposition, but submission. Here I accept the predicates and concomitant heuristic efficacy of the SF/fantasy distinction, and from there attempt an immanent critique.

The paradigm's lacunae and possible strategies for overcoming them arise precisely from following its own logic, through its nuancing particularly in the hands of Freedman. The conclusions to be drawn are, I hope, not so much paradoxical as – perhaps camply – dialectical. I will argue that the position's logic not only demands and offers a too-often unnoticed auto-*ideologikritik*, but ends up collapsing the supposed 'specificity' and superiority of SF derived from it. This is not so much an argument against as a sublation of this tenacious generic antithesis, an apparent rebuke to Suvinianism reached precisely through fidelity to the Suvin event.

Cognition and Possibility

It is nothing new, of course, to point out that much of the supposed science in SF is precisely that – supposed. More than that, it is often mistaken, spurious or 'pseudo'. Nor is it new to raise the question of whether and how such inaccurate predicates disqualify a work from being SF. Remarkably, the debate in fact pre-exists the genre proper, and is inherited by it, as evidenced by Jules Verne's irritation at H.G. Wells' straight-faced flim-flam as compared to his own supposed scientific accuracy, and his sense that this excluded Wells' work from a rigorous literature of extrapolation.[12] This drive to disqualify can still be seen among some of the more unforgiving readers and writers of so-called 'hard SF', for whom scientific inaccuracies can count more or less definitionally as literary flaws.

That such fallacies are embedded in countless SF texts, and that this might raise theoretical questions about the nature of a genre of 'cognitive estrangement', is clear. Caveats about the possible nonisomorphism of the one to the other notwithstanding, 'cognition' is generally conceived of in terms of, or at least intimately related to, a rigorous and rational – 'scientific' – relationship to material reality itself.[13] This lies behind the repeated classic distinction that SF's worlds are 'possible', whereas fantasy's are 'impossible' – which itself locates the *science* in science fiction.[14] But, as Adam Roberts points out, 'several of the frequently deployed "nova" of SF are things that "science" has specifically ruled out of court as literally impossible',[15] so scientific 'possibility' cannot be the grounds of 'cognition' for the post-Suvinian definition to hold.

The paradigm can, however, recover from this. '[I]t is not the "truth" of science that is important to SF', in Roberts' words, 'it is the scientific method', and it is this that is the 'cognitive logic' in 'cognitive estrangement'.[16] Recognising the lack of clarity on this point as a 'serious' problem in a paradigm to which he is rigorously committed, Carl Freedman goes further than any other writer in theorising this nuanced sense of cognition as 'cognitive logic' as being at the heart of SF. According to his reformulated Suvinianism,

> cognition proper is *not*, in the strictest terms, exactly the quality that defines science fiction. What is rather at stake is what we might term … the *cognition effect*. The crucial issue for generic discrimination is not an epistemological judgment external to the text itself on the rationality or irrationality of the latter's imaginings, but rather … the attitude *of the text itself* to the kind of estrangements being performed.[17]

This is an ingenious move, one that is simultaneously innovative and a systematisation of something *un*surprising – a certain generic common-sense that has allowed generations of readers and writers to treat, say, faster-than-light drives as science-fictional in a way that dragons are not, despite repeated assurances from the great majority of physicists that the former are no less impossible than the latter.

That is not, however, the end of the story. Despite the elegance of this solution, it raises as many problems as it solves. With his focus on the attitude of 'the text itself', Freedman laudably attempts to retain some taxonomic rigour by evading the subjectivity concomitant with theories based on reader response or authorial intent. However, strictly speaking 'the text itself', of course, has *no* attitude to the kind of estrangements it performs, nor indeed to anything else.

Taken literally, Freedman's insistence that C.S. Lewis' SF trilogy, starting with *Out of the Silent Planet* (1938), 'considers that principles it regards as cognitively valid cannot exclude events like the action fictionally portrayed from occurring within the author's actual environment'[18] makes little sense. Lewis' trilogy considers no such thing: it does nothing, in fact, but sit there. Of course that is not the end of the matter, because i) despite any such uncharitable literalism, taken in context as distinguishing the register of Lewis' work (here deemed science-fictional) from that of Tolkien (here paradigmatic of fantasy), *one knows what Freedman means*; and ii) the reason that one does so is that Lewis' trilogy does not in fact just sit there: it sits there in its having-been-written-ness, and its being-read-ness.

In other words, our fidelity to Freedman's own fidelity to Suvin necessarily, in its very focus on the text itself, involves not just a reminder of but a necessary theoretical engagement with the fact that the text does not exist in an a-sociological vacuum. Though they certainly cannot be reduced to intent or opinion, and must be considered in terms of social structure and mediation, questions of human social agency vis-à-vis and relations to the text are inevitable and central.

On this basis, the question, then, becomes, *whose* cognition effect? More pertinently, whose cognition? And whose effect?

Doing Things With Words

This reformulated approach to the specificity of SF, in terms of a written-and-read text, means considering SF not in terms of a text's relationship to its own supposed 'cognitive logic' but as *something done with language by someone to someone*.

This implication of our re-socialised conception of the shift from cognition to 'cognition effect' is again not a new insight, but has in various articulations been a common-sense understanding since at least Wells, who conceived of his task as a writer of 'fantastic stories' as being 'to help the reader to play the game properly', and to 'domesticate the impossible hypothesis' with 'some plausible assumption'.[19]

It was the potential incommensurability of the text's 'cognition' and reality that led Freedman to his formulation of the cognition effect. However, Wells sees his job not as *convincing* anyone of a spurious claim but of helping *'domesticate' an impossibility*: this cheerful and perspicacious admission makes clear that within these texts, not only the 'cognition' but the 'cognition effect' too is *radically contingent* to any actually accurate facticity. Of course that effect *may* be derived from empirical reality and rigorous and rational science: but it is vital to insist, as Wells does, on the potentially absolute discontinuity between the two, on the fact that the effect is the result of a strategy, or a *game*, played by writer and, often, reader, based not on reality-claims but plausibility-claims that hold purely within the text.

Descriptively, this is perfectly obvious, and regularly noted; but its radical implications for the theory of the cognition effect have not been sufficiently remarked. It forces the theorist away from the comforting implication that the 'attitude of the text itself', to put it in Freedman's terms, is necessarily one of good faith. It is perhaps an implicit hankering for such clear-cut cases that lies behind the common focus in the literature on texts predicated on science that is seemingly accurate but that has later been disproved, and behind a certain conceptual privileging of that category over, or its elision with, SF built instead on deliberate falsehoods.

Roberts, for example, considers those '[m]any early SF novels [that] followed the scientific thinking of the day' to argue that the later overturning of those nostrums 'does not invalidate these novels because the point about the science in SF is not "truth" but the entry into a particular material and often rational discourse'.[20] Even if one agrees, it is a somewhat weak argument that SF is not predicated on scientific 'truth' that starts with those texts that *were* predicated on what was held to be true. Scientific accuracy as a conceptual foundation of SF here sneaks back in even as it is dismissed.

Freedman explicitly insists that 'overwhelmingly' SF *is* a 'genuinely cognitive literature',[21] but it is telling that, even discussing the harder cases where it appears not so to be, he stacks the deck. For example, he recalls that Isaac Asimov humorously refused to change his story 'The Dying Night' (1956), which was predicated on 'common astronomical wisdom at the time of the story's composition' that was later disproved, to 'suit the "whims" of astronomers'.[22] Freedman rightly insists that this in no way undermines the cognition effect – indeed, that the astronomical facts had 'nothing to do' with it.[23] However, it is rather startling that his admission of the necessity of the disaggregation of cognition and cognition effect comes in a discussion of a text for which the cognition effect *was* in fact a corollary of actual cognition – just one that was later revised as erroneous.

The case of SF constructed on 'some plausible assumption' that is *always known* by the writer (and very possibly the reader) to be untrue is, contrary to Freedman's assertion, extremely common. Indeed, to Wells it is foundational to the genre. It is also far more theoretically troublesome. The theorist might simply dismiss such work from the genre, but not only would that delineate an extraordinarily depleted field (no Wells!), but, having done so, it would reduce theory to the job of a mere border guard. Mindful that there are always taxonomic grey areas, it seems sensible, in constructing a theory of SF, to have it be a theory of actually-existing SF, rather than of some tautologous ideal-type.

Following Wells, the question then arises: If cognition and the cognition effect are sometimes radically discontinuous, then what is the source of that cognition effect? Definitionally, it is not cognitive logic. One must insist on this: *pace* Freedman, even if, in a particular case, a particular set of cognition-effect-producing claims *are* 'cognitive' and accurate, the cognition effect *tout court* is a category existentially necessary precisely because it is *not* reducible to a logic derived from cognition. What is more, the cognition effect is a category shared across the spectrum of SF, from works based on the scientifically correct, through those based on the believed-but-mistaken, to those based on the wildly spurious. The effect's fundamental driver cannot be cognitive logic itself.

Having split the cognition effect from cognition and its logic, we must add to the formulation of SF as something done with language by someone(s) to someone(s) the question *how*? Again, the answer has been known for decades.

Wells, in his rather scandalous defence of invented science, has it that the writer 'must trick [the reader] into an unwary concession ... and get on with his story while the illusion holds'.[24] The method, then, is a *trickery* effected by the author – or, if it is preferred, author-function – through the text. In SF *sensu stricto*, an *apparently* cognitively logical and rigorous 'scientific' register is invaluable to this; but, crucially, that register is *already mediated* and is not the source of the cognition effect.

As Gwyneth Jones points out, for SF, what is necessary is not accuracy but 'appearance of command over the *language* of science'.[25] The emphasis within her formulation, however, best lies elsewhere: SF relies above all not on the language of science, nor on the command of that language, but on the *appearance* of that command.

The cognition effect is a *persuasion*. Whatever tools are used for that persuasion (which may or may not include actually-cognitively-logical claims), the effect, by the testimony of SF writers for generations and by the logic of the very theorists for whom cognition is key, is a function of (textual) *charismatic authority*. The reader surrenders to the cognition effect to the extent that he or she surrenders to the authority of the text and its author function.

This persuasion, even though 'trickery', is doubtless generally ludic on both sides. Indeed, an awareness of that game-like nature of the interaction can take us a step beyond even a new clarity as to how 'pseudo-science' known to be such by the *author* can still be SF in a meaningful fashion: now, by focusing on consensual authority, we can see how the cognition effect can inhere where the reader, too, knows that the 'cognitive' claims made are specious.

Nor is this a marginal concern for SF. Wells' is not a theory of SF as hoodwinking: it is extremely unlikely that many of his readers would ever have been convinced of the possibility of gravity-repellent cavorite,[26] but because of the particular kind of authority in the text, a cognition effect is created even though neither writer nor reader finds cognitive logic in the text's claims. Instead, they *read/write as if they do.*

This understanding makes sense also of how the presence of the even more preposterous pseudo-science of, say, 1950s B-movie SF does not disqualify a text from membership of the SF genre-cluster. Indeed, there is nothing so specious that a reader may not be persuaded to surrender to it as-if cognitively – which, though it is not the same as believing it, pretends that it is.

There is an experienced bundle of understandings about what it is that makes some texts SF rather than fantasy – a generic folk-understanding. Given that how that specificity is perceived is part of whatever quiddity that specificity has, any attempt to theorise actually-existing SF has to take those understandings seriously. There is little doubt that the Freedman/Suvin theory is accurate in asserting that, for that folk-understanding of SF-not-fantasy, SF-ness is a function of the cognition effect – an embedded relation in the text between cognition and the reality function. However, any claim that the effect is a function of embedded cognitive rational rigour is untrue. To the extent that the cognition effect is about cognition, it is precisely *about* it, *about* a putatively logical way of thinking, not a function of it. And inasmuch as the experienced effect is in fact a function of authority, the 'cognition effect', in deriving supposed cognitive logic from external authority, is not only fundamentally a-rational but also intensely ideological.

The Degradation of Science

The cognition effect – a term which grows more sinister the more the phenomenon is critically interrogated – surrenders the terrain of supposed conceptual logic and rigour to the whims and diktats of a cadre of 'expert' author-functions. This is a translation into meta-literary and aggrandising terms of the very layer of technocrats often envisaged in SF and its cultures as society's best hope. This fond fantasy of a middlebrow–utopian bureaucracy – what Wells called Samurai – is a vaguely Fabian sociological articulation of the traditional SF hero, the *engineer*,[27] deploying narrowly (and ideologically) conceived instrumental rationality, often in the form of applied science, to the bettering of the world. In light of this, and of the uncomfortably patrician and anti-democratic class politics of which this tendency was and is an expression, Suvin's passing claim that the fictional 'novum' operates by 'hegemony'[28] is invested with rather unhappy connotations.

There is no call to be po-faced about this: ideological this 'suspension of disbelief' may be, but as a literary-level 'consensual' surrender, it is inextricable from enjoyment of the genre, and strictly in and of itself at the level of form (i.e. irrespective of the concrete ideologies of specific texts) inherent genocidal apology or the maintenance of capitalism it is not. Nor, however, is it innocent – not even of all relation to those most extreme articulations of modern barbarity.[29]

As this immanent *ideologikritik* of SF and of the Suvinian paradigm – derived, to reiterate, not in opposition but fidelity to that paradigm – reminds us, these structuring levels of textual ideology at the level of SF-as-form (which go beyond those specific to a text's content) include this surrender of cognition to authority. There is also, and derived from this, the level of the ideology of the theory: the Suvinian–Freedmanite paradigm itself.

Even before any dialectical negation of the so-called 'cognitive logic' central to the model, the constant and explicit privileging of SF over fantasy is based on the supposedly self-evident grounds of that 'cognitive logic'. Here, a peculiar nostalgia is clear. As the link to the Edisonian engineer above is intended to illustrate, this supposed logic is repeatedly, if not explicitly, related to a strangely prelapsarian, often instrumentalised, science and bureaucratic rationality. To the extent that SF claims to be based on 'science', and indeed on what is deemed 'rationality', it is based on capitalist modernity's ideologically projected self-justification: not some abstract/ideal 'science', but capitalist science's bullshit about itself. This is not, of course, to argue in favour of some (perhaps lumpen-postmodernist) irrationalism, but that the 'rationalism' that capitalism has traditionally had on offer is highly partial and ideological – 'could not', as Suvin himself has put it, 'but give reason a bad name'.[30] The desire is for a richer, socially embedded rationality, which would not be a degraded embarrassment.

In the aftermaths of two world wars and a holocaust which saw 'hard' *and* social science harnessed to mass industrial slaughter – an epoch which unsurprisingly shattered the bourgeois reformist daydreams of ineluctable progress-through-rationality – and following the aesthetic upheavals of the radical modernisms (including their pulp-fantastic wings) that were born out of a repudiation of that species of capitalist–comprador rationalism that was all that had been officially on offer, one might expect Marxist theory, which has for several generations drawn out these connections, to exhibit a certain caution about claims of the self-evident progressiveness of self-styled rationalism. One might consider, with apologies for the thickets of scare-quotes to stress the point, that the model of a 'scientific rationality' that is 'progressive' in opposition to 'reactionary' 'irrationalism' is, generously, roughly nine decades out of date – a bad joke after World War I, let alone after the death camps. Yet this model is at the heart of the *grundnorm* of mainstream Marxist theory of SF. Astonishingly, as I have argued, it has been so in full knowledge that the claims about 'cognitive logic' *are specious*, as when Jameson explicitly privileges SF utopias over 'generic fantasy' on the grounds of the gravity granted by the former's 'scientific *pretensions*'.[31]

In fact, this simultaneous adoption by the genre's writers, readers and theorists of SF's self-declared 'rationalist' agenda, and their clear-sightedness about the spuriousness of its predicates, is an important reminder of the fact that the purchase of ideology, in all spheres, is dependent on the persuasive power not of its specific and explicit truth-claims, but of the ideological project as a self-sustaining totality. The lies of ideology, in other words, do not necessarily do their job by being believed, but by hegemonising a conceptual agenda irrespective of whether they are believed.[32]

In ideology, charisma and authority become autotelic – that is their point. In mediated microcosm, this is how SF can easily and with some justification end up being defined as that which is written by an SF writer.

Specificity *Contra* Specificity

This immanent reformulation should act to puncture the science-fictional scorn at fantasy, and the still-prevalent sense among Marxist SF critics that fantasy, the projected Other of a supposedly rationalist SF, is intrinsically, in its literary form, 'theoretically illegitimate'.[33] If SF itself is *at the level of form* ideology, the contrast no longer has teeth.

This is not, it should but perhaps does not go without saying, to suggest a simple inversion of the traditional Marxist hierarchy of SF and fantasy. It might, for example, be tempting and excitingly flattering to analogise from the model above that SF operates as a corralling of the utopian spirit by a secular literary priesthood, whereas fantasy – for which no such ideological and constraining cognition effect inheres, and through which therefore the reader experiences an unmediated relation to the radical estrangement – mimics the radical democratisation of vision effected by ecstatic sects, for which the repudiation of a priestly caste was an emancipatory act.

It might be tempting, but it would be utterly ridiculous. For one thing, as certain wings of fantastic fiction (especially classic 'weird fiction') illustrate well, whatever the radicalism of actual ecstatic sects in their revolutionary periods, the structuring of literature around an unmediated numinous is often not merely reactionary but crypto- or even openly fascist.[34]

The idea that, because SF is deep-structured by an ideological conception of the world, fantasy is less so, is foolish. The claim that fantasy is in some systematic way resistant to ideology or rebellious against authority is, as anyone who knows the genre can attest, laugh-out-loud funny.

Apart from anything else, it is of course not in fact the case that, for fantasy, the estrangement, radical or otherwise, is unconstrained. In fact, precisely what distinguishes genre fantasy from the more freeform alienation of, say, surrealism and other avant-gardes is that the genre's integration of that alienation from reality with pulp exigency leads to its control and 'domestication' by the logic of *narrative*. This narrative logic, while perhaps in various ways enabling, and endlessly celebrated in mainstream culture and even by radical critics,[35] is also without question both constraining and ideological. Considered thus, the ideology of the cognition effect is but one particular organising principle behind that structurating temporo-moral ideology of narrative itself, which demands further critical investigation.

Fantasy, then, in its form as well as its many contents, is no less an ideological product than SF is. However, nor is it more so.

In recent years there has been a creeping Marxist *rapprochement* with fantasy, and concomitant new approaches to the sub-genre's specifics.[36] It is beyond the remit of this intervention to examine these, or indeed fantasy itself, in any detail. Two things, however, are clear.

One is that, at the sociological level of production and consumption, the distinction between SF and fantasy continues to be pertinent, and that there are specificities to the fantastic, as well as to the science-fictional, side of the dyad (the deployment of magic, most obviously), which theory would do well to investigate further. It is perfectly plausible, then, that SF and fantasy might still sometimes be usefully distinguished: but if so, it is not on the basis of cognition, nor of some fundamental epistemological firewall, but as different ideological iterations of the 'estrangement' that, even in high Suvinianism, both sub-genres share.

The specifics of that estrangement need unpicking. One potential pitfall of the focus among Marxists on the sub-sub-genre of utopian fiction, the sense that the fundamental *differentia specifica* of fantastic fiction, and certainly what gives it any political teeth, is a utopia-function (which can easily, of course, encompass dystopias), is an implicit, sometimes explicit, claim that non-utopian SF and fantasy are in some way at best *attenuated utopias*. But we should not be seduced by the long and honourable tradition of left utopias and utopian studies into foreclosing the reverse possibility (which better serves the project of theorising *actually-existing* SF and fantasy, rather than ring-fencing segments of the fields): that utopias (including dystopias) are, rather, specific articulations of *alterity*, and that it is of that that SF/fantasy is the literature. In this model, the atom of SF's *and* fantasy's estrangement, in other words, is their unreality function, of which utopia is but one – if highly important – form.

Taking alterity as a starting point might allow us to trace structural relations between fantastic genres and the anti-realist avant-garde. It might also allow a revisiting with critical rigour of a traditional – and traditionally denigrated as woolly and anti-theoretical – notion of the 'sense of wonder', as intrinsic to the field.[37]

Of course this is highly tentative. Whatever we deem the irreducible unit of fantastic estrangement to be, and wherever that might lead us theoretically, all of this underlines a second point. At the same sociological level at which SF and fantasy continue to be distinguished, the boundaries between them also – if anything at an accelerating pace – continue to erode. Where that has hitherto been seen as pathological in SF theory, it is to be hoped that, by undermining the supposedly radical distinction between the two on the basis of cognition, that erosion can now be seen as perfectly legitimate.

One could go further. It might be claimed that the continual efforts to parcel out a separate realm of estranging fiction corralled by a nostalgic, neo-Fabian and ideological conception of legitimate and illegitimate modes of cognition has been a stunting factor in the development of a radical, aesthetically estranging and narratologically rigorous literature of literalised metaphor and alterity.

Of course that might be hogwash. Or, trivially and most likely, both the boundaries and their breaching might continue both to enable and constrain creativity and innovation in fantastic fiction. At the very least, however, it is to be hoped that the theoretical focus might shift from the conventional but epiphenomenal distinctions that have long been deemed definitional to the field, to the fundamental alterity-as-estrangement shared *across* the field: what it does; how it does it; and what we might do with it. For that, Marxist theory needs to continue its thaw towards fantasy

It may be too early to effect that thaw by the insistence on a shared generic substance with SF. Even if, as I hold, this claim is accurate, it is perhaps strategically inadequate. Here I have attempted to undermine the supposed specificity of SF by respecting and interrogating that specificity. A mirror-image operation might work, too. To blur the boundaries further, it might be efficacious to respect the unstable specifics – but specifics nonetheless – of that contingently bundled sub-genre, 'fantasy'. Precisely to continue the project of theorising a conjoined SF and fantasy, in other words, SF, with its tendency to hegemonise the conversation, might have to be temporarily excluded.

Red Planets we have. We should not neglect the red dragons.

Notes

1. Darko Suvin, *Metamorphoses of Science Fiction: On the Poetics and History of a Literary Genre* (New Haven: Yale University Press, 1979), p. 8.
2. Ibid., p. 9.
3. Ibid., p. 69.
4. Ibid., p. 9.
5. Horst Pukallus, 'An Interview with Darko Suvin', *Science Fiction Studies* 18: 2 (1991), available at www.depauw.edu/sfs/interviews/ suvin54.htm (accessed 17 July 2008).
6. Darko Suvin, 'Considering the Sense of "Fantasy" or "Fantastic Fiction": An Effusion', *Extrapolation* 41: 3 (2000), p. 211. This fascinating, fecund and infuriating constellation of insights and questionable extrapolations deserves an extended and dedicated engagement that is beyond my scope here.
7. The two are still constitutively opposed, and there are still 'more obstacles to liberating cognition' in fantasy (Suvin, 'Considering the Sense of "Fantasy"', p. 211).
8. Suvin, 'Considering the Sense of "Fantasy"', p. 210.
9. Fredric Jameson, *Archaeologies of the Future: The Desire Called Utopia and Other Science Fictions* (London: Verso, 2006), pp. 57, 60. Christopher Kendrick (personal communication) points out that 'though Jameson does endorse the Suvin thesis, his actual position on the fantasy question is different from Suvin's. Jameson basically casts fantasy as backward in relation to SF because it "goes back to" romance, and so tends to "believe in" good and evil, or in other words to be ethical; SF, on the other hand, he associates with a "mode

of production aesthetic", which is presumably economic–political rather than ethical in basic orientation.' While Jameson's position is closely related to Suvin's, Kendrick speculates that, to the extent that it is to be *equated* with it, it is perhaps 'as an attempt to rationalise what in Suvin tends to appear as prejudice'. This extremely intriguing formulation demands further investigation.

10. Carl Freedman, *Critical Theory and Science Fiction* (Hanover: Wesleyan University Press, 2000), p. 43.

11. For example, John Newsinger, 'Fantasy and Revolution: An Interview with China Miéville', *International Socialism* 88 (2000), available at www.marxists.de/culture/sci-fi/newsinger.htm.

12. See China Miéville, 'Introduction' to H.G. Wells, *First Men in the Moon* (London: Penguin, 2005).

13. Quite how evasive a term 'cognition' is is something few of its deployers engage with sufficiently. In his reconsideration of fantasy, Suvin states that 'cognition is much richer than, and in some ways even opposed to, scientific rationalism' (Suvin, 'Considering', p. 239). However, this suggestive qualification is not fleshed out, the model(s) of 'cognition' rather nebulously emerging as a function of whether it 'include[s] people' rather than being dominated by abstractions (p. 239), is narratively coherent with 'richness of figures' (p. 240) and is 'pleasantly useful' (p. 211). Alongside these intriguing fragments of an alternative theory of (what is increasingly unhelpful to term) cognition, however, sits the traditional underlying claim that 'the epistemology of SF can appeal to the cognitive universalism of natural and/or social laws' as opposed to the 'occultism, whimsy or magic' models of fantasy (p. 238). This puts Suvin back in accord with his earlier self, for whom SF takes a fictional hypothesis 'and develops it with extrapolating and totalizing "scientific" rigor' (Darko Suvin, 'On the Poetics of the Science Fiction Genre', *College English* 34: 3 (1972), p. 374).

14. See for example Suvin's own mention of the fairytale as escaping the empirical world 'into a closed collateral world indifferent toward cognitive possibilities' as part of his very definition of 'cognition', and his argument that '[a]nything is possible in a folktale, because a folktale is manifestly impossible' (*Metamorphoses*, pp. 6–8). Robert Conquest goes so far as to suggest that science fiction is not the best name for the field, and that '"Possibility Fiction" might have been better' (Robert Conquest, 'Science Fiction and Literature', *The Critical Quarterly* V: iv (1963), p. 358).

15. Adam Roberts, *Science Fiction* (London: Routledge, 2000), p. 8.

16. Ibid., p. 10.

17. Freedman, *Critical Theory*, p. 18; emphases in original.

18. Ibid., p. 18.
19. Cited in Miéville, 'Introduction', p. xvii.
20. Roberts, *Science Fiction*, p. 9.
21. Freedman, *Critical Theory*, p. 19.
22. Ibid., p. 18.
23. Ibid., p. 18.
24. Cited in Miéville, 'Introduction', p. xvii.
25. Gwyneth Jones, *Deconstructing the Starships: Science, Fiction and Reality* (Liverpool: Liverpool University Press, 1999), p. 16; emphasis in original.
26. Indeed, that they would not is, according to Lewis, 'a merit not a defect', central to the text's success. C.S Lewis, 'On Science Fiction', in *Of Other Worlds: Essays and Stories* (London: Harcourt, 1967), p. 64.
27. See Roger Luckhurst, *Science Fiction* (Cambridge: Polity, 2005).
28. Suvin, *Metamorphoses*, p. 63.
29. See John Rieder, *Colonialism and the Emergence of Science Fiction* (Middletown: Wesleyan University Press, 2008).
30. Suvin, 'Considering the Sense of "Fantasy"', p. 214. This extended critique of 'impoverished pseudo-rationality' is one of the best sections of Suvin's 'effusion', though one of which the full implications are not fully fleshed out.
31. Jameson, *Archaeologies*, p. 57; my emphasis.
32. I have argued this in 'The Lies that aren't Meant to Deceive Us', available at www.socialistreview.org.uk/article.php?articlenumber=9870.
33. Freedman, *Critical Theory*, p. 17.
34. This argument is developed in China Miéville, 'Weird Fiction', in Mark Bould, Andrew M. Butler, Adam Roberts and Sherryl Vint, eds, *The Routledge Companion to Science Fiction* (London: Routledge, 2009).
35. According to Suvin, 'storytelling is a privileged cognitive method' and '[i]n my pantheon, narrative ... is one of the Supreme Goods' ('Considering the Sense of "Fantasy"', p. 233).
36. For the most important recent revisionist Marxist position, see Mark Bould, 'The Dreadful Credibility of Absurd Things: A Tendency in Fantasy Theory', *Historical Materialism* 10: 4 (2002), pp. 51–88.
37. The most productive avenues for research on this basis are probably those that relate the 'sensawunna' (as it has been derisively rendered) via the conceptual shift occasioned by its problematic of discordant *scale*, as John Clute has argued, to the tradition of the sublime (and perhaps, and perhaps concomitantly, with traditions of – often religious – ecstatic and visionary writing). Scale is an invaluable optic, predicated as it is on the uneasy familiarity of supposed

radical strangeness, rather than any truly fundamental break with any known. This is a topological translation of something I would consider key to the 'wonder' in the 'sense of wonder': precisely the necessary *failure* of alterity, the inevitable stains and traces of the everyday in whatever can be thought from within it, including its estranged/estranging other. Without such guilty stains, there could be no recognition or reception – true alterity would be inconceivable, thus imperceptible. We gasp not just at the strangeness but at the misplaced familiar within it. Class analysis here might include, among other projects: conceiving the (always-already failing) fantastic as a combined and uneven development of a conceived totality as reality and its rebuke; articulating the sublime and numinous as a misspoken emancipatory telos; a Benjaminian/Beckettian attempt to fail better and better at thinking an unthinkable.

APPENDICES

Left SF: Selected and Annotated, If Not Always Exactly *Recommended*, Works
Mark Bould

These lists of recommended reading and viewing take a deliberately broad view of what constitutes left SF. Not all of the authors and directors listed below would call themselves leftists, and some works are not so much leftist as of interest to leftists. None are completely unproblematic and some are not very good at all.

1. Reading

Edward Abbey, *The Monkey Wrench Gang* (1975). Eco-saboteurs take on colluding business and government. Sequel: *Hayduke Lives!* (1990). See also *Good Times* (1980).

Abe Kobo, *Inter Ice Age 4* (1959). The most overtly science-fictional of Abe's absurdist explorations of contemporary alienation. See also *Woman in the Dunes* (1962), *The Face of Another* (1964), *The Ruined Map* (1967), *The Box Man* (1973), *The Ark Sakura* (1984), *Beyond the Curve* (1991), *The Kangaroo Notebook* (1991).

Chingiz Aitmatov, *The Day Lasts Longer than a Hundred Years* (1980). Surprisingly uncensored mediation of Central Asian tradition, Soviet modernity and the possibilities presented by an alien world.

Brian Aldiss, *HARM* (2007). A British muslim author, imprisoned and tortured for making a joke, hallucinates another – very resonant – world.

Benjamin Appel, *The Funhouse* (1959). Satire on commodity-hedonism and nuclear anxiety.

Eleanor Arnason, *A Woman of the Iron People* (1991). Post-revolutionary humans and humanoid aliens face the problems of interspecies communication and colonial encounter. See also *To the Resurrection Station* (1986), *Ring of Swords* (1993), *Ordinary People* (2005).

Brian Attebery and Ursula K. Le Guin, eds, *The Norton Book of Science Fiction* (1994). Notoriously 'unrepresentative' anthology of North American literary and feminist SF from 1960 to 1990.

Margaret Atwood, *The Handmaid's Tale* (1985). Fundamentalist dystopia reduces women to their reproductive function. See also *The Blind Assassin* (2000), *Oryx and Crake* (2003).

Wilhelmina Baird, *Crashcourse* (1993). Self-reflexive post-feminist cyberpunk. Sequels: *Clipjoint* (1994), *Psykosis* (1995).

J.G. Ballard, *Crash* (1973). Everything you need to know about sex, technology and commodity fetishism. See also *The Atrocity Exhibition* (1970).

Iain M. Banks, *Consider Phlebas* (1987). Vivid space opera set in a (possibly) utopian, post-scarcity future. Sequels: *The Player of Games* (1988), *The Use of Weapons* (1990), *Excession* (1996), *Inversions* (1998), *Look to Windward* (2000), *Matter* (2008).

Max Barry, *Jennifer Government* (2003). Knockabout shenanigans in the consolidated world market.

John Barth, *Giles Goat-Boy* (1966). The Cold War as allegorical campus novel.

John Calvin Batchelor, *The Birth of the People's Republic of Antarctica* (1983). A berserker on a ship of fools amid the fleet of the damned and the wretched of the earth.

Robert Bateman, *When the Whites Went* (1963). A plague eradicates all non-black people.

Barry Beckham, *Runner Mack* (1972). Fabular account of an attempted black revolution.

Andrea L. Bell and Yolanda Molina Gavilán, eds, *Cosmos Latinos: An Anthology of Science Fiction from Latin America and Spain* (2003). Technoscientific empire experienced from the other side.

Edward Bellamy, *Looking Backward, 2000–1887* (1888). Extremely popular, not-exactly socialist utopia that prompted the eruption of late-nineteenth century utopias. Sequel: *Equality* (1897).

Margaret Bennett, *The Long Way Back* (1954). Representatives of post-holocaust Africa visit primitive Britain.

J.D. Beresford, *Revolution: A Story of the Near Future in England* (1921). Curiously muted account of a British socialist revolution. See also *Goslings* (1913), 'What Dreams May Come...' (1941), *A Common Enemy* (1942), *The Riddle of the Tower* (1944).

Adolfo Bioy Casares, *The Invention of Morel* (1940). Exploring the psychosexual power of the image in the age of mechanical reproduction. See also *Asleep in the Sun* (1973).

Terry Bisson, *Fire on the Mountain* (1988). John Brown and Harriet Tubman's *successful* raid on Harper's Ferry leads to a global socialist utopia.

Michael Blumlein, *The Movement of Mountains* (1987). A doctor recognises the humanity of a lab-made slave species and joins them in revolution. See also *The Brains of Rats* (1990).

Alexander Bogdanov, *The Red Star* (1908, 1913). The first Bolshevik utopia, featuring Martian technocracy and free love.

Leigh Brackett, *The Long Tomorrow* (1955). Civil Rights-era post-apocalyptic critique of religious intolerance and instrumentalist rationality.

Ray Bradbury, *Fahrenheit 451* (1953). Dyspeptic, nostalgic satire on commodity culture.

Gerd Brantenberg, *Egalia's Daughters* (1977). In the land of the wim, masculist menwim raise consciousness among housebounds, burn their pehoes and organise gender revolution.

Max Brooks, *World War Z: An Oral History of the Zombie War* (2006). The Multitude as apocalyptic globalised zombie horde.

Rosel George Brown, *Sibyl Sue Blue* (1968). Interstellar adventure featuring a sexy, kick-ass … middle-aged single mother. Sequel: *The Waters of Centaurus* (1970).

John Brunner, *The Sheep Look Up* (1972). An overpopulated world drowning in its own pollution. See also *Stand on Zanzibar* (1968), *The Jagged Orbit* (1969), *Total Eclipse* (1974), *The Shockwave Rider* (1975).

Mikhail Bulgakov, *Heart of a Dog* (1925). Satire on NEP-era USSR. See also 'Diaboliad' (1925).

Edward Bulwer Lytton, *The Coming Race* (1871). Hysterical vision of the rising proletariat.

Katherine Burdekin, *Swastika Night* (1937). Dystopia set 500 years after Hitler's victory. See also *The Rebel Passion* (1929), *The End of this Day's Business* (1990).

Octavia Butler, *Kindred* (1979). African-American woman pulled backwards in time to the antebellum plantation on which her ancestors slaved. See also *Patternmaster* (1976), *Dawn* (1987), *The Parable of the Sower* (1993) and their sequels.

Eugene Byrne, *ThiGMOO* (1999). Virtual constructs of fictional characters develop (class-)consciousness and start a revolution. See also *Back in the USSA* (1997), co-written with Kim Newman.

Pat Cadigan, *Synners* (1989). Brings a richer sense of human and social complexity to cyberpunk, mapping the relationships between street subcultures and corporate systems. See also *Fools* (1992).

Karen Cadora, *Stardust Bound* (1994). Against the wishes of the post-apocalyptic state, women rebuild the science of astronomy.

Ernest Callenbach, *Ecotopia: The Notebooks and Reports of William Weston* (1975). West Coast ecological utopia. Sequel: *Ecotopia Emerging* (1981).

V.F. Calverton, *The Man Inside: Being the Record of the Strange Adventures of Allen Steele among the Xulus* (1936). Anti-fascist, anti-Stalinist, prematurely Althusserian genius experiments on animals and humans to prepare the way for post-socialist posthumanity.

Karel Čapek, *War with the Newts* (1936). Hilarious, bitter fantasia, dripping with irony, about colonial/proletarian development and insurrection.

Angela Carter, *The Passion of New Eve* (1977). Delirious, profane encounters in a US transformed by race and gender wars. See also *Heroes and Villains* (1969), *The Infernal Desire Machines of Doctor Hoffman* (1972), *Nights at the Circus* (1984).

Margaret Cavendish, *The Blazing World* (1668). Royalist, visionary–reactionary – but feminist – utopia.

Philip George Chadwick, *The Death Guard* (1939). Apocalyptic anti-war story featuring a species of artificially created brute warriors.

Suzy McKee Charnas, *Walk to the End of the World* (1974). Post-apocalyptic women rebel in the cracks of institutionalised misogyny and gender essentialism. Sequels: *Motherlines* (1978), *The Furies* (1994), *The Conqueror's Child* (1999).

Flynn Connolly, *The Rising of the Moon* (1993). In the twenty-first century, a group of feminists lead a revolution against Catholic tyranny.

Edwin Corley, *Siege* (1969). Black revolutionaries seize Manhattan.

György Dalos, *1985* (1983). Post-war Hungarian history reworked as Orwell sequel.

Dennis Danvers, *The Fourth World* (2000). Cyberpunk meets Zapatismo and finds another world *is* possible. See also *The Watch* (2002).

Camilla Decarnin, Eric Garber and Lyn Paleo, eds, *Worlds Apart: An Anthology of Lesbian and Gay Science Fiction and Fantasy* (1986). Queer anthology.

Allan de Graeff, ed., *Human and Other Beings* (1963). Collection of mid-century anti-racist US magazine SF (1949–61).

Samuel Delany, *Stars in My Pockets Like Grains of Sand* (1984). Sprawling space opera/planetary romance/neo-slave narrative, set in a radically decentred Galactic civilisation modelled on Derrida's notion of *différance*. See also *Babel-17* (1966), *The Einstein Intersection* (1967), *Nova* (1968), *Dhalgren* (1975), *Triton: An Ambiguous Heterotopia* (1976).

Don DeLillo, *White Noise* (1985). Deadpan black comedy about the society of the spectacle.

Philip K. Dick, *A Scanner Darkly* (1977). Atypical yet quintessential Dick novel about commodification and its destruction of communities and individuals. See also *The Man in the High Castle* (1962), *Martian Time-Slip* (1962), *The Three Stigmata of Palmer Eldritch* (1965), *Do Androids Dream of Electric Sheep?* (1968), *Ubik* (1969) and five-volume collected short stories.

Thomas Disch, *334* (1972). Everyday life in a twenty-first century not much better, not much worse than our own. See also *The Genocides* (1965), *Camp Concentration* (1968), *Getting into Death* (1973), *On Wings of Song* (1979). Disch edited the ecological anthology *The Ruins of Earth* (1973) and *The New Improved Sun: An Anthology of Utopian Science Fiction* (1975).

Esmé Dodderidge, *The New Gulliver or, The Adventures of Lemuel Gulliver Jr in Capovolta* (1979). Gulliver's descendant in a feminist utopia.

Ignatius Donnelly, *Caesar's Column* (1890). Inequality and oppression escalate into war. See also *Doctor Huguet* (1891), *The Golden Bottle* (1892).

Candas Jane Dorsey, *Learning About Machine Sex and Other Stories* (1988). Title story ridicules cyberpunk's inherent phallocentrism.

W.E.B. Du Bois, *Dark Princess: A Romance* (1928). Messianic Hegelian world-historical African-American joins the Great Central Committee of Yellow, Brown and Black's global revolution.

L. Timmel Duchamp, *Alanya to Alanya* (2005). Aliens and feminists intervene to save the Earth. Sequels: *Renegade* (2006), *Tsunami* (2007), *Blood in the Fruit* (2008), *Stretto* (2008). See also *Love's Body, Dancing in Time* (2004), *The Red Rose Rages (Bleeding)* (2005).

Gordon Eklund, *All Times Possible* (1974). Hopeful, despairing alternative history of an American workers' state.

M. Barnard Eldershaw (Marjorie Barnard and Flora Eldershaw), *Tomorrow and Tomorrow and Tomorrow* (1947; censored text restored, 1983). Naturalistic account of Australian life, from the 1920s until an alternative ending of World War II, written by a future socialist utopian.

Suzette Haden Elgin, *Native Tongue* (1984). Reduced to childlike wards of their menfolk, women develop a secret language to express their perception of, and change, the world. Sequels: *The Judas Rose* (1987), *Earthsong* (1993).

Ralph Ellison, *Invisible Man* (1952). Classic afrofuturist account of phantasmagoric, apocalyptic modernity and futures yet unborn.

Roger Elwood and Virginia Kidd, eds, *Saving Worlds* (1973). Ecological SF anthology.

David Ely, *A Journal of the Flood Year* (1992). The forced proletarianisation of a diligent bureaucrat.

Carol Emshwiller, *Carmen Dog* (1988). Animals transform into human women, and vice versa, challenging masculinist reason and rationality. See also *The Mount* (2002).

Zöe Fairbairns, *Benefits* (1979). Follows the ebb and flow of feminist resistance as the backlash state introduces increasingly draconian 'benevolent' measures.

Russell B. Farr and Nick Evans, eds, *The Workers' Paradise* (2008). Stories about the future of work, collected in protest against Australian anti-worker legislation. Dedicated to 144 union activists murdered worldwide in 2006.

Claude Farrère, *Useless Hands* (1920). Worker's resistance to exploitation and mechanisation ends in a defeat which (unintentionally) indicts capitalist brutality.

Minister Faust, *The Coyote Kings of the Space-Age Bachelor Pad* (2004). African-Canadian satire about life in the margins. See also *From the Notebooks of Dr Brain* (2007).

Eric Flint, *1812: The Rivers of War* (2005). Alternate history, resulting in the foundation of the Native American Confederacy of Arkansas by long-time left activist and Socialist Workers Party member – an unlikely blend of Modes-of-Production Trotskyism with militarist SF. Sequel: *1824: The Arkansas War* (2006). See also *1632* (2000; numerous ongoing sequels).

Caroline Forbes, ed., *The Needle on Full: Lesbian Feminist Science Fiction* (1985). Lesbian–feminist SF anthology.

Katherine V. Forrest, *Daughters of the Coral Dawn* (1984). Blithely audacious comedy of interstellar colonisation and lesbian separatism. Sequels: *Daughters of an Amber Noon* (2002), *Daughters of an Emerald Dusk* (2005).

Karen Joy Fowler, *Sarah Canary* (1991). In the American West, a mysterious woman, who might be an alien, finds unlikely companions.

Anatole France, *The White Stone* (1905). *Conte philosophique* excoriating the barbarism of colonialism and envisioning a collectivist future. See also *Penguin Isand* (1908), *The Revolt of the Angels* (1914).

Sally Miller Gearheart, *The Wanderground: Stories of the Hill Women* (1980). Lesbian–feminist utopia set after Nature has restricted men to the cities.

Amitav Ghosh, *The Calcutta Chromosome* (1996). Postcolonial SF about the limits of western science.

William Gibson, *Pattern Recognition* (2003). Non-SF SF novel mapping the commodity-image. Sequel: *Spook Country* (2007). See also *Neuromancer* (1984), *Count Zero* (1986), *Mona Lisa Overdrive*

(1988), *Virtual Light* (1993), *Idoru* (1996), *All Tomorrow's Parties* (1999).

Charlotte Perkins Gilman, *Herland* (1914). Separatist utopia by leading American feminist and socialist. Sequel: *With Her in Our Land* (1916). See also 'Moving the Mountain' (1911).

Molly Gloss, *The Dazzle of the Day* (1997). From the community of an interstellar vessel emerges a commitment to low-impact colonisation. See also *Wild Life* (2000).

Lisa Goldstein, *The Dream Years* (1985). Time-slip romance featuring Paris in the Surrealist 1920s and May 1968, with the future of revolutionary consciousness in the balance.

Jen Green and Sarah Le Fanu, eds, *Despatches from the Frontier of the Female Mind* (1985). Feminist SF anthology.

Sam Greenlee, *The Spook Who Sat by the Door* (1969). The CIA's first black field agent trains street gangs to form a revolutionary army.

George Griffith, *The Angel of the Revolution* (1893). Airborne anarchist terrorists create a world government. See also *Olga Romanoff* (1894).

Nicola Griffith, *Slow River* (1995). A wealthy, young lesbian's forced proletarianisation in a dark near-future. See also *Ammonite* (1993). Griffith co-edited the queer anthology *Bending the Landscape: Science Fiction* (1998).

Sutton E. Griggs, *Imperium in Imperio* (1899). The rise and betrayal of revolutionary black secessionism.

Emil Habibi, *The Secret Life of Saeed, the Ill-Fated Pessoptimist: A Palestinian who Became a Citizen of Israel* (1974). Candide-like protagonist recounts his fantastical life during the establishment of modern Israel.

Joe Haldeman, *The Forever War* (1974). Disorientated, alienated soldiers, suffering from time-dilation, return to a rapidly changing Earth. Sequels: *Forever Peace* (1997), *Forever Free* (1999).

Patrick Hamilton, *Impromptu in Moribundia* (1939). Satire on middle-class world-views and capital's fantasy that it, not labour, produces wealth.

Nick Harkaway, *The Gone-Away World* (2008). Black comic phantasmagoria on military–corporate Empire.

Jacqueline Harpman, *I Who Have Never Known Men* (1995). Ambiguous feminist fable about 40 women, abducted and imprisoned underground for a decade, who emerge into an empty world.

Harry Harrison, *Make Room! Make Room!* (1966). Classic vision of an overpopulated future.

M. John Harrison, *Signs of Life* (1996). Machismo meets free-marketeering on biotech's cutting edge. See also *Light* (2002), *Nova Swing* (2006).

Milo Hastings, *City of Endless Night* (1920). Confused, ambivalent anti-socialist dystopia, acutely prescient of Nazism.

Robert A. Heinlein, *For Us, The Living: A Comedy of Customs* (2004). Following the failure of Upton Sinclair's EPIC campaign, on which he volunteered, Heinlein wrote this long-unpublished anti-racist, anti-clerical, nudist utopian novel, advocating a Social Credit system with which to moderate capitalism. Sadly, he became an increasingly right-wing libertarian, wavering in the anti-racism and already problematic feminism of this first novel.

Zenna Henderson, *Ingathering: The Complete People Stories* (1995). Humanoid aliens with psychic powers struggle to fit into our world.

John Hersey, *My Petition for More Space* (1974). Dark comic fable of overpopulation. See also *The Child Buyer* (1960), *White Lotus* (1965).

Theodor Hertzka, *Freeland* (1890). Socialistically inclined utopian fantasy in which capitalism, stripped of exploitation and competition, forms the basis of an ideal society.

Chester Himes, *Plan B* (1983). Anguished Himes ends his hyperreal Harlem crime cycle with black revolution.

Russell Hoban, *Riddley Walker* (1980). Linguistically inventive novel in which, 2000 years after the nuclear holocaust, gunpowder is reinvented.

T. Shirby Hodge (Roger Sherman Tracy), *The White Man's Burden: A Satirical Forecast* (1915). Disentimed visitor to future African anarchist utopia learns of the triumph of peoples of colour, and witnesses the destruction of a white American invasion.

Cecilia Holland, *Floating Worlds* (1976). Ambiguously feminist, anti-colonialist space opera.

Pauline Hopkins, *Of One Blood* (1901–03). A technologically advanced, ancient African civilisation is poised to retake the world.

Nalo Hopkinson, *Midnight Robber* (2000). Interplanetary colonisation, told in the voices of the colonised. Hopkinson co-edited *So Long Been Dreaming: Postcolonial Visions of the Future* (2004).

William Dean Howells, *A Traveler from Altruria* (1892–93). Visitor from a truly socialist, christian land exposes the contradictions between capitalism and democracy. Sequels: *Letters of an Altrurian Traveller* (1893–94), *Through the Eye of the Needle* (1907).

W.H. Hudson, *The Crystal Age* (1887). Semi-matriarchal, ecological–pastoral utopia.

Julian Huxley, 'The Tissue-Culture King' (1926). Anti-colonial adventure about cloning, telepathy and commodity fetishism.

Blyden Jackson, *Operation Burning Candle* (1973). Black revolutionaries plan a symbolically resonant outrage to shatter dominant ideology.

K.W. Jeter, *Noir* (1998). In a future of indentured posthumous labour and *extreme* penalties for copyright infringement, a corporation might have perfected capitalism.

Michel Jeury, *Chronolysis* (1973). Disorientated agent of an anarchosocialist near-future finds himself at the centre of a conflict with multinational corporations trying to alter history so as to take over the future.

Gwyneth Jones, *White Queen* (1991). Ironic green–socialist–feminist–postcolonial revision of the alien invasion narrative. Sequels: *North Wind* (1994), *Phoenix Café* (1997). See also *Escape Plans* (1986), *Kairos* (1988), *Bold as Love* (2001; four sequels), *Life* (2004).

Anthony Joseph, *The African Origins of UFOs* (2007). Afropsychedelic SF noir.

William Melvin Kelley, *A Different Drummer* (1959). The black population desert a southern state.

John Kendall, *Unborn Tomorrow* (1933). Young couple flee 1995's 'unnatural' global socialist utopia.

Damon Knight, *Hell's Pavement* (1955). Madcap satire on 1950s US.

Cyril Kornbluth, *His Share of Glory* (1997). Satirises militarist/consumerist 1950s US. See also *The Syndic* (1953), *Not This August* (1955) and collaborations listed under Judith Merril and Frederik Pohl.

Nancy Kress, *Beggars in Spain* (1993). Ostensibly about genetically engineered superhumans, but demonstrating the ways in which capital already makes us posthuman. Sequels: *Beggars and Choosers* (1994), *Beggars Ride* (1996).

Larissa Lai, *Salt Fish Girl* (2002). Magic realist SF exploring the marginalisation of labour, immigrants and women.

Mary E. Bradley Lane, *Mizora: A Prophecy* (1880–81). High-tech, hollow earth, female utopia.

Herrmann Lang, *The Air Battle: A Vision of the Future* (1859). Technologically advanced African state fights to end the enslavement of whites. Not exactly anti-racist, it champions miscegenation.

Justine Larbalestier, ed., *Daughters of Earth: Feminist Science Fiction in the Twentieth Century* (2006). Feminist SF anthology.

Alice Laurence, ed., *Cassandra Rising* (1978). Feminist SF anthology.

J.M.G. Le Clézio, *The Giants* (1973). Poetic, mildly experimental jeremiad against modernity, rationalisation, consumerism and Americanisation.

Ursula K. Le Guin, *The Dispossessed: An Ambiguous Utopia* (1974). Anarchism in a world of scarcity is compared to capitalism in a world of artificial scarcity as a scientist attempts to understand sequence, simultaneity and determinism. See also *The Left Hand of Darkness* (1969), *The Word for World is Forest* (1972), *Always Coming Home* (1985).

Doris Lessing, *The Memoirs of a Survivor* (1974). An outsider watches the collapse of civilisation from her window. See also *The Four-Gated City* (1969), *The Fifth Child* (1988), *Re: Colonised Planet 5, Shikasta* (1979; four sequels).

Roy Lewis, *The Extraordinary Reign of King Ludd: An Historical Tease* (1990). A century after the victorious 1848 revolution, global Darwinian–Malthussian Luddite guild socialism is at risk.

Sinclair Lewis, *It Can't Happen Here* (1935). Always timely, if oddly comical, account of America's turn to fascism.

A.M. Lightner, *The Day of the Drones* (1969). African expedition discovers the remnants of white civilisation.

Anna Livia, *Bulldozer Rising* (1988). A group of older women plot survival in a future predicated on youthfulness.

Alun Llewellyn, *The Strange Invaders* (1933). A post-apocalyptic, USSR-derived feudal theocracy is challenged by the migration of giant lizards.

Jack London, *The Iron Heel* (1907). Bloody revolution against a capitalist oligarchy. See also 'A Curious Fragment' (1908), 'Goliah' (1908), 'The Dream of Debs' (1909), 'The Red One' (1918).

Simon Louvish, *Resurrections From the Dustbin of History: A Political Fantasy* (1992). Fifty years after Luxemburg and Liebknecht founded the Socialist German State, Hitler's grandson is a heartbeat away from the US presidency.

Ian McDonald, *Sacrifice of Fools* (1996). Aliens settle in Belfast in the midst of future Troubles. See also *Desolation Road* (1988), *Necroville* (1994), *Chaga* (1995), *Kirinya* (1988), *Tendeléo's Story* (2000), *River of Gods* (2004), *Brasyl* (2007).

Maureen F. McHugh, *China Mountain Zhang* (1992). Everyday life in a not-too-distant future dominated by Communist China.

Vonda McIntyre, *Dreamsnake* (1978). Post-apocalyptic feminist SF about sexuality, gender and healing, as well as power and its abuses.

Ken MacLeod, *The Execution Channel* (2007). The war on terror rolls on into a grim (alternative) future. See also *The Star Fraction* (1995; four sequels).

Barry Malzberg, *Galaxies* (1975). Bitter commentary on writing for US SF markets, presented as notes towards an unfinished novel. See also *Screen* (1968), *The Falling Astronauts* (1971), *Revelations* (1972),

Beyond Apollo (1972), *Overlay* (1972), *Herovit's World* (1973), *Scop* (1976), *Cross of Fire* (1982), *The Remaking of Sigmund Freud* (1985).

Andrew Marvell, *Minimum Man* (1938). Overthrowing a fascist state depends upon the cooperation of posthuman midgets (another ambivalently self-conscious proletariat).

Lisa Mason, *Summer of Love* (1994). A time-traveller returns to 1967 San Francisco to preserve the future, only to learn that history is contingent and potential.

Vladimir Mayakovsky, *The Bedbug* (1929). Satirical play in which a Soviet bureaucrat is kept in a zoo.

Shepherd Mead, *The Big Ball of Wax* (1954). Near-future anti-corporate satire.

Farah Mendlesohn, ed., *Glorifying Terrorism* (2006). Collection published in contravention of the UK's draconian, Kafka-esque 2006 Terrorism Act.

Judith Merril, *Homecoming and Other Stories* (2005). Short fiction developing traditional SF materials from a broadly feminist, Trotskyist-inflected angle. See also *Shadow on the Hearth* (1950) and her collaborations with Cyril M. Kornbluth: *Outpost Mars* (1952), *Gunner Cade* (1952). Merril edited *Year's Best SF* anthologies (1956–68) and *England Swings SF* (1968), which played a key role in the New Wave.

China Miéville, *Iron Council* (2004). Revolution comes to New Crobuzon, ending with a remarkable image of revolutionary potential. Follows *Perdido Street Station* (2000) and *The Scar* (2002).

Warren Miller, *The Siege of Harlem* (1964). A veteran recounts the Harlem secession to his grandchildren.

Misha, *Red Spider White Web* (1990). Grim cyberpunk about art and commodification.

Adrian Mitchell, *The Bodyguard* (1970). In totalitarian Britain, an elite bodyguard recounts his life, unaware of the revolution going on around him.

J. Leslie Mitchell, *Gay Hunter* (1934). Flung into a post-apocalyptic pastoral Britain, the eponymous heroine fights the re-emergence of 'civilisation' (i.e. the imposition of a class system by technocratic fascism).

Naomi Mitchison, *Memoirs of a Spacewoman* (1962). Delightful adventures in embracing otherness. See also *We Have Been Warned* (1935).

Judith Moffett, *The Ragged World* (1991). Aliens force humans to save Earth from ecocatastrophe, regardless of the cost. Sequels: *Time, Like an Ever-Rolling Stream* (1992), *The Bird Shaman* (2008). See also *Pennterra* (1987).

Michael Moorcock, *Behold the Man* (1969). Deliciously blasphemous time-travel story. See also *Breakfast in the Ruins* (1972), *The Final Programme* (1968; three sequels), *The Black Corridor* (1969), *The Warlord of the Air* (1971; two sequels). Moorcock was the driving editorial force behind the New Wave – see *New Worlds: An Anthology* (1983).

Alan Moore, *V for Vendetta* (1982–88). An anarchist takes on British totalitarianism. See also *Watchmen* (1986–87), *The League of Extraordinary Gentlemen* (1999–).

Robert Morales and Kyle Baker, *Truth: Red, White and Black* (2002). Reworked Captain America origin story in which the 'supersoldier' experiments were conducted on African-Americans.

Julian Moreau, *The Black Commandos* (1967). Super-scientific black super-warriors, complete with flying saucers, crush white supremacism.

William Morris, *News from Nowhere* (1890). Socialist utopia without distinctions between work, life and art.

Grant Morrison, *The Invisibles* (1994–2000). The Invisible College oppose the Archons of the Outer Church, aliens who have enslaved humanity. See also *Zenith* (1987–92), *Animal Man* (1988–90), *St Swithin's Day* (1989), *Doom Patrol* (1989–92), *Big Dave* (1993–94), *Flex Mentallo* (1996), *The Filth* (2002–03) and *We3* (2004).

Walter Mosley, *Blue Light* (1998). A cosmic light hits mid-1960s San Francisco, prompting a peculiar apocalyptic story about race, sex, identity, death, transformation and possibility. See also *Futureland: Nine Stories of an Imminent Future* (2001).

Pat Murphy, 'Rachel in Love' (1987). Intelligence-boosted chimpanzee flees the patriarchal technoscientific institution which created her. See also *The City, Not Long After* (1988).

Alice Nunn, *Illicit Passage* (1992). In a besieged, class-ridden space colony, women foment revolution unseen.

Barbara O'Brien, *Operators and Things* (1958). Satire on corporations, patriarchy and alienation, published as a schizophrenic's autobiography.

E.V. Odle, *The Clockwork Man* (1923). Comic encounter with a future of mechanism, dialectically conceived as hopeful *and* terrible.

Joseph O'Neill, *Land Under England* (1935). Anti-Nazi subterranean adventure about a totalitarian society of people reduced to mindless automata. See also *Day of Wrath* (1936).

Rebecca Ore, *Gaia's Toys* (1995). Underground eco-warriors genetically engineer Earth's survival. See also *Becoming Alien* (1988; two sequels), *The Illegal Rebirth of Billy the Kid* (1991), *Slow Funeral* (1994).

George Orwell, *Nineteen Eighty-Four* (1949). Renowned anti-Stalinist dystopia.

Jane Palmer, *The Planet Dweller* (1985). Menopausal single mother ditches tranquillisers for interstellar adventures.

Severna Park, *Hand of Prophecy* (1998). Lesbian–feminist post-colonial space opera.

Olivier Pauvert, *Noir* (2005). In near-future fascist France, a killer returns to life to solve a murder he has no memory of committing.

Marge Piercy, *Woman on the Edge of Time* (1976). Drawn across time to a utopian future, impoverished, institutionalised Connie Ramos must fight in the present to ensure it emerges. See also *He, She, and It* (1991).

Doris Piserchia, *Star Rider* (1974). Interstellar adventure proves far more enticing than marriage and motherhood.

Frederik Pohl, 'The Midas Plague' (1954) and 'The Tunnel Under the World' (1954). Among the very best 1950s SF satires. See also collaborations with Cyril M. Kornbluth: *The Space Merchants* (1953), *Search the Sky* (1954), *Gladiator-at-Law* (1955), *Wolfbane* (1957).

Ishmael Reed, *Mumbo Jumbo* (1972). Monotheism, white supremacism and order vs jazz and liberation. See also *Flight to Canada* (1976).

Kit Reed, *Weird Women, Wired Women* (1998). Collects stories (1958–97) charting patriarchy's demands upon post-war (white, middle-class) American women.

Mack Reynolds, *Looking Backward, From the Year 2000* (1973). Socialist Labor Party supporter Reynolds wrote prolifically for the often right-wing US SF magazines; here, inspired by Bellamy, he imagines a post-scarcity future en route to a utopia it knows is definitionally unattainable. Sequel: *Equality: In the Year 2000* (1977). See also *Black Man's Burden* (1972; two sequels), *Commune 2000 A.D.* (1974; two sequels), *Satellite City* (1975), *After Utopia* (1977), *Perchance to Dream* (1977), *Lagrange Five* (1979; two sequels).

Adam Roberts, *Salt* (2000). Conflict between totalitarian and anarchistic colonisers. See also *Stone* (2002), *Polystom* (2003), *The Snow* (2004), *Gradisil* (2006), *Slowly* (2008).

Albert Robida, *The Twentieth Century* (1881). Postmodern capital, simulacral architecture and the thematisation of daily life are among the many anticipations in this unexpectedly (if problematically) feminist vision of future Paris.

Kim Stanley Robinson, *Red Mars* (1992), *Green Mars* (1993), *Blue Mars* (1995). Monumental trilogy charting the tensions between red and green politics as Mars is terraformed into a utopian homeworld. See also *The Wild Shore* (1984; two sequels), *Antarctica* (1997), *The Years of Rice and Salt* (2002), *Forty Signs of Rain* (2004; two sequels). Robinson edited the ecological anthology, *Future Primitives: The New Ecotopias* (1994).

Spider Robinson, *Night of Power* (1985). Black Power revolutionaries take New York.

Mordecai Roshwald, *Level 7* (1959). Grim tale of 'surviving' a nuclear war. See also *A Small Armageddon* (1962).

Joanna Russ, *The Female Man* (1975). Key work of feminist SF blends aesthetic and political radicalism. See also *We Who Are About To...* (1977), *The Two of Them* (1978), *On Strike against God* (1982), *(Extra)Ordinary People* (1984).

Eric Frank Russell, *The Great Explosion* (1962). Gandhian passive resistance thwarts terrestrial imperialism.

Geoff Ryman, *Air or Have not Have* (2004). The information age arrives like a flood in a small Asian village. See also *The Unconquered Country* (1986), *The Child Garden; or, A Low Comedy* (1989), *Lust* (2000).

James Sallis, ed., *The War Book* (1969). Anti-war SF anthology.

Sarban, *The Sound of His Horn* (1952). 500 years after Hitler's victory, a timeslipped POW finds a world of baroque Nazi sentiment and dehumanisation.

Pamela Sargent, *The Shore of Women* (1986). In a gender-separatist post-apocalypse, an exiled woman from a high-tech city and a subsistence tribesman fall in love. Sargent edited three groundbreaking collections of SF with female protagonists by women, *Women of Wonder* (1975), *More Women of Wonder* (1976) and *The New Women of Wonder* (1978); collated and expanded as *Women of Wonder: The Classic Years* (1996) and *Women of Wonder: The Contemporary Years* (1996).

Rob Sauer, ed., *Voyages: Scenarios for a Ship Called Earth* (1971). Ecological SF anthology.

George Saunders, *Civilwarland in Bad Decline* (1996). Stories set in a minimum-wage, simulacral US. See also *Pastoralia* (2000), *The Brief and Frightening Reign of Phil* (2005), *In Persuasion Nation* (2006).

Josephine Saxton, *The Travails of Jane Saint and Other Stories* (1986). Resisting reprogramming of her revolutionary tendencies, Jane adventures in other realities. Sequel: *Jane Saint and the Backlash* (1989). See also *The Power of Time* (1985), *Queen of the States* (1986).

George Schuyler *Black No More* (1931). African-Americans' adoption of a perfect whitening treatment destroys white supremacism. See also *Black Empire* (1936–38).

Jody Scott, *I, Vampire* (1984). Feminist satire on contemporary capitalism. See also *Passing for Human* (1977).

Melissa Scott, *Trouble and Her Friends* (1994). Queer cyberpunk. See also *Shadow Man* (1995), *Night Sky Mine* (1996), *Dreaming Metal* (1997), *The Shapes of Their Hearts* (1998), *The Jazz* (2000).

Alan Seymour, *The Coming Self-Destruction of the USA* (1969). Agonised depiction of an African-American revolution.

eluki bes shahar, *Hellflower* (1991). Postfeminist cyberpunkish space opera. Sequels: *Darktraders* (1992), *Archangel Blues* (1993).

Mary Shelley, *Frankenstein, or The Modern Prometheus* (1818). Among many other things, a vision of a rising, rebellious proletariat. See also *The Last Man* (1826).

Lucius Shephard, *Life During Wartime* (1987). *Heart of Darkness* replayed in near-future US-occupied Latin America.

Lewis Shiner, *Deserted Cities of the Heart* (1988). Magic-realist SF about US imperialism. See also *Frontera* (1984), *Slam* (1990), *Glimpses* (1993). Shiner edited the anti-war anthology, *When the Music's Over* (1991).

John Shirley, *Eclipse* (1985). After World War III, a ragtag, tech-savvy resistance fights a neo-fascist regime and its corporate sponsors. Sequels: *Eclipse Penumbra* (1988), *Eclipse Corona* (1990).

Robert Silverberg, *Dying Inside* (1972). Contemporary alienation explored through a man with slowly-fading mind-reading powers. See also *Thorns* (1967), *A Time of Changes* (1971), *The Stochastic Man* (1975).

Clifford Simak, *Ring Around the Sun* (1953). Mutant humans destroy capitalism so as to end the Cold War. See also *City* (1952).

Upton Sinclair, *The Millennium: A Comedy of the Year 2000* (1914). Global catastrophe leaves a dozen of the world's wealthiest to recapitulate in microcosm the shifts from slavery to feudalism to capitalism to socialism. See also *Prince Hagen* (1903; play version, 1921), *The Industrial Republic: A Study of the America of Ten Years Hence* (1907), *Roman Holiday* (1931), *I, Governor of California, and How I Ended Poverty* (1933), *We, People of America, and How We Ended Poverty: A True Story of the Future* (1934), *I, Candidate for Governor: And How I Got Licked* (1934–35).

Eduard Skobolev, *Catastrophe* (1983). Manic, talkative postcolonial adventure about the intertwined madness of imperialism and nuclear war.

Joan Slonczewski, *A Door into Ocean* (1986). Feminist separatist utopia of sorts, in which indigenous non-violence struggles to understand and heal colonial invasion. Sequels: *Daughter of Elysium* (1993), *Brain*

Plague (2000). See also *The Forms on Foxfield* (1980), *The Children Star* (1998).

Cordwainer Smith, *The Rediscovery of Man* (1988). In the far future, animals engineered into sentience revolt against human enslavers. See also *Norstrilia* (1975).

Kent Smith, *Future X* (1990). A time-travelling descendant of Malcolm X must prevent his ancestor's assassination and his own dystopian future.

Edmund Snell, *Kontrol* (1928). A decent chap overcomes technocratic quasi-fascism.

Norman Spinrad, *The Iron Dream* (1972). In 1919, Adolf Hitler emigrated to the US to become a pulp SF author; this is the novel he wrote in the weeks before his death from syphilis. See also *Bug Jack Barron* (1969), *Other Americas* (1988), *Russian Spring* (1991).

Olaf Stapledon, *Star Maker* (1937). Breathtaking, unrelenting cosmic epic about embracing otherness to form community. See also *Last and First Men* (1930), *Odd John: A Story Between Jest and Earnest* (1935), *Sirius: A Fantasy of Love and Discord* (1944).

Neal Stephenson, *Quicksilver* (2003). The rise of mercantilism told from an information-age perspective posits capital as the first global information technology. Sequels: *The Confusion* (2004), *The System of the World* (2004). See also *Cryptonomicon* (1999).

Boris and Arkady Strugatsky, *The Second Invasion from Mars* (1968). This time the Martians win by economic means; no-one much seems to notice or care. See also *Hard to be a God* (1964), *Monday Begins on Saturday* (1965), *The Ugly Swans* (1966–67), *Noon: 22nd Century* (1967), *Tale of a Troika* (1968), *Roadside Picnic* (1972).

Theodore Sturgeon, *Venus Plus X* (1960). A post-gender utopia – full of yearning and all the hang-ups of 1950s magazine SF. See also *More than Human* (1953), 'The World Well Lost' (1953); his short fiction is collected in *The Ultimate Egoist* (1994) and multiple subsequent volumes.

Tricia Sullivan, *Maul* (2004). Post-feminist riot grrl shopping 'n' fighting spree, with a second-wave twist.

Lucy Sussex, *My Lady Tongue and Other Tales* (1990). Lesbian, postcolonial SF and fantasy.

Jonathan Swift, *Gulliver's Travels* (1726). Satire on the excesses of reason and unreason.

Sheri S. Tepper, *The Gate to Women's Country* (1988). Post-apocalyptic separatist utopia featuring a secret feminist project for the survival of humanity and the world. See also *Grass* (1989; two sequels), *Beauty* (1991), *Gibbon's Decline and Fall* (1996), *The Fresco* (2000), *The Visitor* (2002), *The Companions* (2003), *The Margarets* (2007).

Sheree R. Thomas, ed., *Dark Matter: A Century of Speculative Science Fiction from the African Diaspora* (2000). Mostly African-American SF. See also *Dark Matter: Reading the Bones* (2004).

James Tiptree, Jr, *Her Smoke Rose Up Forever: The Great Years of James Tiptree, Jr* (1990). Collects Alice Sheldon's best stories about gender, identity, sex and death, including 'The Women Men Don't See' (1973) and 'Houston, Houston, Do You Read?' (1976).

Sue Thomas, *Correspondence* (1991). A disaffected woman slowly transforms herself into a machine, which begins to flourish.

Alexei Tolstoy, *Aelita* (1922). Two Soviet visitors to Mars back a worker's revolt. See also *Engineer Garin and His Death Ray* (1927).

Mark Twain, *A Connecticut Yankee in King Arthur's Court* (1889). Anti-clerical, republican if ultimately ambivalent time-travel narrative about the transition from feudalism to industrial capitalism.

Thomas F. Tweed, *Rinehard* (1933). Brain-damaged – or divinely inspired – president overthrows the constitution and US institutions so as to alleviate the Depression.

Jules Verne, *Paris in the Twentieth Century* (written 1863; 1994). 'Lost' dystopian comic romance unlocks the ambivalence towards modernity and mechanisation of Verne's more famous works. See also *Twenty Thousand Leagues under the Seas* (1870; transl. William Butcher), *The Begum's Millions* (1879; transl. Stanford L. Luce).

Élisabeth Vonarburg, *In the Mothers' Land* (1992). A post-apocalyptic matriarchy is rocked by archaeological discoveries. See also *The Silent City* (1981), *Reluctant Voyagers* (1994), *Dreams of the Sea* (1996), *A Game of Perfection* (1997), *Slow Engines of Time and Other Stories* (1999).

Kurt Vonnegut, Jr, *Player Piano* (1952). Dystopian satire on cybernetic automation.

Rex Warner, *The Aerodrome* (1941). Comic jeremiad against the fascistic forces of modernity and the security state. See also *The Wild Goose Chase* (1936).

Ian Watson, *Slow Birds* (1985). Collection of ironic stories, several of them directed against Cold War escalations.

E.L. White, *Lukundoo, and Other Stories* (1927). Title story is an (ambiguously) anti-colonialist colonial fantasy.

Colson Whitehead, *The Intuitionist* (1999). In an alternate America, race relations are articulated through the science and art of elevator construction and maintenance.

Kate Wilhelm, *Where Late the Sweet Birds Sang* (1976). Feminist post-apocalyptic tale of cloning and posthuman becoming.

John A. Williams, *The Man Who Cried I Am* (1967). A novel of African-American insurgency. See also *Sons of Darkness, Sons of Light* (1968), *Captain Blackman* (1972), *Jacob's Ladder* (1987).

Raymond Williams, *The Volunteers* (1978). Near-future thriller, prescient of the Thatcher–Blair state, about resistance and revolution.

Tess Williams, *Sea as Mirror* (2000). Interspecies communication offers a key to surviving ecological and nuclear disasters.

Connie Willis, 'All My Darling Daughters' (1985). Grim tale of an abused girl in an orbital boarding school, where the boys rape aliens. See also *Doomsday Book* (1992).

Monique Wittig, *The Guérillères* (1969). Incantatory account of women's armed resistance to patriarchy and men.

Bernard Wolfe, *Limbo* (1952). Dystopian satire digging deep into cybernetics and psychoanalysis, by Trotsky's one-time bodyguard. See also 'The Bisquit Position' (1972).

Jack Womack, *Random Acts of Senseless Violence* (1993). The best of the six-book *Dryco* series (1987–2000) tells the story of a young woman's descent into poverty and abandonment of middle-class standards unsuited to her new life. See also *Let's Put the Future Behind Us* (1996).

Ivan Yefremov, *Andromeda* (1957). Soviet adventures in a future socialist galaxy.

Yevgeny Zamyatin, *We* (1924). Prematurely anti-Stalinist dystopian satire on mechanism and order written by 1921.

Pamela Zoline, 'The Heat Death of the Universe' (1967). Central to New Wave and feminist SF, it brings together the drudgery of a housewife's daily life and the entropic universe.

2.   Viewing

Aelita (Protazonov, 1924). Adaptation of Alexei Tolstoy's novel emphasises the importance of building the revolutionary state.

Alien (Scott, 1979). Monster-on-the-loose-in-a-spaceship hokum. Noteworthy for its production design, anti-corporatism and 'feminist' protagonist.

Alligator (Teague, 1980). John Sayles-scripted monster movie. Eponymous giant creature eats corrupt officials and polluting corporate miscreants.

Alphaville (Godard, 1965). Dystopian satire on bureaucracy and com-modification, betraying a genuine affection for popular culture. See also *RoGoPaG* (1963), *The Seven Deadly Sins* (1967), *Week End* (1967), *Germany Year 90 Nine Zero* (1990).

Andromeda (Sherstobitov, 1967). The first part of a never-completed adaptation of Ivan Yefremov's novel of space exploration.

Á Nous la liberté (Clair, 1931). Popular front utopia, in which mechanisation frees workers for love, play, fishing and tramping.

La Antenna (Sapir, 2007). Mr TV plots to enslave a city where everyone has lost their voices.

The Atomic Café (Loader, Raferty and Raferty, 1982). Compilation of US pro-nuclear propaganda.

The Bedford Incident (Harris, 1965). A cat-and-mouse game between a US destroyer and a Soviet nuclear submarine exposes Cold War mentality.

Born in Flames (Borden, 1983). Ten years after the US socialist revolution, radical feminists foment a further revolution to eradicate sexism. Made over five years, and thus shaped by the transition from second- to third-wave feminisms.

The Brother from Another Planet (Sayles, 1984). Escaped black alien slave on the run finds community in Harlem.

Conquest of the Planet of the Apes (Thompson, 1972). The studio neutered the conclusion of this depiction of worker/slave revolt, which resonated too strongly with Black Power.

CQ (Coppola, 2001). The spirit of May 1968 lurks somewhere between an aspiring director's Godardian short and the camp Italian SF movie he is hired to complete.

CSA: The Confederate States of America (Willmott, 2004). Alternative history pseudo-documentary in which slavery is not abolished reveals how deeply the tendrils of racism extend into the present.

Cube (Natali, 1997). Eponymous device models the logic of capital for those trapped within it. See also *Cypher* (2002), *Nothing* (2003).

The Damned (Losey, 1963). A warning that the only way to live in a nuclear world is to cease to be human.

Dark City (Proyas, 1998). In a noirish city in space, aliens experiment on humans, offering a phantasmagorical image of life under capital.

The Day the Earth Stood Still (Wise, 1951). Anti-nuclear film (or a celebration of the pax Americana).

Death of a President (Range, 2006). Pseudo-documentary about the state's response to the assassination of George W. Bush.

District 13 (Morel, 2004). Free-running as individual utopia.

Dr Strangelove or: How I Learned to Stop Worrying and Love the Bomb (Kubrick, 1964). Arms race satire. See also *2001: A Space Odyssey* (1968), *A Clockwork Orange* (1971).

Dust (Loban, 2005). Satire on contemporary Russia and elegy for the things lost with the end of the USSR.

Edge of Darkness (Campbell, 1985). Fabulist chiller about British nuclear policies.

Face of Another (Teshigahari, 1966). Haunting adaptation of Abe Kobo's novel of alienation, in which a man whose face is disfigured in a fire is given an amazingly lifelike mask. See also *Pitfall* (1962), *Woman of the Dunes* (1964), *The Ruined Map* (1968).

Fail-Safe (Lumet, 1964). Cold War tensions accidentally escalate into a nuclear exchange. Based on Eugene Burdick and Harvey Wheeler's novel; remade on period equipment and broadcast live in 2000.

First on the Moon (Fedorchenko, 2005). Mockumentary about the pre-war Soviet space programme.

Five (Oboler, 1951). Racial and sexual tensions threaten the survivors of nuclear apocalypse.

4 (Khrjanovsky, 2005). The apocalypse has already happened in this tale of clones and conspiracies in contemporary Russia.

Gas! – or It Became Necessary to Destroy the World in Order to Save It (Corman, 1971). Countercultural fun and games after a gas kills everyone over 25.

Godzilla (Honda, 1954). Mournful, pacifistic, anti-nuclear monster movie.

Hail (Levinson, 1973). The president introduces extreme measures to suppress the counterculture.

Hey Happy (Gonick, 2001). Outré queer comedy about sex, raves, UFOs and the apocalypse.

The Invasion of the Body Snatchers (Siegel, 1956). A satire on mechanical reproduction, commodification, alienation and McCarthyism. Based on Jack Finney's novel; Kaufman's 1978 version is the best of the three remakes.

Island of Lost Souls (Kenton, 1932). The best adaptation of H.G. Wells' *The Island of Doctor Moreau* draws out colonialism's hysterical sadism.

La Jetée (Marker, 1962). Dystopian meditation on memory, desire and identity.

Jubilee (Jarman, 1977). Elizabeth I time-travels into the depressed, depressing future of Elizabeth II's jubilee.

Last Angel of History (Akomfrah, 1995). Science-fictionalised documentary about funk and afrofuturism.

Last Night (McKellar, 1998). Low-budget comedy-drama riposte to *Armageddon* (Bay, 1998), focused on the lives of ordinary people during the six hours before the end of the world.

King Kong (Cooper and Schoedsack, 1933). Powerful – if accidental – fantasy of colonial revolt.

The Man in the White Suit (McKendrick, 1951). A revolution in manufacturing threatens the whole system of capitalism, including organised labour.

The Man Who Fell to Earth (Roeg, 1976). Hyperbolic parable about alienation in the dawning information era. Based on a novel by Walter Tevis.

Max Headroom (Jankel and Morton, 1985). TV ratings are everything, even at the cost of viewers' lives. Punky dystopian drama later sanitised as a US primetime series.

Metropolis (Lang, 1926). Workers vs capitalists in a monumentalist dystopia. See also *The 1000 Eyes of Dr Mabuse* (1960).

Mon Oncle (Tati, 1958). Comedy about the absurdity of ultramodernity. See also *Play Time* (1967).

Mr Freedom (Klein, 1969). The eponymous American superhero must destroy France in order to save it from Red Chinaman. See also *The Model Couple* (1977).

Night of the Living Dead (Romero, 1968). Something from space zombifies the dead in this anti-racist movie. See also *The Crazies* (1973), *Dawn of the Dead* (1978).

The Parallax View (Pakula, 1974). Journalist investigating a Robert Kennedy-style assassination uncovers a conspiracy involving a sinister corporation.

Piranha (Dante, 1978). John Sayles-scripted monster movie indicts the military–industrial complex.

Poison (Haynes, 1991). New Queer Cinema adaptation of Jean Genet includes a mad-science parody of AIDS hysteria.

Primer (Carruth, 2004). Dystopian vision of the inescapable here-and-now.

Punishment Park (Watkins, 1971). Young radicals and counterculturals are given a potentially lethal alternative to prison. See also *The War Game* (1965), *Privilege* (1967), *Gladiators* (1969), *The Trap* (1975), *Evening Land* (1977).

Repo Man (Cox, 1984). Punk fable about the alienation of contemporary American life, including televangelists, small-time crooks, repo men, ufologists, government conspiracies and the Roswell aliens. See also *Death and the Compass* (1992), *Revengers Tragedy* (2002).

RoboCop (Verhoeven, 1987). Violent, anti-corporate satire. See also *Starship Troopers* (1997).

The Rocky Horror Picture Show (Sharman, 1975). Unlocks the queerness of popular SF.

Rollerball (Jewison, 1975). One man vs the global corporations.

The Spook Who Sat by the Door (Dixon, 1973). Independent adaptation of Sam Greenlee's novel about black urban revolution.

Sankofa (Gerima, 1993). Self-centred fashion model time-travels to the era of plantation slavery and Maroon resistance.

Save the Green Planet (Jang, 2003). Capitalists *are* aliens!

Seconds (Frankenheimer, 1966). A corporation enables the discontented rich to take on new identities in lives designed to fulfil their desires. Based on David Ely's novel. See also *The Manchurian Candidate* (1962), *Seven Days in May* (1964).

Seven Days to Noon (Boulting brothers, 1950). A nuclear scientist tries to blackmail Britain into unilateral disarmament.

The Silent Star (Maetzig, 1960). East German paean to international cooperation, featuring a trip to Venus, *Alien*-style gender equality and a dire nuclear warning. Based on Stanislaw Lem's novel.

The Sleepwalker (Spiner, 1998). In totalitarian future Buenos Aires, thousands of people have no memory of their real identities. A Dickian conceit articulates the trauma of Argentina's *desaparecidos*.

Southland Tales (Kelly, 2007). Science-fictionalised depiction of the era of Homeland Security; preceded by the comics collected as *Southland Tales: The Prequel Saga* (2007).

The Stuff (Cohen, 1985). Low-budget satire on commodity fetishism. See also *God Told Me To* (1976), the *It's Alive* trilogy (1974–87).

Tetsuo (Tsukamoto, 1989). Re-embodying the fantasy of cyberspace, as if the Angel of History were a Japanese cyberpunk filmmaker.

They Live (Carpenter, 1988). Yuppies *are* aliens!

Tribulation 99: Alien Anomalies Under America (Baldwin, 1992). Alternative history in which US incursions into Latin America disturb a subterranean extraterrestrial society. See also *RocketKitKongoKit* (1986), *Spectres of the Spectrum* (1999).

Twenty Thousand Leagues under the Sea (Paton, 1916). The only adaptation of Jules Verne's novel to emphasise Nemo's anticolonialism.

A Very British Coup (Jackson, 1988). A working-class socialist prime minister dismantles Britain's nuclear arsenal. Based on Chris Mullin's novel. See also *Threads* (1984).

Watermelon Man (Van Peebles, 1970). A white racist wakes up one morning to find he is black.

Welcome II the Terrordome (Onwurah, 1995). British hip-hop story of life, death and revolution in a future black ghetto.

White Man's Burden (Nakano, 1995). Role-reversed race melodrama in an alternative US.

Wild in the Streets (Shear, 1968). Countercultural under-thirties take over the government.

The World, the Flesh and the Devil (MacDougall, 1959). Racial and sexual tensions threaten the survivors of the apocalypse.

The Year of the Sex Olympics (Elliott, 1968). Nigel Kneale's satire on ubiquitous media as a distraction from the operations of power 'predicts' reality TV.

Critical and Theoretical Works

1.   Selected Marxist SF Theory and Criticism

Marc Angenot, 'The Absent Paradigm: An Introduction to the Semiotics of Science Fiction', *Science Fiction Studies* 6: 1 (1979), pp. 9–19.

Marc Angenot and Darko Suvin, 'Not Only But Also: Reflections on Cognition and Ideology in Science Fiction and SF Criticism', *Science Fiction Studies* 6: 2 (1979), pp. 168–79.

——'A Response to Professor Fekete's "Five Theses"', *Science Fiction Studies* 15: 3 (1988), pp. 324–33.

Raffaella Baccollini and Tom Moylan, eds, *Dark Horizons: Science Fiction and the Dystopian Imagination* (London: Routledge, 2003).

Matthew Beaumont, 'Red Sphinx: Mechanics of the Uncanny in *The Time Machine*', *Science Fiction Studies* 33: 2 (2006), pp. 230–50.

——*Utopia Ltd: Ideologies of Social Dreaming in England, 1870–1900* (Leiden: Brill, 2005).

Mark Bould, 'Come Alive By Saying No: An Introduction to Black Power SF', *Science Fiction Studies* 34: 2 (2007), pp. 220–40.

——'The Dreadful Credibility of Absurd Things: A Tendency in Fantasy Theory', *Historical Materialism* 10: 4 (2002), pp. 51–88.

——'On the Boundary between Oneself and the Other: Aliens and Language in *AVP*, *Dark City*, *The Brother from Another Planet* and *Possible Worlds*', *Yearbook in English Studies* 37: 2 (2007), pp. 234–54.

——and Sherryl Vint, 'Learning from the Little Engines That Couldn't: Transported by Gernsback, Wells, and Latour', *Science Fiction Studies* 33: 1 (2006), pp. 129–48.

William J. Burling, ed., *Kim Stanley Robinson Maps the Unimaginable: Critical Essays* (Jefferson: McFarland, 2009).

——'Reading Time: The Ideology of Time Travel in Science Fiction', *Kronoscope* 6: 1 (2006), pp. 5–28.

——'The Theoretical Foundation of Utopian Radical Democracy in Kim Stanley Robinson's *Blue Mars*', *Utopian Studies* 16 (2005), pp. 75–96.

Istvan Csicsery-Ronay, Jr, 'Science Fiction and Empire', *Science Fiction Studies* 30: 2 (2003), pp. 231–45.

Samuel R. Delany, *The American Shore: Meditations of a Tale of Science Fiction* (Elizabethtown: Dragon Press, 1978).

——*The Jewel-Hinged Jaw: Notes on the Language of Science Fiction* (Elizabethtown: Dragon Press, 1977).

——*Starboard Wine: More Notes on the Language of Science Fiction* (Pleasantville: Dragon Press, 1984).

John Fekete, 'The Stimulations of Simulations: Five Theses on Science Fiction and Marxism', *Science Fiction Studies* 15: 3 (1988), pp. 312–23.

Peter Fitting, 'The Modern Anglo-American SF Novel: Utopian Longing and Capitalist Cooptation', *Science Fiction Studies* 6: 1 (1979), pp. 59–76.

——'Reality as Ideological Construct', *Science Fiction Studies* 10: 2 (1983), pp. 219–36.

——'*Ubik*: The Deconstruction of Bourgeois SF', *Science Fiction Studies* 2: 1 (1975), pp. 47–54.

H. Bruce Franklin, 'America as SF: 1939', *Science Fiction Studies* 9: 2 (1982), pp. 38–50.

——*Robert A Heinlein: America as Science Fiction* (Oxford: Oxford University Press, 1980).

——'The Vietnam War as American SF and Fantasy', *Science Fiction Studies* 17: 3 (1990), pp. 341–59.

——*War Stars: The Superweapon and the American Imagination* (Oxford: Oxford University Press, 1988).

Carl Freedman, *Critical Theory and Science Fiction* (Hanover: Wesleyan University Press, 2000).

——*George Orwell: A Study in Ideology and Literary Form* (New York: Garland, 1988).

——*The Incomplete Projects: Marxism, Modernity, and the Politics of Culture* (Middletown: Wesleyan University Press, 2002).

Donna J. Haraway, *Modest_Witness@Second_Millennium.FemaleMan©_Meets_Oncomouse™: Feminism and Technoscience* (London: Routledge, 1997).

——*Primate Visions: Gender, Race, and Nature in the World of Modern Science* (London: Routedge, 1989).

——*Simians, Cyborgs, and Women: The Reinvention of Nature* (London: Free Association Books, 1991).

Fredric Jameson, *Archaelogies of the Future: The Desire Called Utopia and Other Science Fictions* (London: Verso, 2005).

Rob Latham, *Consuming Youth: Vampires, Cyborgs and the Culture of Consumption* (Chicago: University of Chicago Press, 2002).

Pierre Macherey, *A Theory of Literary Production*, transl. Geoffrey Wall (London: Routledge & Kegan Paul, 1978).

China Miéville, 'The Conspiracy of Architecture: Notes on a Modern Anxiety', *Historical Materialism* 2 (1998), pp. 1–32.

——'Editorial Introduction', *Historical Materialism* 10: 4 (2002), pp. 39–49.

——ed., *Historical Materialism* 10: 4 (2002) – 'Marxism and Fantasy' special issue.

Andrew Milner, 'Utopia and Science Fiction in Raymond Williams', *Science Fiction Studies* 30: 2 (2003), pp. 199–216.

——and Robert Savage, 'Pulped Dreams: Utopia and American Pulp Science Fiction', *Science Fiction Studies* 35: 1 (2008), pp. 31–47.

Tom Moylan, *Demand the Impossible: Science Fiction and the Utopian Imagination* (London: Methuen, 1986).

——*Scraps of the Untainted Sky: Science Fiction, Utopia, Dystopia* (Boulder: Westview, 2000).

——and Raffaella Baccolini, eds, *Utopia Method Vision: The Use Value of Social Dreaming* (Bern: Peter Lang, 2007).

Annalee Newitz, *Pretend We're Dead: Capitalist Monsters in American Pop Culture* (Durham: Duke University Press, 2006).

Yusuf Nurudin, Alcena M.D. Rogan and Victor Wallis, eds, *Socialism and Democracy* 20: 3 – 'Socialism and Social Critique in Science Fiction' special issue.

Patrick Parrinder, ed., *Learning from Other Worlds: Estrangement, Cognition and the Politics of Science Fiction and Utopia* (Liverpool: Liverpool University Press, 2000).

John Rieder, 'Embracing the Alien: Science Fiction in Mass Culture', *Science Fiction Studies* 9: 1 (1982), pp. 26–37.

——*Colonialism and the Emergence of Science Fiction* (Middletown: Wesleyan University Press, 2008).

Glenn Rikowski, 'Alien Life: Marx and the Future of the Human', *Historical Materialism* 11: 2 (2003), pp. 121–64.

Kim Stanley Robinson, *The Novels of Philip K. Dick* (Ann Arbor: UMI Research Press, 1984).

Shaviro, Steven (1993) *The Cinematic Body* (Minneapolis: University of Minnesota Press, 1993).

——*Connected, or What it Means to Live in the Network Society* (Minneapolis: University of Minnesota Press, 2003).

——*Doom Patrols: A Theoretical Fiction about Postmodernism* (London: Serpent's Tail, 1997).

Vivian Sobchack, *Screening Space: The American Science Fiction Film* (New York: Ungar, 1987).

Suvin, Darko, 'Considering the Sense of "Fantasy" or "Fantastic Fiction"', *Extrapolation* 41: 3 (2000), pp. 209–47.

——*Metamorphoses of Science Fiction: On the Poetics and History of a Literary Genre* (New Haven: Yale University Press, 1979).

——*Positions and Presuppositions in Science Fiction* (Houndmills: Macmillan, 1988).

——'Reflections on What Remains of Zamyatin's *We* after the Change of Leviathans: Must Collectivism Be Against People?' in Marleen Barr, ed., *Envisioning the Future: Science Fiction and the Next Millennium* (Middletown: Wesleyan University Press, 2003), pp. 51–81.

——'Science Fiction Parables of Mutation and Cloning as/and Cognition', in Domna Pastourmatzi, ed., *Biotechnological and Medical Themes in Science Fiction* (Thessaloniki: University Studio, 2002), pp. 131–51.

——'Utopianism from Orientation to Agency: What Are We Intellectuals under PostFordism To Do?' *Utopian Studies* 9: 2 (1998), pp. 162–90.

——*Victorian Science Fiction in the UK: Discourses of Knowledge and Power* (Boston: G.K. Hall, 1983).

——ed., *Fictions* 3 (2005) – 'US Science Fiction and War/Militarism' special issue.

Sherryl Vint, 'Double Identity: Interpolation in Gwyneth Jones' *Aleutian Trilogy*', *Science Fiction Studies* 28: 3 (2001), pp. 399–425.

——and Mark Bould, 'All That Melts Into Air Is Solid: Rematerialising Capital in *Cube* and *Videodrome*', *Socialism and Democracy* 20: 3 (2006), pp. 217–43.

Phillip Wegner, *Imaginary Communities: Utopia, the Nation, and the Spatial Histories of Modernity* (Berkeley: University of California Press, 2002).

Raymond Williams, 'Science Fiction', *The Highway* 48 (1956), pp. 41–5. Reprinted in *Science Fiction Studies* 15: 3 (1988), pp. 356–60.

——'Utopia and Science Fiction', *Science Fiction Studies* 5: 3 (1978), pp. 203–14. Reprinted in Patrick Parrinder, ed., *Science Fiction: A Critical Guide* (London: Longman, 1979).

2   Other Critical and Theoretical Works

Anglophone Journals

Extrapolation (1959–).
Femspec (1999–).
Foundation: The International Review of Science Fiction (1972–).
Journal of the Fantastic in the Arts (1988–).
Science Fiction Film and Television (2008–).
Science Fiction Studies (1973–).
Utopian Studies (1988–).

Selected Reference and Introductory Works

Brian Aldiss with David Wingrove, *Trillion Year Spree: The History of Science Fiction* (London: Gollancz, 1986).

Paul K. Alkon, *Science Fiction Before 1900: Imagination Discovers Technology* (New York: Twayne, 1994).

Neil Barron, ed., *Anatomy of Wonder 5: A Critical Guide to Science Fiction* (Westport: Libraries Unlimited, 2004); four earlier editions (1976, 1981, 1987, 1995) with substantially different contents.

Mark Bould, *The Routledge Film Guidebook: Science Fiction* (London: Routledge, forthcoming).

——Andrew M. Butler, Adam Roberts and Sherryl Vint, eds, *The Routledge Companion to Science Fiction* (London: Routledge, 2009).

——Andrew M. Butler, Adam Roberts and Sherryl Vint, eds, *Fifty Key Figures in Science Fiction* (London: Routledge, 2009).

——and Sherryl Vint, *The Routledge Concise History of Science Fiction* (London: Routledge, forthcoming).

John Clute and Peter Nicholls, eds, *The Encyclopedia of Science Fiction*, second edn (London: Orbit, 1993). Third edn forthcoming.

Phil Hardy, ed., *The Aurum Film Encyclopedia: Science Fiction*, second edn (London: Aurum, 1995).

Edward James, *Science Fiction in the Twentieth Century* (Oxford: Oxford University Press, 1994).

Edward James and Farah Mendlesohn, eds, *The Cambridge Companion to Science Fiction* (Cambridge: Cambridge University Press, 2003).

Brooks Landon, *Science Fiction after 1900: From the Steam Man to the Stars* (New York: Twayne, 1997).

Sarah Lefanu, *In the Chinks of the World Machine: Feminism and Science Fiction* (London: The Women's Press, 1989).

Roger Luckhurst, *Science Fiction* (Cambridge: Polity, 2005).

Robin Anne Reid, ed., *Women in Science Fiction and Fantasy* (Westport: Greenwood, forthcoming)

Patrick Parrinder, *Science Fiction: Its Criticism and Teaching* (London: Methuen, 1980).

Adam Roberts, *The History of Science Fiction* (Basingstoke: Palgrave Macmillan, 2005).

——*Science Fiction*, second edn (London: Routledge, 2006).

Mark Rose, *Alien Encounters: Anatomy of Science Fiction* (Cambridge: Harvard University Press, 1981).

David Seed, ed., *A Companion to Science Fiction* (Oxford: Blackwell, 2005).

Brian Stableford, *Science Fact and Science Fiction* (London: Routledge, 2006).

Selected Monographs, Collections and Anthologies

Paul K. Alkon, *The Origins of Futuristic Fiction* (Athens: University of Georgia Press, 1987).

Lucie Armitt, ed., *Where No Man Has Gone Before: Women and Science Fiction* (London: Routledge, 1991).

Mike Ashley, *The Time Machines: The Story of the Science-Fiction Pulp Magazines from the Beginning to 1950* (Liverpool: Liverpool University Press, 2000).

——*Transformations: The Story of the Science-Fiction Magazines from 1950–1970* (Liverpool: Liverpool University Press, 2005).

Gateways to Forever: The Story of the Science-Fiction Magazines from 1970–1980 (Liverpool: Liverpool University Press, 2007).

——*The Eternal Chronicles: The Story of the Science-Fiction Magazines since 1980* (Liverpool: Liverpool University Press, forthcoming).

Brian Attebery, *Decoding Gender in Science Fiction* (London: Routledge, 2002).

Anne Balsamo, *Technologies of the Gendered Body: Reading Cyborg Women* (Durham: Duke University Press, 1996).

Marleen Barr, ed., *Future Females: An Anthology* (Bowling Green: Bowling Green University Popular Press, 1981).

——*Alien to Femininity: Speculative Fiction and Feminist Theory* (Westport: Greenwood, 1987).

——*Feminist Fabulation: Space/Postmodern Fiction* (Iowa: Iowa University Press, 1992).

——ed., *Future Females, The Next Generation: New Voices and Velocities in Feminist Science Fiction Criticism* (Boulder: Rowman & Littlefield, 2000).

Daniel Leonard Bernardi, *Star Trek and History: Race-ing Toward a White Future* (New Brunswick: Rutgers University Press, 1998).

Christopher Bolton, Istvan Csicsery-Ronay, Jr, and Takayuki Tatsumi, eds, *Robot Ghosts and Wired Dreams: Japanese Science Fiction from Origins to Anime* (Minneapolis: University of Minnesota Press, 2007).

Damien Broderick, *Reading by Starlight: Postmodern Science Fiction* (London: Routledge, 1995).

Scott Bukatman, *Terminal Identity: The Virtual Subject in Postmodern Science Fiction* (Durham: Duke University Press, 1993).

I.F. Clarke, *Voices Prophesying War: Future Wars, 1763–3749*, second edn (Oxford: Oxford University Press, 1992).

Istvan Csicsery-Ronay, Jr, *The Seven Beauties of Science Fiction* (Middletown: Wesleyan University Press, 2008).

Jane L. Donawerth, *Frankenstein's Daughters: Women Writing Science Fiction* (Syracuse: Syracuse University Press, 1997).

——and Carol A. Kolmerten, eds, *Utopian and Science Fiction by Women: Worlds of Difference* (Liverpool: Liverpool University Press, 1994).

Kodwo Eshun, *More Brilliant Than the Sun: Adventures in Sonic Fiction* (London: Quartet, 1998).

Thomas Foster, *The Souls of Cyberfolk: Posthumanism as Vernacular Theory* (Minneapolis: University of Minnesota Press, 2005).

Colin Greenland, *The Entropy Exhibition: Michael Moorcock and the British 'New Wave' in Science Fiction* (London: Routledge & Kegan Paul, 1983).

Taylor Harrison, Sarah Projansky, Kent A. Ono and Elyce Rae Helford, eds, *Enterprise Zones: Critical Positions of Star Trek* (Boulder: Westview, 1996).

N. Katherine Hayles, *Chaos Bound: Orderly Disorder in Contemporary Literature and Science* (Ithaca: Cornell University Press, 1990).

——*How We Became Posthuman: Virtual Bodies in Cybernetics, Literature and Informatics* (Chicago: University of Chicago Press, 1999).

——*My Mother was a Computer: Digital Subjects and Literary Texts* (Chicago: University of Chicago Press, 2005).

——ed., *Chaos and Order: Complex Dynamics in Literature and Science* (Chicago: University of Chicago Press, 1991).

Veronica Hollinger and Joan Gordon, eds, *Edging into the Future: Science Fiction and Contemporary Cultural Transformation* (Philadelphia: University of Pennsylvania Press, 2002).

John Huntington, *Rationalizing Genius: Ideological Strategies in the Classic American Science Fiction Short Story* (New Brunswick: Rutgers University Press, 1989).

Henry Jenkins, *Textual Poachers: Television Fans and Participatory Culture* (London: Routledge, 1992).

Gwyneth Jones, *Deconstructing the Starships: Science, Fiction and Reality* (Liverpool: Liverpool University Press, 1999).

De Witt Douglas Kilgore, *Astrofuturism: Science, Race, and Visions of Utopia in Space* (Philadelphia: University of Pennsylvania Press, 2003).

Gill Kirkup, Linda Janes, Kathryn Woodward and Fiona Hovenden, eds, *The Gendered Cyborg: A Reader* (London: Routledge, 2000).

Rob Kitchin and James Kneale, eds, *Lost in Space: Geographies of Science Fiction* (New York: Continuum, 2002).

Damon Knight, *The Futurians: The Story of the Science Fiction 'Family' of the 30s That Produced Today's Top SF Writers and Editors* (New York: John Day, 1977).

Annette Kuhn, ed., *Alien Zone: Cultural Theory and Contemporary Science Fiction Cinema* (London: Verso, 1990).

——ed., *Alien Zone II: The Space of Science Fiction* (London: Verso, 1999).

Brooks Landon, *Aesthetics of Ambivalence: Rethinking Science Fiction in the Age of Electronic (Re)production* (Westport: Greenwood, 1992).

Justine Larbalestier, *The Battle of the Sexes in Science Fiction* (Middletown: Wesleyan University Press, 2002).

Ursula K. Le Guin, *The Language of the Night: Essays on Fantasy and Science Fiction* (New York: Perigee, 1979).

——*Dancing at the Edge of the World: Thoughts on Words, Women, Places* (New York: Grove, 1989).

Graham Lock, *Blutopia: Visions of the Future and Revisions of the Past in the Work of Sun Ra, Duke Ellington, and Anthony Braxton* (Durham: Duke University Press, 2000).

Roger Luckhurst, *The Invention of Telepathy* (Oxford: Oxford University Press, 2002).

Larry McCaffery, ed., *Storming the Reality Studio: A Casebook of Cyberpunk and Postmodern Science Fiction* (Durham: Duke UP, 1991).

Louis Marin, *Utopics: Spatial Play*, transl. Robert A. Vollrath (London: Macmillan, 1984).

Graham J. Murphy and Sherryl Vint, eds, *Beyond the Reality Studio: Cyberpunk in the New Millennium* (forthcoming).

Alondra Nelson, ed., *Social Text* 71 (2002) – 'Afrofuturism' special issue.

Wendy Gay Pearson, Veronica Hollinger and Joan Gordon, eds, *Queer Universes: Sexualities and Science Fiction* (Liverpool: Liverpool University Press, 2006).

Constance Penley, *NASA/Trek: Popular Science and Sex in America* (London: Verso, 1997).

Constance Penley, Elisabeth Lyon, Lynn Spigel and Janet Bergstrom, eds, *Close Encounters: Film, Feminism and Science Fiction* (Minneapolis: University of Minnesota Press, 1991).

David Porush, *Soft Machine: Cybernetic Fiction* (London: Methuen, 1984).

Sean Redmond, ed., *Liquid Metal: The Science Fiction Film Reader* (London: Wallflower, 2004).

Joanna Russ, *To Write Like a Woman: Essays in Feminism and Science Fiction* (Bloomington: Indiana University Press, 1995).

——*The Country You Have Never Seen: Essays and Reviews* (Liverpool: Liverpool University Press, 2007).

Ziauddin Sardar and Sean Cubitt, eds, *Aliens R Us: The Other in Science Fiction Cinema* (London: Pluto, 2002).

Robert Scholes, *Structural Fabulation: An Essay on the Fiction of the Future* (Notre Dame: Notre Dame University Press, 1975).

David Seed, *American Science Fiction and the Cold War: Literature and Film* (Keele: Keele University Press, 1999).

Alan N. Shapiro, *Star Trek: Technologies of Disappearance* (Berlin: Avernus, 2004).

George Slusser and Tom Shippey, eds, *Fiction 2000: Cyberpunk and the Future of Narrative* (Athens: University of Georgia Press, 1992).

Claudia Springer, *Electronic Eros: Bodies and Desire in the Postindustrial Age* (London: Athlone, 1996).

Brian Stableford, *Scientific Romance in Britain, 1890–1950* (London: Fourth Estate, 1985).

——*The Sociology of Science Fiction* (San Bernadino: Borgo, 1987).

J.P. Telotte, *Replications: A Robotic History of Science Fiction Film* (Chicago: University of Illinois Press, 1995).

——*A Distant Technology: Science Fiction Film and the Machine Age* (Middletown: Wesleyan University Press, 1999).

——*Science Fiction Film* (Cambridge: Cambridge University Press, 2001).

——ed., *The Essential Science Fiction Television Reader* (Lexington: University Press of Kentucky, 2008).

John Tulloch and Henry Jenkins, *Science Fiction Audiences: Watching Doctor Who and Star Trek* (London: Routledge, 1995).

Sherryl Vint, *Bodies of Tomorrow: Technology, Subjectivity, Science Fiction* (Toronto: University of Toronto Press, 2006).

Gary Westfahl, *The Mechanics of Wonder: The Creation of the Idea of Science Fiction* (Liverpool: Liverpool University Press, 1998).

Martin Willis, *Mesmerists, Monsters, and Machines: Science Fiction and the Cultures of Science in the Nineteenth Century* (Kent: Kent State University Press, 2006).

Gary K. Wolfe, *The Known and the Unknown: The Iconography of Science Fiction* (Kent: Kent State University Press, 1979).

Jenny Wolmark, *Aliens and Others: Science Fiction, Feminism and Postmodernism* (Hemel Hempstead: Harvester Wheatsheaf, 1993).

——ed., *Cybersexualities: A Reader on Feminist Theory, Cyborgs and Cyberspace* (Edinburgh: Edinburgh University Press, 1999).

Lisa Yaszek, *Galactic Suburbia: Recovering Women's Science Fiction* (Columbus: Ohio State University Press, 2008).

ABOUT THE CONTRIBUTORS

Matthew Beaumont is a Senior Lecturer in the Department of English Language and Literature at University College, London and the author of *Utopia Ltd: Ideologies of Social Dreaming in England 1870–1900* (2005). He is the editor of *Adventures in Realism* (2007) and the Oxford World Classics edition of Edward Bellamy's *Looking Backward* (2007), and a co-editor of *As Radical as Reality Itself: Essays on Marxism and Art for the 21st Century* (2007) and *The Railway and Modernity: Time, Space, and the Machine Ensemble* (2007).

Mark Bould is Reader in Film and Literature at the University of the West of England and co-editor of *Science Fiction Film and Television*. He is the author of *Film Noir: From Berlin to Sin City* (2005) and *The Cinema of John Sayles: Lone Star* (2009) and a co-editor of *Parietal Games: Critical Writings By and On M. John Harrison* (2005), *The Routledge Companion to Science Fiction* (2009), *Neo-noir* (2009) and *Fifty Key Figures in Science Fiction* (2009). He is currently co-writing *The Routledge Concise History of Science Fiction* and writing *The Routledge Film Guidebook: Science Fiction*.

William J. Burling is Professor of English at Missouri State University and is the editor of *Kim Stanley Robinson Maps the Unimaginable: Critical Essays* (2009). He has recent essays in *Utopian Studies*, *Kronoscope*, *Extrapolation*, *The Routledge Companion to Science Fiction* and *Fifty Key Figures in Science Fiction*.

Carl Freedman is Professor of English at Louisiana State University. He is the author of *George Orwell: A Study in Ideology and Literary Form* (1988), *Critical Theory and Science Fiction* (2000) and *The Incomplete Projects: Marxism, Modernity and the Politics of Culture* (2002), and the editor of *Conversations with Isaac Asimov* (2005), *Conversations with Ursula K. Le Guin* (2008) and *Conversations with Samuel R. Delany* (forthcoming).

Darren Jorgensen is a lecturer in art history at the University of Western Australia. In addition to publishing on Aboriginal representations and their implications for leftist politics, he is currently drafting a study of SF and the sublime, and co-editing with Helen Merrick special issues of *Extrapolation* (on the histories of SF) and *Reconstruction* (on the transformation of genre).

Rob Latham is Associate Professor of English at the University of California at Riverside. A co-editor of *Science Fiction Studies* since 1997, he is the author of *Consuming Youth: Vampires, Cyborgs, and the Culture of Consumption* (2002) and is currently working on a book on New Wave SF.

Iris Luppa is Senior Lecturer in Film Studies at London South Bank University. She is the author of *Weimar Cinema* (2009) and has published several articles on the films of Fritz Lang.

China Miéville is the author of *King Rat* (1998), *Perdido Street Station* (2000), *The Scar* (2002), *Iron Council* (2004), *Looking for Jake and Other Stories* (2005), *Un Lun Dun* (2007) and *The City & The City* (2009). An editor of *Historical Materialism* and the author of *Between Equal Rights: A Marxist Theory of International Law* (2005), he is Honorary Research Fellow at Birkbeck School of Law and Associate Professor of Creative Writing at Warwick University.

Andrew Milner is Professor of Cultural Studies at Monash University. His most recent books are *Re-Imagining Cultural Studies* (2002), *Literature, Culture and Society* (2005), *Postwar British Critical Thought* (2005) and *Imagining the Future: Utopia and Dystopia* (2006).

John Rieder is a Professor of English at the University of Hawai'i at Manoa, where he teaches courses on Marxist cultural theory and SF. He is the author of *Colonialism and the Emergence of Science Fiction* (2008).

Steven Shaviro is the DeRoy Professor of English at Wayne State University. He is the author of *The Cinematic Body* (1993), *Doom Patrols: A Theoretical Fiction about Postmodernism* (1997), *Connected, or, What It Means to Live in the Network Society* (2003) and *Without Criteria: Kant, Whitehead, Deleuze, and Aesthetics* (2009). His blog is *The Pinocchio Theory* (www.shaviro.com/blog).

Sherryl Vint is Assistant Professor of English at Brock University and a co-editor of *Extrapolation, Humanimalia* and *Science Fiction Film and Television*. The author of *Bodies of Tomorrow* (2007) and a co-editor of *The Routledge Companion to Science Fiction* (2009) and *Fifty Key Figures in Science Fiction* (2009), she is currently completing *Animal*

Alterity: Science Fiction and the Question of the Animal and co-writing *The Routledge Concise History of Science Fiction*.

Phillip Wegner is an Associate Professor in English at the University of Florida. He is the author of *Imaginary Communities: Utopia, the Nation, and the Spatial Histories of Modernity* (2002) and *Life Between Two Deaths, 1989–2001: US Culture in the Long Nineties* (2009), and is currently completing *Periodizing Jameson; or, the Adventures of Theory in Post-Contemporary Times* and *Ontologies of the Possible: Utopia, Science Fiction, and Globalization*.

INDEX

Printed and bound by CPI Group (UK) Ltd, Croydon, CR0 4YY

13/04/2025

14656490-0004